CONTENTS

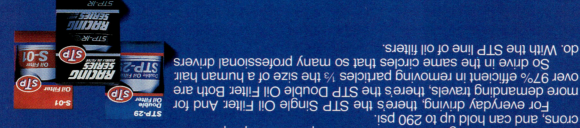

INDIANAPOLIS
500
YEARBOOK

PENNZOIL

25

MONROE

GOOD YEAR

cademartori

Our compliments to the Champ!

PPG proudly salutes super-star Bobby Rahal, champion of the 1986 PPG Indy Car World Series.

And our compliments, too, to Steve Horne, president of TrueSports Inc., owner of Bobby's car, to Budweiser, his sponsor, and to the exceptional crew of designers, car builders, engineers and mechanics who constructed and maintained his Budweiser Special.

Bobby captured the respect and admiration of the entire racing world by emerging from a pack of the world's greatest drivers, competing in the world's richest racing series, to win six races, including the greatest of them all - the Indianapolis 500 - on his way to the championship.

In a series that demands extraordinary skills, versatility, concentration and courage, he proved once again that the Indy Cars are the world's fastest and most sophisticated racing machines.

And his car, like the entire starting field at all races in the series, including the Indianapolis 500, was painted with PPG's tough urethane finishes.

Just one more reason why PPG automotive finishes are the leading choice of auto makers worldwide.

ITS POWER WILL MOVE YOU. ITS BEAUTY WILL STOP YOU. THE ALL-NEW CHRYSLER LE BARON CONVERTIBLE.

The sky is your roof...the wind echoes your own breathless excitement. This is the all-new LeBaron convertible. Beauty...with a passion for driving.

Slip into rich, supportive leather,* sense the power of command at your fingertips, grip the cushioned wheel...your driving instincts come alive.

Powered by fuel-injected turbo,* LeBaron's response is immediate. Engineered with advanced front-wheel drive and positive-response suspension, LeBaron gives you confidence and control at every turn.

LeBaron is beauty and grace in motion. For it is designed and built as a true convertible...from start to finish. Thus, it rides with a smooth, quiet strength.

And because we build it like no other, we back it like no other. With Chrysler's new 7/70 Protection Plan** that covers engine, powertrain and turbo for 7 years or 70,000 miles and against outer body rust-through for 7 years or 100,000 miles. Whether you buy or lease.

Its power will move you. Its beauty will stop you. The all-new LeBaron convertible. At Chrysler-Plymouth dealers.

Chrysler 7/70
Division of Chrysler Motors

Chrysler. Driving to be the best.

Ever see A.J. Foyt so euphoric? The occasion is U.S. Tobacco's recognition of A.J.'s 30th consecutive "500" and the lad getting his undivided attention is Larry Roberds, A.J.'s 10-year-old grandson. (IMS-Spargur)

Al Unser seemed destined to join brother Bobby on the sidelines for this one but in storybook fashion he landed a car at the last minute and rode to a record-tying 4th win. (Wendt)

Roberto Guerrero is fit to be tied when the "500" is plucked from his grasp, but his mood will soon change when he sees his wife and baby son. (IMS-Seidman)

VOLUME XV
Unequalled in Coverage of the World's Most Famous Automobile Race

Publisher	Carl Hungness
Editor	Donald Davidson
Art & Production Director	Steve Miller
Secretaries	Wilma Steffy
	Terri Gunn
Advertising	Jo Hungness
Litho Preparation	Whitt Photo Service
Typesetting	Tim Davidson
Copy Editor	Sherry Davidson
Cover Artist	Hector Cadematori

Our special thanks to Bill Donaldson, Kurt Hunt, Bob Laycock, Roger Deppe, and Bill York, of the Indianapolis Motor Speedway, for their continuing assistance in the compilation of this book. Thanks also to Ron McQueeney and Pat Jones of the IMS Photo Department, and Tammie Phillips for assistance in the photo selection from IMS, Brenda Stafford for transcribing the winner's interview, and Director of Timing and Scoring, Art Graham, who provided much valuable information used in the preparation of the race story.

IMS—Staff Photographers:
Ron McQueeney, Tammie Phillips, Bill Watson, David Thomas, Jim Haines, Steve Lingenfelter, Dan Francis, Larry Seidman, Frank Newman, Dave Willoughby, Harlen Hunter, Bob Scott, Tom Lucas, Charles Duffy, Ed Kackley, Jack Schofer, Debbie Young, Steve Snoddy, Dave Dwiggins, Jeff Stephenson, Mag Binkley, Harry Goode, Mike Young, Lance Sellers, Denis Sparks, Harold Bergquist, Steve Voorhees, Larry Smith, Todd Hunter, Mark Reed, Loretta Young, Pat Taylor, Steve Swope, Leigh Spargur, Del Neal, Kay Totten Spivey, Steve Ellis, Sam Scott, Bob Poynter, Linda Zimmerman

Contributing Photographers:
Doug Wendt, Phil Whitlow, John Mahoney, John Strauser, Gerald Walker, Arnie deBrier, Jim Adams, Bob Mount, David Scoggan, Steve Weaver, Bill Ferguson, Bill Ridley, Pat Pinkley, Larry Van Sickle, Dan Bonwell, Rex Van Zant, Rodney Margison, Mike Grider, Harry Dunn, Bob Ellis, Lisa Little, Robert Eakins, Michael Katsoff, Jack Ackerman

Contributing Writers:
Donald Davidson, David Scoggan, Jep Cadou, Al Stilley, Philip LeVrier, Bob Watson

Library of Congress Catalog Card Number: 76-84562
Library Binding 0-915088-47-9
Paperbound 0-915088-46-0

Printed by Webcrafters, Inc., Madison, Wisconsin

Book trade distribution by:

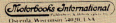
Motorbooks International
Osceola, Wisconsin 54020, USA

Bobby Rahal's 1986 Indianapolis 500-winning March/Cosworth.
Tires: Goodyear racing Eagles.

The fact that both of these Indy cars are on Goodyear Eagles is no coincidence.

The 1987 Indianapolis 500 Chrysler LeBaron pace car.
Factory specified tires: Goodyear Eagle GT street radials.

For the past 15 years, every Indianapolis 500 has been won on Goodyear tires.

Over the years, as the teams and the drivers became aware of Goodyear's superiority, they changed. To Goodyear.

So it's not surprising that every car in this year's Indianapolis 500 will compete on Goodyear racing Eagles.

Or that, once again, the Indianapolis 500 pace car—the Chrysler LeBaron Convertible—will also be on Goodyear Eagles: Eagle street radials.

The success of both the Eagle street radials and the racing Eagles has a common source: Goodyear's ability to make better high-performance tires.

For the track. For the street. For virtually every performance car.

So it's really no coincidence that Goodyear racing Eagles will be found on the car that wins this year's Indianapolis 500.

Or that Goodyear Eagle street radials are found on more high-performance cars than any other tire in the world.

In fact, when you consider how the Eagles perform, it's really no coincidence at all.

GOODYEAR

Take me home. *The quick way.*

THE MONTH OF MAY, DAY BY DAY

A rash of mysterious accidents punctuates the two-week search for speed.

By David Scoggan

Even the defending winner is back on square one when the track opens for practice each May. Truesports, having switched from March to Lola, unload to begin a new campaign. (IMS-D. Young)

After years of futile attempts to curtail ever-climbing Indy Car Speeds, CART and USAC settled on a fine-tuning of their existing car specifications for the 1987 season. Combined with projected horsepower increases and the promise of radial tires from Goodyear, a 220 MPH lap at the Indianapolis Motor Speedway was projected as a distinct possibility.

Bobby Rahal maintained the momentum from his emotional Indy 500 victory to claim the 1986 CART/PPG Indy Car World Series points title. Rahal's Budweiser/Truesports March team clinched the $331,000 bonus at the season finale in Miami when sole championship challenger Michael Andretti retired his Kraco March. (This insured that the legitimate national champion would wear 1 at Indy for the first time since 1982.)

An ominous threat to Rahal's opportunity to fly the number 1 loomed in the visage of one Sir James Goldsmith. The British corporate raider masterminded a hostile takeover of the Goodyear Tire and Rubber Company, placing many segments of automobile racing in jeopardy. Fortunately, Goodyear extracted Goldy's fangs with a mere $2.6 billion buyback. (Wouldn't it have been simpler just to hire a hit man?)

Rick Mears set two American closed-course speed records during the '86 season. Mears and the Pennzoil March 86C/Cosworth turned a lap of 223.401 MPH while qualifying for the August 2 Michigan 500. The Penske team returned to MIS on November 17 and Mears took an Ilmor-Chevy-powered 86C (with an extra dosage of turocharger boost) to an astonishing 233.934 MPH.

While Roger Penske's organization was the only one to campaign the Chevrolet Indy engine last year, two additional teams would carry the powerplant full-time in 1987. Pat Patrick would have Ilmor-Chevies in his twin Marlboro Marches for Emerson Fittipaldi and Kevin Cogan. (Incidentally, Patrick Racing did test the motor periodically through '86, with Cogan's 86C topping 214 MPH in a November IMS session.) Lola-mounted Mario Andretti's Newman/Haas team completed the '87 roster, giving the "bowtie brigade" a representative from each new chassis make (Penske PC-16, March 87C, and Lola T8701).

Technical Director Jack Beckley and Steward Art Meyers are two of the key officials. (Whitlow)

The beautiful Chrysler LeBaron pace car. (IMS-McQueeney)

This walkway between the back of the grandstands and the Garage Area will be wall-to-wall people come first qualifying day. (Pinkley)

The rumors finally became fact: Porsche is coming to Indy in 1988. At a February 3 press conference in New York City, the basics of a four-year program were presented. Quaker State will be the major sponsor of the V-8 powered machine, which is expected to compete in the final three CART races of the '87 season. The effort will be directed by Al Holbert, head of Porsche Motorsports-North America. Speculation to potential drivers fell on Al Unser (Senior and Junior), Chip Robinson, A.J. Foyt, Mario and Michael Andretti, and any other person with previous Stuttgart connections.

Once more the insidious stench of drugs pervaded Indy Car racing. Randy Lanier, '86 Indy 500 Rookie of the Year, was charged on October 15 as part of a smuggling ring that allegedly brought more than 100,000 pounds of marijuana into Florida between 1980 and 1986. As of this writing, Lanier's whereabouts are unknown; he is presumed dead or out of the country.

Frank Arciero hoped to replace the fugitive with '86 fill-in drivers Jeff MacPherson and/or Eddie Cheever. (Lanier had sustained a broken leg in the Michigan 500.) MacPherson, however, signed with Rick Galles and Cheever jumped at the chance to return to Formula One with the USF&G Arrows team, so Arciero merely gave his American Racing Series driver Fabrizio Barbazza a promotion. Barbazza's move created a vacancy in the Buick-powered Indy 500 entry provided by ARS chairman Pat Patrick as a reward for the '86 series point champion. An offer to runner-up Jeff Andretti was nixed by poppa Mario, so Buick test driver Jim Crawford became the logical replacement. In numerous tests at the Speedway between August and November, Crawford had logged well over 2,000 miles in the March 86C "mule".

Three other drivers placed their eggs in the Buick V-6 basket. Tom Sneva's Skoal Bandit March would make the one-race switch (Tom had been quoted as stating, "The first Buick to finish 500 miles will win the race."), joining Derek Daly's Pace Racing March and the Ron Hemelgarn March to be driven by Rich Vogler.

Vogler was part of an ambitious effort from LivingWell fitness center impresario Ron Hemelgarn. Arie Luyendyk came aboard as lead driver after Provimi Veal Racing folded (though Aat Groenevelt retained sufficient funds to make Provimi Arie's primary sponsor). Former IMS one-lap record holder Scott Brayton hustled enough Amway and Autostyle dollars to cinch a last-minute deal for a third Hemelgarn March; his hopes of carrying traditional Buick propulsion were dashed by the factory — such gratitude! (Plans to put team ARS driver Steve Millen through Rookie Orientation were scrapped when the New Zealander broke his leg in a March IMSA crash.)

Three-time Indy winner Al Unser joined the unemployment ranks when newspaper heir-turned-movie mogul Ted Field procured the third Penske seat for his long-time "key grip", Danny Ongais. Big

Al was heavily courted by the Cahill brothers — motel magnates from Iowa who wanted to advance from ARS to Indy Car ownership —but the project died for want of corporate finances.

After earning the number two starting position for the Miami CART race, Raul Boesel was axed from the Dick Simon team. Simon blamed outrageous contractual demands, while Boesel contended Ludwig Heimrath, Junior's sponsorship money (Mackenzie Financial and Tim Horton Donuts) bought the ride. Regardless, Boesel was snapped up by Tom Walkinshaw and his potent Silk Cut Jaguar Sports prototype organization.

Winter testing created an additional burden for some. A collapsed rear wing on Arie Luyendyk's just-(and first)- delivered March 87C caused heavy contact with the Phoenix International Raceway wall; the March factory immediately shipped a replacement tub and shelved the experimental triple-element device. Also tasting the PIR concrete were Kevin Cogan (scratch one Patrick 86C), Jim Crawford (he also wrinkled the battle-scarred, but repaired ARS 86C/Buick at the Atlanta oval), and Rick Mears. Front suspension failure on late-arriving Penske PC-16 chassis number one put Mears and crew even further behind schedule.

Mario Andretti was another "defective wing victim", trashing his spanking new Lola in a Laguna Seca tumble. Mario (and the others) emerged uninjured, but the crash further lessened the already remote possibility of Frenchman Patrick Tambay joining the Newman/Haas team.

Most team alignments were set by the March 2 kickoff of IMS spring testing. Seventeen drivers and sixteen different machines ran practice laps before the April 5 shutdown.

Pacesetter of the early action was Kevin Cogan, who pushed his Patrick Racing March 87C/Ilmor-Chevy to a day's ending lap of 214.3 MPH on a sunny, 58 degree March 20. Teammate Emerson Fittipaldi managed a best of 211.7 in his similarly-unmarked white and day-glo red 87C during the two- day session.

Jim Crawford continued the marathon Buick testing program, appearing for 14 of 25 available test days. While most of his laps were in the 208-209 range, he did rip off a 213.1 circuit on March 26. Unfortunately, the bulk of Jim's miles came on last year's bias-ply tires, so when the ARS crew finally converted to radials, all their chassis info became worthless. (By this time, the patchwork white, red, and black March 86C was nearing the 4,000 mile mark.)

Goodyear's traditional pre-May tire test featured three former Indy winners and some erroneous speed reports. Mario Andretti battled high winds and mechanical gremlins to reach a confirmed

Al Unser spends the first week and a half in civvies. (IMS- D. Young)

TWO AMERICAN LEGENDS.

DANNY SULLIVAN AND MILLER BEER.

It takes more than desire to become a legend. It takes a will to win. A determination to be clearly superior to the competition.

These are the qualities that drove Danny Sullivan and the Penske/Miller American to victory at the 1985 Indianapolis 500.

And these are the qualities that are making Danny Sullivan one of the newest legends in American racing.

For over 130 years, we've been brewing Miller Beer with the same kind of desire, the same kind of determination to be clearly superior.

And today, the legend of Miller Beer lives on. Miller High Life is brewed darker with a special roasted malt. For richness you can see. Quality you can taste.

And Miller contains no additives or preservatives.

So when you want a beer that's made to be the best, ask for Miller High Life.

Because just like Danny Sullivan, it's a legend made the American way.

MADE THE AMERICAN WAY.

Defending winner Bobby Rahal and Chief Steward Tom Binford flank Five Hundred Festival Queen Pam Jones. That's pace car driver Carroll Shelby with the red tie. (Walker)

213.1 MPH in the 5 Hanna Car Wash Lola T8701/Ilmor-Chevy. Johnny Rutherford struggled in the 208 bracket for two days before pushing his 21 Vermont American March 87C/Cosworth to 211.6 before rain cut short the third and final day (March 18).

Defending Indy and Cart champion Bobby Rahal turned an observed best of 212.2 in the 1 Budweiser/Truesports entry. For 1987, Rahal and crew forsook five years of loyalty to March equipment and jumped over to the Lola camp. "I think [Lola] got a little complacent over the last year or two," stated Rahal, "and I felt in talking to them at the end of last year that they were very committed to producing the best car."

Some of you may have read headlines in the racing weeklies of 215-216 MPH laps by Rahal and Rutherford. Well, that just didn't happen. According to Johnny Capels, crew chief for the Alex Morales team, the aforementioned numbers were actually straight-away speeds that were misconstrued by second and third parties. What would put an end to the constant flow of bogus test speeds? How about one person — armed with an accurate stopwatch — located in the tower to serve as Chief Test Timer? Sure, it's cold in March, but people are out there anyway! And don't tell me no one cares, because someone should.

Al Unser, Junior cleared 212 MPH on two separate occasions. Al's 30 Domino's Pizza Hot One posted a 212.3 clocking on March 6, then returned on March 19 and hit 212 flat (blowing the engine the following day). Doug Shierson had returned to March chassis for the first time since 1983 and Little Al liked the switch. Comparing the Lola and March, he commented, "It's like the difference between a Ford and a Chevy . . passenger car. . . . . hopefully it will be that little bit that will make a difference in the race. I think now we have a car that we can run with them."

Closing on the 212 mark was new Machinists Union hire Pancho Carter. The '85 Indy polesitter came aboard to drive the 29 Hardee's March 87C/Cosworth after Scott Brayton reportedly turned down the deal. Pancho's 211.8 lap on March 28 bettered the 208's turned by West Coast-bound Josele Garza in the same car two days earlier.

Michael Andretti arrived on a frigid March 12, approached 211 MPH in the 18 Kraco 87C and by 4 o'clock was en route to Pennsylvania to become a father. Wife Sandra gave birth to son Marco the next day; strict orders followed as grandfather Mario demanded to be referred to as "uncle".

Sharing time with Kraco was the reorganized Raynor Motorsports group. Dennis Firestone reached the mid-210 MPH level with the attractive dark orange and silver 10 '87 Lola now being wrenched by 1986 Indy qualifier Phil Krueger.

Carroll Shelby with Steward Keith Ward and Registrar Bob Cassaday, who'll ride with Shelby in the pace car at the start. (B. Mount)

The new message boards greatly enhance the enjoyment of the race-goers. (deBrier)

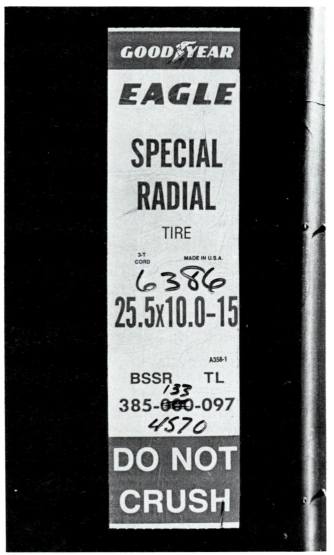

Goodyear radials come to the Speedway for the first time in competition. (Whitlow)

This circa 1957-58 golf cart was restored last year. (Strauser)

The transporters are housed on the east side of the Garage Area throughout May. (Walker)

Rich Vogler was the second-busiest driver (behind fellow Buickite Jim Crawford), running on eight different days with a best lap of 205 flat. Vogler was the only test "casualty"; on March 14, he lost control exiting turn 2 and spun crazily down the backstretch. Slight wall contact with both nose and rear wing inflicted minor damage on the red and white Kentucky Fried Chicken 86C. Hemelgarn stablemate Arie Luyendyk's brief (March 5/6) stint found him nearing 208 MPH in the short-track-bodied 71 Provimi/LivingWell 87C/Cosworth.

The weather was so abysmal from March 9 to 11 that Truesports left the Speedway without turning a wheel, but rookie Fabrizio Barbazza couldn't afford to be choosy. His Indy introduction began in the 130 MPH range and had progressed over 201 when his engine let go on the main straightaway. A small fire on the rear bodywork of the red, unlettered Arciero Racing 87C/Cosworth was eventually extinguished by the safety crew.

Veteran Gary Bettenhausen put in an appearance with the dark red March 87C of Dick Hammond, reaching 206.3 on March 26. The Buffalo-based Genesee Beer group finally switched to Cosworth power in mid-'86, abandoning the stock-blocks (Chevy V-8 and Buick V-6) used by the team since its inception in 1981.

Last cars to test were the similar-appearing, all-white March 87C machines of Derek Daly and Steve Chassey. Battling the gales of April 5, Daly hit 207.0 in the Pace Electronics Buick. Chassey neared 204 MPH with the March/Cosworth of Laughrey Racing, a new team formed by a rarity in Indy Car racing — the female car owner. Local medical supplies distributor Lydia Laughrey also signed Huey Absalom as crew chief for the unsponsored effort.

A few teams missed out on valuable early IMS practice. Rick Galles canceled his March 9-11 dates, losing needed development miles on the Brabham-Honda V-8 engine. The harried Penske organization missed Goodyear's tire test while thrashing to prepare two PC-16 chassis for the rapidly- approaching first two CART races. (A.J. Foyt adopted his usual anti-testing stance, which seemed odd, considering his switch from trusty Marches to an unfamiliar Lola.)

While Daly and Chassey (and Crawford — of course) were lapping the Speedway, the '87 CART/PPG Indy Car World Series opened with the Toyota Grand Prix of Long Beach. Mario Andretti dominated the California streets, giving the Ilmor- Chevy racing engine its initial win with a flag-to-flag run from pole position. Trailing the Hanna Car Wash '87 Lola by one lap were runner-up Al Unser, Junior and third place Tom Sneva. Emerson Fittipaldi dogged Mario until wastegate problems sidelined him just past halfway.

Katy and Marco Guerrero find Daddy. (IMS-Spargur)

Finally! In his 49th career start, Roberto Guerrero claimed a much-deserved first Indy Car victory in the Phoenix International Raceway Checker 200 on April 12. Starting last because his March 87C/Cosworth came up 2 1/2 pounds light in post-qualifying inspection, the rapid Colombian overcame a stop-and-go penalty to elude number two finisher Bobby Rahal by 8 seconds. Arie Luyendyk's third-place drive was also his best CART achievement. Pole-sitter Mario Andretti faded to fifth, but maintained the points lead heading into Indianapolis.

Last winter, the Dan Cotter operation was taken over by Vince Granatelli, son of Andy (AKA ''Mr. 500''); Guerrero's True Value machine had thus been rechristened with STP co- sponsorship and corresponding day-glo red livery. Some expected the team to suffer from the off-season departure of chief mechanic Phil Casey, but the addition of long-time Patrick Racing engine builder (and now unretired) Sonny Meyer provided a stabilizing influence.

Mike Nish and his wife were seriously injured in a highway accident while returning home from the Phoenix race. The part-time Machinists Union driver and two-time Indy non- qualifier sustained a crushed vertebra, fractures of both ankles, a broken rib, and lacerations to his face and abdomen. Wife Sandi escaped with a fractured hip.

When the last entry had trickled into the Speedway after the midnight April 3 postmark deadline, the complete tally was an encouraging 76 — eight more than last year's total. One name missing from the roster was All-American racers; for the first time since 1966, there would be no Eagle chassis at Indy. Without financial backing, Dan Gurney was free to concentrate his talents on the AAR factory Toyota IMSA GTO program featuring Chris Cord and Willy T. Ribbs.

The entry list contained some surprises. Dick Ferguson, absent from Indy Car racing since May of 1985, signed to drive the ex-Wilke '85 March of California car dealer Elmer Fields. George Walther (father of the incarcerated Salt) ended a six-year track sabbatical and nominated Rocky Moran to pilot his year-old March. Midget and ARS shoe Stan Fox ('84 Indy DNQ) appeared as an A.J. Foyt team member, then was joined by road racing phenom Davy Jones. Johnny Parsons vacillated on his assignment with John Buttera's Pontiac- powered March 86C, so World of Outlaws sprint car superstar Sammy Swindell assumed the seat. Two-time Indy

winner Gordon Johncock began yet another comeback effort; an outfit called Gold Racing registered an '87 March/Cosworth for Johncock while he honed his dormant skills in the Phoenix ARS race.

Three CART teams planning limited schedules for '87 decided to skip Indy. Russell Newman Teamworks driver Didier Theys of Belgium ('86 Super Vee champ) finished seventh at Long Beach in their ex-Doug Shierson '86 Lola. Bob Tullius and his Group 44 organization, renowned for their awesome IMSA Jaguars, purchased an '86 March from Roger Penske so protege Chip Robinson could compete in four of this season's CART events (grabbing 6th at Long Beach). The legendary Dale Coyne and his ex-Menard March 86C/stock-block Chevy probably couldn't have mustered the 180 MPH needed to start his rookie test anyway.

A few embryonic (or perhaps downright fictitious) combinations failed to materialize by deadline. The invisibile Savoy International team claimed to be negotiating with Canadian John Jones, the '85 IMSA GTO champ who ran Formula 3000 last year. John Andretti, son of Mario's twin brother Aldo, was supposedly courted by both CMS Racing of Plainfield, Indiana and Wayne Decker (of Black and Decker power tools) without results. Al Unser was also mentioned in conjunction with the Decker scheme, then big Al reportedly just missed a deal with Maxwell House coffee that could have reunited him with George Bignotti. (Was it with the Cahill brothers? Who knows?)

Eight first-year drivers participated in the seventh annual Rookie Orientation Program from Friday, April 24 to Sunday, April 26. Six of the Indy neophytes completed all four available test phases (180-184 MPH, 185-189, 190-194, and 195-199).

Fabrizio Barbazza paced this year's group. After hitting 197.4 on Friday with the 12 Arciero March 86C (96 laps total), Barbazza returned on Sunday with their 1987 March to turn a program-best 205.949 in 60 laps. George Walther's 76 ex-Morales '86 March (with unchanged red and beige paint scheme) took sometime-executive jet pilot Rocky Moran to a second-quick 201.748 after 110 total circuits.

New Leader Cards hire Randy Lewis overcame a temperamental smoking turbocharger to post a best lap of 199.991 out of 188 trips

Vince Granatelli almost won as a rookie car owner. (Strauser)

233.9 MPH

One Man.

Rick Mears has set so many records, he's out of wall space. His latest was November 17, at the Michigan International Speedway. 233.934 Miles Per Hour. The new American closed-course speed record. Officially timed by CART. Sanctioned by SCCA. And recognized by the Automobile Competition Committee of the United States/FIA.

One Machine.

His car—the Pennzoil Z-7 Special. His engine—the revolutionary new Penske-prepared Chevrolet Indy V8.

One Motor Oil.

His motor oil—Pennzoil. Rick always uses it. And he wouldn't think of setting a new record without it.

He had the talent. The team. The engine. And the protection of a quality motor oil in the car that's now called the fastest in CART racing history.

PENNZOIL®

The Standard of Protection
Since 1889.™

The Hoosier Dome can be seen beyond the turn two VIP suites in this mainstraight control tower view of the changing downtown Indianapolis skyline. (IMS-S. Scott)

in the 24 Western Digital/Oracle March 86C. The 41-year-old Californian might have driven here in 1984, but his scheduled gig with Rattlesnake Racing and GAF film sponsorship fell through.

Ludwig Heimrath, Jr. took over the 23 Tim Horton Donuts '87 Lola after boss Dick Simon shook it down and reached 198.456 in his 109-lap education. A.J. Foyt worked a transaction with Simon to provide wheels for his new understudy Davy Jones, and the '86 IMSA BMW GTP chauffeur hit 197.758 in 100 laps with the 22 Mackenzie '86 Lola. (Simon also dialed in the 22 for Jones.)

Sammy Swindell overcame a multitude of mechanical problems to finish his test late Sunday. Right front brake woes limited Swindell's Friday action to a mere 8 laps; the next day the 59 Center Line March 86C blew its normally- aspirated, stock-block Pontiac V-8 engine. The evil-sounding beast held together long enough on Sunday to compile a three- day total of 109 laps at a best speed of 196.936.

Poor Jeff MacPherson had a miserable IMS initiation. The former off-road racer managed only 26 laps (at around 185 MPH) in his assigned ride — the gremlin-infested 11 Honda- powered March 87C of Rick Galles. He then borrowed Frank Arciero's '86 March and completed two phases on Saturday afternoon (192.554 in 33 laps), only to have a front wheel bearing seize while warming up on Sunday morning. Number 12 came in on the hook and Jeff's weekend was finished.

German-born Dominic Dobson, last year's CART/Vandervell Rookie of the Year, accomplished only 185.950 before losing the engine in Dick Simon's 22 Lola loaner after a paltry 24 laps. Dobson lost his '86 ride with Ralph Wilke to the financial backing of Randy Lewis, and his eleventh-hour program with Zephyr Racing (his entered ex-Kraco March 86C) was still forming on the West Coast.

As the start of official practice drew near, one driver switch came down. Rick Miaskiewicz replaced Tom Bigelow in the 97 March 86C/Cosworth entered by Sandy Racing of West Lafayette, Indiana (Bigelow's USAC midget owners). It seems Miaskiewicz and backers didn't have enough cash to purchase his assigned 32 M-Group/J.

Kattman 1987 Lola, but Bigelow's Pizza Hut sponsorship money was considerably shy of what had been promised, so '86 Indy non-qualifier Miaskiewicz took over 97 for a reported $50,000.

It appeared Gordon Johncock's Return to Indy would again be nipped in the bud. His new March was sitting at O'Hare Airport in Chicago, but no one from ''Gold Racing'' showed up to pay for it. (Perhaps it was prophetic that Johncock's car was located at the bottom of the 500 entry list — without a number.)

Ex-McLaren executive-turned Newman-Haas team manager Tyler Alexander evidently poses a real corker to Roger Penske. (Strauser)

Why Passport is the most expensive* radar detector in the world

What sets Passport above other detectors is the technical reach of our engineers, and their insistence on excellence at every design step. *Road & Track* called us "the industry leader in detector technology." Here's why:

Double-ridge waveguide: It was always taken as gospel that miniaturizing a detector would hurt performance. Passport proved this wrong. The miniaturized horn antenna feeds into a double-ridge waveguide. Dual compound chokes are required, and the notch filters are press fit to exact depth. The design process was incredibly complex. But the payoff is indisputable. Passport's performance is uncompromised by its discreet size.

Rashid rejection: In another engineering first, our detectors have been made immune to K-band signals transmitted by the

RADAR   RASHID

Rashid VRSS collision warning system. Other detectors produce false alarms in the presence of Rashid. Our AFR™ (Alternating Frequency Rejection) circuitry isolates and neutralizes Rashid signals, yet leaves the radar detection capability undiminished for your protection.

X-K differentiation: Passport has separate warning tones to distinguish X-band from K-band. The difference is important. Traffic radar is just one of many transmitters assigned to X-band by the FCC. Motion detectors, burglar alarms and microwave door openers also share this frequency. When you hear the X-band warning, you respond accordingly.

But just two transmitters operate on K-band — radar and Rashid. K-band radar's short effective range requires immediate response. Since our AFR circuitry rejects Rashid, Passport's K-band warning is positively radar, and you always know how to respond.

Variable-rate warning: On radar contact, Passport's bar graph of eight Hewlett-Packard LEDs indicates radar strength, and you

will hear the audible warning — pulsing slowly at first, quicker as you approach, then constant as you near effective radar range. Our engineers have preprogrammed the warning system to tell you everything you need to know about radar. Passport asks no further programming of you, unlike many lesser detectors.

SMD circuitry: Passport's miniaturization was made complete by the use of SMD's (Surface Mounted Devices), micro-electronics common in satellites but long considered too exotic for radar detectors. SMD circuit boards also provide ruggedness unobtainable with conventional technology.

Compact dimensions: Passport was designed to be the most discreet detector ever — only 0.75″ H x 2.75″ W x 4.50″ L. On guard, it never draws attention to itself.

Die-cast aluminum housing: The antenna is integrated into Passport's die-cast SAE 308 aluminum housing. This way no amount of abuse can ever shake the antenna

loose, and Passport's precision electronics are protected by a rugged metal vault for durability under extreme conditions.

Nextel finish: The alloy housing is finished in charcoal Nextel — a light-absorbing coating — to eliminate all possibility of reflection and glare.

Twin speakers: A fully adjustable volume control allows you to set the loudness of the audible warning from twin speakers. The warning tone is 1024 Hz, identical to that used for Morse code, for maximum clarity yet minimum annoyance.

All accessories included: Passport comes complete with everything needed for installation in any car, including coiled cord,

straight cord, windshield mount bracket, visor mount bracket, hook-and-loop fastener, lighter adapter, direct-wire power adapter, and comprehensive owners manual. A leather travel case is also included.

Satisfaction guaranteed: We engineered Passport, we build it, and we sell direct to you. We take full responsibility for your satisfaction. If you're not completely satisfied within 30 days, return Passport. We'll refund all your money, including postage.

Now... same-day shipping: Call us toll free with your questions. If you decide to buy, orders in by 3:00 pm eastern time Monday through Friday go out the same day by UPS, and we pay for shipping. Overnight delivery is guaranteed by Federal Express for $10 extra.

Passport's price reflects the exacting standards of our engineers... and of our customers.

* Based on lowest price offered for dash-mounted detectors in leading auto magazines.

Call Toll Free 800-543-1608
(Phone Mon-Fri 8am-11pm, Sat 9-5:30, Sun 10-5 EST)

RADAR · RECEIVER

$295 (OH res. add $16.23 tax)
Slightly higher in Canada

Cincinnati Microwave
Department 61817
One Microwave Plaza
Cincinnati, Ohio 45249-9502

© 1987 CMI

CUMMINS 444

NTC-400

CUMMINS
MAKES YOU

At Indy, and On the Interstate

■ In the 1987 Indy 500, Al Unser drove his Cummins-sponsored race car, with a Cummins turbocharger, into Victory Circle, and into the record books as a four-time winner of racing's Greatest Spectacle. ■ Experience, quality engineering and total commitment make the winning difference at Indy and on the Interstate. ■ Over 1 million Cummins-powered trucks are running today.

■ **Cummins has new Big Power NT engines at 365, 400 and 444 horsepower. When you buy these engines rated at 2100 RPM, you get free, 5 year/500,000 mile major component coverage.** Every day, every mile, you win with dependable, fuel efficient, high performance, high resale value engines. ■ Call your Cummins Distributor or Truck Dealer today. ■ Let Cummins make you a winner!

A WINNER

You can bet that Dick Simon is preparing his 1988 sponsorship presentation. (IMS-Lingenfelter)

Saturday, May 2
Partly Sunny and Muggy

With Chief Steward Tom Binford's 1:28 announcement, "Gentlemen, the track is now open for practice," Ludwig Heimrath, Jr. became the initial participant of May, 1987 and upheld the legacy of Dick Simon Racing (three first-outs in the last four years).

Simon hoped to accompany his rookie, but a start-up backfire from Heimrath's 23 Mackenzie Spirit '87 Lola caused chief mechanic Peter Roband to vault into Simon's path. The slight hesitation allowed Josele Garza's 55 Schaefer/Machinists Union March 87C (co-sponsored by another publicity hound: Phil Hedback of Bryant Heating and Cooling) to split the teammates.

"We had a little plan in mind and I guess it worked out for us," said Heimrath, a 30-year-old Canadian whose namesake father raced Indy Cars periodically between 1969 and 1971 but never made it to the Brickyard.

Four of Heimrath's classmates finished their rookie tests under the observation of veteran drivers and were cleared for unrestricted practice. Fabrizio Barbazza in the 12T (52) Arciero March 87C, Sammy Swindell in John Buttera's 59 Center Line/Machinists March 86C/Pontiac, and Randy Lewis in the 42 Western Digital/Oracle March 86C (renumbered after the ROP) all repeated their final phase, while Jeff Mac-Pherson finished the last two test segments with the 11 MacHoward Leasing/Galles March 87C/Honda. (Never before had four rookies passed their exams on Opening Day, but a successful ROP now cuts the May process down to a bare minimum.)

Top speed on a somewhat uncomfortable Saturday was the 210.772 by Michael Andretti's 18 Kraco/STP March 87C/Cosworth. After having a rear wing side plate fly off entering turn one at 2:24 (the piece sailed through the air like a frisbee and landed on the track), Andretti returned with his repaired mount to turn his quick trip at 4:51. Not a bad mark, but a little disappointing to "numbers freaks" who expected speeds to start at the private test level of 212-214 and go straight up.

"If there's going to be quicker times, I think you're going to need a good day with no wind and cool temperatures," opined the new father. At least Michael didn't have to worry about his father snatching away top-speed honors at the last minute like last year; Mario and crew stayed in the barn.

Pancho Carter's first hot lap of 208.429 in the 29 Hardee's March 87C stood for second best, while Arie Luyendyk's 71 Provimi/LivingWell 87C and Dick Simon's 22 Soundesign '87 Lola tied for third at 208.188 (but Arie did it first). Luyendyk also worked his identical 71T (43) backup 87C over 206, trailing Josele Garza's 207.7 on the speed list.

Michael Andretti had the 18T (38) Kraco 87C above 206 MPH, while defending champ Bobby Rahal "checked for leaks" in his 1 Budweiser '87 Lola at an easy 203.8 MPH. Fabrizio Barbazza hit 200.4 after polishing off his rookie test.

Rich Vogler had both of his Kentucky Fried Chicken/ValPak March/Buicks out for work; after mechanical problems arose in the 81 primary 87C model, Vogler turned to the 81T (51) year-old machine. Hemelgarn stablemate Scott Brayton debuted his strikingly-painted (blue and white with shocking pink on top) Amway/Autostyle March 87C/Cosworth. Scott's car wore 91T, but the ID "tub number" near the roll bar was the traditional Brayton family number of 37. (Perhaps Mr. Brayton was granted 91 against his wishes?)

Little Al Unser brought out the backup 30 Domino's Pizza March 87C for some leisurely laps (no "T" was found on the car, but the ID number gave its true identity). Former Can-Am champion Rick Miaskiewicz practiced in the ex-Machinists 97 Pizza Hut/RCV March 86C. Last of the 19 cars to make Saturday runs was the 15 Hon-

da-powered Team Valvoline/Galles March 87C of Geoff Brabham (sneaking out at 5:55).

The traditional Mayor's Breakfast morning festivities drew 3,200 revelers to the downtown Convention Center. Then the caravan of 750 vehicles headed to the Speedway for their yearly One Lap of Indy . . . Among those present at the postbreakfast IMS opening ceremonies were Indianapolis Mayor William Hudnut; '86 winner Bobby Rahal; Michael Howe, national merchandising manager of Chrysler; LeBaron pace car driver Carroll Shelby; and the lovely and zany Miss Pamela Jane Jones, 500 Festival queen from Speedway City and IUPUI . . . The 185 MPH speed limit was lifted after only 11 minutes of green time (at 1:39), even though the first few cars created such dust roostertails that they resembled landlocked hydroplanes . . . A total of 39 cars were housed at the track.

Sunday, May 3
Sunny and Mild; then Overcast, Windy, and Cool

A freakish, one-car crash that saw Pancho Carter's Hardee's March take flight, then slide upside down like a 1,500 pound toboggan overshadowed a strong speed showing from Mario Andretti.

Carter had just turned his day's best lap of 210.035 when (with but two minutes remaining before the 6:00 shutdown), the 29 orange and white 87C swapped ends in turn 3. As it was spinning, the car lifted through the short chute and into turn four; there it finally nudged the outer wall—still upside down. Carter sustained only a case of "race

Cousins Robbie and Al Unser, Jr. (Strauser)

18

track rheumatism;'' amazing, considering the large holes ground through his Simpson helmet caused by the roll bar's departure.

"I more or less have to blame it on the driver, probably running a little harder than what the conditions allow,'' explained the '85 Indy polesitter. "It could have been a combination of running in spoiled air behind cars, the gusty day, and getting out of the throttle a little bit. All of these together caused it to get sideways.''

Mario Andretti was about six seconds behind Carter and witnessed the wild ride. "It looked to me like Pancho was trying to compensate for the wind and he started spinning. When the air got underneath, it flipped him right over.'' (The wind was gusting out of the northeast—from the outside of turn three towards the infield.)

Carter was conscious through the entire escapade and said it "never really hit real hard upside down. It just picked itself up and sat itself down.'' His main objective became moving his head around enough to salvage his rapidly disappearing helmet. "The roll bar had to collapse pretty early because it was pushing me down in the cockpit the whole time. I saw sparks for a while, then I didn't see any, so I knew the roll bar was gone.''

Considering the potential for carnage, the car got off easy, too. "It wrinkled some of the front suspension A-arms, tore the rear wing up, and scraped the bodywork,'' said Carter. Then he suggested, "If you could run the car without a roll bar, the crew could repair it tonight and be ready to run tomorrow at 11:00.''

Mario Andretti overcame both the wind

Pancho Carter gets airborne and completely inverts, amazingly enough, without injury to himself and with comparatively little damage to the car. (sequence by Steve Weaver)

More mental calculations for the fastest man at the track. (IMS-Spargur)

and electrical problems that caused him to twice be towed in (in the space of 13 minutes) to post quick time of 213.371, fastest ever turned on Day 2. "I was quite surprised that we got the car working fairly solid even though we were getting moved around quite a bit,'' said Mario of the 5:43 jaunt. (He had his identical 5T (6) Hanna Car Wash '87 Lola/Chevy out for its premiere laps as well, topping 208 MPH.)

Bobby Rahal gave Lola the top two slots with his 212.464 in the Budweiser 1. Michael Andretti at 211.7 (in 18), Al Unser, Jr. at 211.5 (in 30T—which now had a "T''), and Arie Luyendyk's primary 71 (and Carter) at 210 flat led the March brigade. Dick Simon and Josele Garza topped 209 MPH, while first-timer Roberto Guerrero hit 209.1 in the 4T (60) STP/True Value March 87C.

The entire Roger Penske fleet was circulating by noon. Rick Mears progressed to 208.5 in the 8 Pennzoil Z-7 PC-16/Chevy. Danny Sullivan managed 205 MPH with his 3 Miller American PC-16. New addition Danny Ongais cleared 204 in the black with yellow trim 25 Panavision PC-16 (Penske's first-ever black Indy entry). Sullivan also made a brief, slow shakedown of the yellow 8T (28) Pennzoil updated version of last year's PC-15/Chevy.

Johnny Rutherford's 21 Vermont American (207.5), the 77 Scheid Tire/Superior Training/Metrolink 1411 (whew!) March 87C/Buick of Derek Daly (205.0), and Dennis Firestone in the 10 Raynor '87 Lola (203.8) all made respectable debuts. Marlboro/Patrick teammates Kevin Cogan (7) and Emerson Fittipaldi (20) practiced their much-too-similar Chevy-powered March 87C's at around 205 MPH.

Rocky Moran completed his rookie test in the 76 George Walther March 87C, still painted in Vermont American colors. (Weren't the Walther entries traditionally white, blue, or a combination of same?) Steve Chassey appeared with the 87 Laughrey/Medi-Span March 87C, sporting a paint scheme reminiscent of the 1986 Benetton Formula One team—white and bluish-green with splashes of other colors streaked about. Gary Bettenhausen brought out the year-old March 86C of Dick Hammond's Gohr Racing; the car had been erroneously registered and numbered as 56, so their primary '87 March would, curiously, have to wear the "T''.

In a rare pre-Monday (or Tuesday) appearance by an A.J. Foyt entry, Davy Jones exited the pits in his unmarked 44 black and coyote-red March 86C with an engine so disabled it sounded more like Foyt's V-6 Chevy than its actual Cosworth. After a few pitiful laps, it self-destructed and caught fire. A.J. himself conducted the bucket brigade and a mere 30 minutes after 44 had arrived, only a large wet spot remained.

A total of $76,370 was raised by the Arnold II project for the Special Olympics. More than 4,000 Special Olympians and their families joined numerous drivers in competition at the Speedway's Flag Lot on Sunday afternoon . . . The weather conditions were very Jekyll-and-Hydeish. At 11:00, there was hazy sunshine with mild temperatures and a slight breeze. By 5:00, the skies were completely overcast, the wind was near gale force and everyone was freezing . . . Arie Luyendyk's day ended prematurely when the fitting to the left side pod came loose and air ripped up the pod

cover . . . Thirty cars practiced today; 35 of the 51 machines on site had done so.

Monday, May 4
Sunny, Windy, and Mild

High winds kept speeds to a modest level, but that didn't keep Dennis Firestone from establishing himself as a dark horse for the pole.

Firestone's 211.565 (at 4:53) in the Raynor Motorsports Lola T8701 stood as Monday's top electric eye clocking until Roberto Guerrero tied that mark with a lap that was completed at least ten seconds after the 6:00 closing yellow light (a definite "no-no").

The Australian-born Firestone didn't complain about having to share the spotlight with a somewhat "illegal" lap. "Our last lap, if we hadn't run out of fuel, would've been 212 or 213," he stated. "I think it's making a statement that we're going to be a contender, and that's neat. We can all use that—some recognition for our efforts."

Guerrero was happy with his progress in 4T: "The wind was a bit of a factor all day today. I think that's what kept the speeds a little bit down from yesterday, but you have to work in all conditions."

Actually, Al Unser, Jr. posted a faster lap of 212.0 during the end-of-day flurry, but his best electric eye speed was an earlier 211.317 (this in the first-time out 30 Domino's 87C). "The car feels good," said Little Al, "and now we just have to nickel-and-dime it to get the most out of it." Mario Andretti was fourth fastest, but managed "only" 211 flat before retiring to the garage at 4:05.

The Buicks were beginning to flex their collective muscles. Derek Daly hit 209.2 and Rich Vogler was over 207 in his March 86C backup car. The other two squad members were making their initial appearances. Tom Sneva cruised at 201.9 with the 33 Skoal Bandit 87C of Mike Curb, while Jim Crawford took some semi-fast laps in the 2T (62) American Racing Series 86C. (With its bland, white with black lettering paint scheme, Crawford's ride reminded one of a giant bag of generic corn chips.)

More backup cars (if you can really call them that) got their first shots among the month-high 35 machines. Bobby Rahal's 1T (31) Budweiser Lola T8701 and Johnny Rutherford's Vermont American '87 March both cleared 205 MPH. Emerson Fittipaldi shook down the 20T (40) Marlboro spare 87C/Chevy, while Geoff Brabham took a few slow laps in his 15T (45) Team Valvo-

George Snider and A.J. Foyt: Close friends and teamates yet again. (IMS-Sellers)

The Marlboro hospitality food was prepared on several different days by accomplished chef Kevin Cogan. (IMS-L. Young)

line 87C/Honda (featuring a top-mounted telemetry device that looked like a weather vane).

Long-time "King watchers" had the A.J. Foyt routine down pat and the man didn't disappoint a soul. Out for its first trot at 5:20, by 5:30 the 14 Copenhagen/Gilmore '87 Lola was rolling back to the barn. No full laps were recorded on the more-black-than-coyote-red steed.

Foyt's two rookies cleared their first hurdles toward qualifying. Davy Jones passed his final test phase, while Stan Fox dusted off his refresher exam in his first day of work with the solid orange-red 41 Kerker Exhaust March 86C/Cosworth. Ludwig Heimrath, Jr. also completed his driver's test today.

Tony Bettenhausen made his first appearance of the month in his maroon and white 16 Call-Free March 86C, the same machine he qualified for the last year's race (then leased to Provimi for the balance of the season). Older brother Gary hit 203 in the debut performance for the "pseudo-backup" 56T (65) Genesee Beer March 87C. Randy Lewis began familiarizing himself with the brand-new, blue and white 24 Leader Cards March 87C (Oracle was the only sponsor name displayed so far).

The environment played havoc with the Penske team. Rick Mears dropped to 202

MPH, while Danny Ongais struggled at 197 and Danny Sullivan could muster only a lowly 194. "We're just trying to learn what it wants and doesn't want," explained Mears. "It's the first time we've run here with [the PC-16] and the wind's really gusty today, so it's making it a little more difficult to tell what the [chassis] changes do—why they're better or worse, or whatever."

The 14th annual Art Pollard Memorial Picnic was conducted in the infield tent area in conjunction with the Larue D. Carter Memorial Hospital Youth Service . . . It didn't take long before Tom Sneva's 33 was wearing a much smaller rear wing than it started the day with . . . Ludwig Heimrath's 23 lost an engine late in the afternoon.

Tuesday, May 5
Partly Sunny and Mild

Mario Andretti: 218.204 MPH; fastest lap in IMS history. Dennis Firestone: crash at 5:58. Ex-pole candidate.

Bobby Rahal's 1:17 run of 213.017 stood as top time until Andretti began his onslaught. Leading off with a 213.5 at 1:55, Mario jumped to 216.0 and 216.710 ten minutes later, then lowered the boom at 2:48. Three consecutive laps caught on the

stopwatch at 216.9, 218.9 (his crew had him at 219.2), and 218.3 put him into no-man's land, although the further up-track electric eye only received the aforementioned 218.204 (41.245 seconds). For an encore, he ripped off laps of 218.101 and 217.9 at 5:37. His straightaway speed was 229 MPH on the best 218, but then hit 230 on the later, "slower" lap.

While other hot dogs were tippy-toeing into turn one, the 5 Hanna Car Wash Lola/Chevy screamed in like Godzilla rising from the sea. With the addition of team manager Tyler Alexander (back from the defunct Beatrice F1 effort) and engineer Adrian Newey (designer of the all-conquering '86 March) to the Newman/Haas roster, it seemed that Mario was blessed with the Total Package.

"There are still a couple of things to try yet," said the new (unofficial) speed king. "It's still early and I don't think we're at the end of our rope. That doesn't mean we're going to improve it, but we're certainly going to try." Crediting "ideal" weather conditions, he admitted, "It was just one of those days where the breeze was light and it was fairly cool, a bit of a hazy overcast—just what we really need to run quick."

When asked if the 220 barrier could fall, Andretti chuckled and said under the right circumstances it was, "doable, of course. I

The best way to get information out of a spark plug is to torture it.

Don Garlits, Garlits/Dodge Top Fuel Dragster

Rod Hall, Dodge Ram Truck

Bobby Rahal, March/Cosworth

Welcome to every spark plug's worst nightmare.

The racing machines you're looking at force Champion spark plugs to operate in temperatures exceeding 4000 degrees Fahrenheit—under pressures as high as 1800 pounds per square inch. Torture that, in some cases, goes on for days.

And like people, spark plugs reveal a lot under stress.

So our ruthless approach to testing has led to numerous improvements in the spark plugs we build for your car: stronger ceramic, tougher electrodes, and superior resistance to heat and pressure, to name a few.

Which is why, at Champion, we believe you have to punish a spark plug to make it good.

MORE PEOPLE RELY ON CHAMPION THAN ANY OTHER SPARK PLUG IN THE WORLD

© 1987 CHAMPION SPARK PLUG CO.

Bobby Rahal ponders the radials. (IMS-D. Young)

226 MPH straightaway shots to post 210.3 marks in their respective Buicks. Crawford's version was the first-time-out 2 American Racing Series 86C. Kevin Cogan topped 210, while Johnny Rutherford's 209.7 just missed. Rick Mears improved to 209.4 before engine problems beset his PC-16/Chevy, which was now sporting winglets mounted just behind the front wheels. Tom Sneva hit 207.6 in the Skoal Buick, but he was completing very few of his practice laps, to the consternation of some.

Roberto Guerrero debuted the 4 STP/True Value 87C at 203 MPH. Guerrero's 4 and Crawford's 2 made a total of 49 cars out for the month . . . Luyendyk's 71 created the day's kookiest yellow light. At 3:06, he rolled through the pits with the wing cover draped across the airfoil. He happened to glance in the mirrors and saw it flapping in the breeze, so he stopped just past the pit exit and waited patiently for the fire crew to figure out what was wrong. They finally spotted the tarp, removed it, and Arie took off . . . 33 cars practiced today . . . Johnny Parsons was reportedly set for the Rich Vogler backup car.

Wednesday, May 6
Sunny and Warm

Strange days at the Brickyard. Four different drivers experienced disturbingly similar war stories today. In order of severity, Kevin Cogan, Scott Brayton, Derek Daly, and Dick Ferguson had their cars inexplicably wander into the danger zone and strike the fence.

At 1:22, Cogan's Marlboro 7 broadsided the first-turn cement after a lap of 203 MPH. Suggesting there may have been fluid on the track, Cogan described the incident: "Steve Chassey went through just before me; [he was] warming up, running slowly, and he did exactly the same thing I did. I just went into the corner . . . turned it, and it just went straight. Basically I was off the throttle the whole way, waiting for the front to take a bite, and it never did." The entire right side of the machine was damaged, but not irreparably so.

Brayton folded the right front wheel and suspension of 91T back to the side pod after tagging the wall while exiting turn four at 4:39. "The car had a push, evidently a little more than I thought," explained Brayton, whose previous lap was a mere 200 flat.

Daly's 5:15 slam-dance against the south chute concrete cracked the right front wheel of his 77 Buick. "That was the only change we made in the pits and not in the garage," he said. "It was my first time around and I got out in the gray stuff."

Approximately three minutes before Daly's problem, Dick Ferguson, in his first day out with the 19 Los Angeles Dry Wall March 85C/Cosworth, got high in the north chute and whitewalled the right side rubber.

A serene Danny Ongais obliges with an autograph. (Ackerman)

He had completed half of his required 20-lap refresher course before the incident halted his progress.

Cogan, Brayton, and Daly were all driving '87 Marches, and the mating of the harder, stiffer Goodyear radial tires to Robin Herd's latest creation (in company with warmer track conditions from spring testing) had become a tenuous proposition for most March teams. Notable exceptions continued to be Roberto Guerrero and Michael Andretti (both hit identical personal-bests of 212.816), and Arie Luyendyk (211.9). The March majority, however, were mired in quicksand: Rutherford, 208.4; Al, Jr., 207.4; Garza, 207.1; Daly, 206.3; Brayton, 204.1; etc.

Once again Mario Andretti paced the pack (a massive 42 cars), but his uninspiring 216.502 was closely trailed by a thought-to-be-obsolete 1986 March. Jim Crawford ended the day's activity with a resounding 215.982 in the 2 ARS 86C/Buick affectionately named "Rosie," for her second-hand status.

"We were lost at 5 o'clock, stuck at 210," exclaimed the gleeful Scotsman. "In desperation, at five till 6, we gave it a big 'tweak' in the pit lane and BANG! it just came right instantly—5 MPH quicker!" Crawford's overall-best gunshot of 231 MPH sounded even more impressive when it was learned he was running one inch shy of allowable turbo boost.

Bobby Rahal made giant strides to 215.879 and advised that, "We learned some good things about the car that will enable us to go quicker." Dick Simon con-

don't know what the 'limit' really is, what that means here, actually. We'll just see what we can get out of the car and that will be the limit for that car." The official track record, by the way, was 217.581 set in 1986 by Rick Mears.

Dennis Firestone's dream of winning the pole position ended against the turn four concrete. After a lap of 212.929, Firestone got too low in four and lost control, doing a 3/4 spin and making hard outer wall contact with the front end. He suffered broken bones in his left foot and a minor fracture of his right leg, but there was a possibility that he could return for the second weekend of time trials. The Raynor Lola, however, was a washout. The accident occurred at exactly the same time as Pancho Carter's odd numbered-day flip. Deja vu, anyone?

Bobby Rahal was satisfied with his 213 lap, since it was run prior to a track-cooling temporary cloud cover. "I think we're getting a handle on it," he commented. "Our best lap got spoiled by traffic, but I think we made some changes that improved it. Our straight line speed is up, and that's really going to help us out."

Arie Luyendyk's 212.665 led the March bunch, and he wasn't overly concerned with Andretti's amazing feats; "If somebody with a March/Cosworth was running 218, then we would be worried; but so far we're the quickest March/Cosworth out there." Dick Simon's 212.164 gave Lola four of the top five spots. Michael Andretti had the 18T Kraco 87C up to 211 flat. A.J. Foyt hit 210.5 in his first day of serious running.

Jim Crawford and Derek Daly both used

Team Up With A Winner!

It's no secret that success on the track is tied to superior effort, a commitment to excellence and an insistance on quality at every point. It's no different on the job or around the home. Whether craftsman or do-it-yourselfer, your finished work reflects both your effort and your access to the right tools for the job. You can get results you'll take pride in when you use long-life tools from Vermont American. Every tool, from saw blade to storage box is precision made to last longer, make your work go easier and look better.

Take a tip from Johnny Rutherford and team up with a winner. Johnny wouldn't settle for less than Vermont American, why should you?

Vermont American Tool Company, P.O. Box 340, Lincolnton, NC 28093-0340, (704) 735-7464

Vermont American®

When the job really counts™

The Tom Sneva team was faced with a myriad of problems. (Walker)

tinued his steady improvement with a 212.7 lap. Rick Mears worked the PC-16 to an encouraging 211.4 (with only a 221 gun speed), but his inability to ascertain the feedback from the chassis was starting to spook him.

Seven cars made first appearances, bringing the monthly total to 56. Raynor Motorsports chief mechanic Phil Krueger shook down the team's 10T (90) '86 Lola backup while a replacement '87 chassis was en route from Carl Haas's shop in Chicago. They hoped to have Dennis Firestone back in the saddle by next Wednesday.

Tom Sneva aired out the 33T (73) Cosworth-powered Skoal March 87C at 205 MPH. Semi-stablemate Ed Pimm warmed up the blue, white, and red 98 March 86C/Cosworth owned by Mike Curb, but operated by RPM Motorsports. Venerable

George "Ziggy" Snider made a rare first-week debut with A.J. Foyt's 84 Calumet Farms March 86C, powered by the potent but temperamental turbo V-6 Chevrolet stock-block.

Pancho Carter reappeared with a brand-new Hardee's March 87C; the 29T (95) carried a much more strongly braced roll bar, just in case. Fabrizio Barbazza sorted out the "primary" 12 Arciero Winery 87C. (Ferguson's elderly 85C was the seventh machine.)

A.J. Foyt cooked a motor big-time at 4:58 . . . Roberto Guerrero lost an engine just 15 minutes after the track opened, but was back out by 2:35 . . . Rookies Stan Fox (208) and Ludwig Heimrath (206) set the neophyte pace . . . Tom Bigelow was rumored to be in line to replace Randy Lewis in the Leader Cards 87C . . . The Cham-

pionship Drivers Association voted unanimously Wednesday night to submit to voluntary drug testing.

Thursday, May 7
Partly Sunny, Breezy, Mild

Mario Andretti did his thing, raising the unofficial speed mark another notch to 218.234. Danny Ongais, unfortunately, did his thing as well, trashing out the 25 Panavision PC-16 in a large way and at least cracking the door for Al Unser to perhaps land a ride.

On the first hot lap of his third practice session (at 11:44), Ongais augered into the fourth turn wall. Was it really a CV joint failure, or the dreaded Radial Effect? The black Penske climbed the wall for 80 feet, then slid to the inner barrier, showering debris, and came to rest at the head of the pits. Ongais suffered a concussion, jeopardizing his chances for driving any backup car.

Immediate speculation turned to Al Unser as a substitute driver. A logical choice, but why take on a replacement when you're having so many problems getting Mears and Sullivan up to speed?

Rocky Moran wiped out the 76 George N. Walther 86C in a "nine minute early" crash. (Remembering the pattern established by Carter and Firestone, it was due at 5:58, but Moran hit at 5:49.) He got high exiting turn two and glanced off the wall with the right rear. The car gyrated down into the inside wall, causing major damage to the rear section, but rookie Moran escaped with minor knee abrasions.

So much for the accidents. Mario Andretti unleashed another patented speed blitz; 218.234 at 1:45 (your writer's stopwatch caught him at 41.08/219.0 at the end of the front stretch), then a 217.812 at 5:45 (on old tires) for good measure. "This is a totally different setup than what we had the other day," said Mario. "It's all a guessing game, obviously."

Bobby Rahal inched forward to 216.502 in his 1T Budweiser Lola. It was a short day for the Truesports team; they started at 11:08 with 1T, ran it until the 216 lap at 11:34, switched to the twin Lola 1 from 12:38 to 1:10, hit 211.7 and quit for the duration.

The March elite continued to chip away at the apparent advantage enjoyed by Lola. Arie Luyendyk worked with 71 until 3:47, topping out at 212.7, then turned to the "fresher-engined" 71T Provimi 87C and ripped off a stout 214.899 minutes before Moran's crash prematurely closed the track. Roberto Guerrero followed suit with a 214.489 in his "comfortable" Granatelli 87C, while Michael Andretti's Kraco version moved up to 213.725.

Dick Simon remained the third fastest active Lola driver with his 214.336 charge

This 1929 Model "A" Sedan Delivery street rod drew many admiring glances from those who passed the Snap-On tool headquarters. (Strauser)

There wasn't much left of the Ongais PC-16. (IMS-B. Scott)

and protege Ludwig Heimrath became the quickest rookie with his 209.2 clocking. Jim Crawford cruised at 210.9; Emerson Fittipaldi and Johnny Rutherford topped 209; Derek Daly, Tom Sneva, Al Unser, Jr., and rookie Davy Jones were all in the 208 MPH bracket.

Roger Penske's great PC-16 commitment was giving way to the known quantity called a March 86C. After a late afternoon do-or-die session in which Rick Mears could only muster 206.1, the call went out to the Reading, Pennsylvania shop—get last year's Marches ready for shipment. Problem was, they were scattered around various parts of the planet, serving as show cars.

Rick Miaskiewicz passed his refresher test in the 97 Pizza Hut/RCV 86C . . . Of the 41 cars on the track, only Phil Krueger's 10T did not surpass 200 MPH . . . Kevin Cogan's 7 was back on track (at 4:50) after his Wednesday crash and found 203 in his brief appearance . . . Randy Lewis and his 24 caused three separate tow-ins (12:36, 2:26, and 4:24) . . . A.J. Foyt had another late mechanical failure; he had slowed down for numerous laps, gesturing at his crew, before a wheel bearing gave out entering turn one, creating his second smokescreen in 24 hours . . . Tom Sneva was trying out some wacky "shark fins" mounted in front of the rear wheels atop the side pods (visually similar to the 1986 Eagle appendages) . . . The Hondas were finally making progress; Jeff MacPherson was over 207 and Geoff Brabham hit 206 . . . While there was some wind today, it stayed consistent from the northeast and didn't gust.

Friday, May 8
Sunny, Breezy, Warm

The scenario remained constant on the eve of time trials. Fast guys were still fast, everyone else was still scratching their collective heads, and more equipment got mangled.

Tom Sneva left for work at 11:18; by 11:22 his 33 Skoal 87C/Buick had been turned into shredded wheat. "We ran through (turns) 2, 3, and 4 pretty hard and the car felt good," said the 3-time Indy pole winner. "Then we got down into one and there was no indication, no warning. The car just never even bothered to try to turn, it just went straight in." The impact knocked off both right side wheels, then the Bandit rolled another 1160 feet across the short chute and bumped the second turn wall as well, but Tom was back out in the Cosworth-powered 33T before 3 o'clock.

Mario Andretti took top time for the fourth day in a row; his 216.242 came at a very warm 2:28. "It was really slippery today and there was an incredible amount of interruptions," lamented Andretti. (There were 20 yellows in all for a total of 3 hours and 33 minutes!) "It was tough to get any consistency and the traffic was heavy too." Andretti also overcame a small oil fire at 3:56 to top 215 MPH during "Happy Hour".

Virtually the same challengers lined up behind the Newman/Haas Lola. Bobby Rahal's 215.568 had him feeling "very much in the hunt" for pole position. Arie

Luyendyk's best lap of 214.951 could have been over 216, he felt, if the car hadn't "pushed so badly coming out of four."

Jim Crawford ran back-to-back laps above 214 (best of 214.438) and predicted, "With the changes we're making tonight we'll either guess right and be up around 218-219, or we'll be wrong and down to around 210." Dick Simon squeaked in a 213.9 lap just before practice ended, while Michael Andretti dropped off slightly to 212.2 MPH. Emerson Fittipaldi and Al Unser, Jr. were the only other runners above 210.

Rick Mears stamped himself as a long-shot front row contender with the just-arrived 8TT (83) Pennzoil Z-7 March 86C/Chevrolet; he rolled onto the track at 3:49 and by 4:54 had hit 209.594. "It was (Roger Penske's) idea," stated the 2-time Indy champ. "He wants to win more than anything. We haven't found the right combination with what we have (PC16), so we decided to see what we can do with something different."

Dick Ferguson felt something break in his 19 Los Angeles Dry Wall 85C as he exited turn four at 3:01. He did one complete spin and pounded the inside wall, wiping out the entire left side of the machine. The car continued into the pit lane, bouncing onto the grassy strip and knocking one of the PA horns onto the main straightaway. Thankfully, no one was injured in the escapade. (Ferguson completed his refresher test earlier today.) More bad news for the Raynor team. Phil Krueger got a little high in the south short chute at 5:21 and tapped the wall with the right rear. The 10T '86 Lola made a violent move into the infield grass, but Krueger kept it away from any solid matter and brought the car home with minor suspension damage.

Gary Bettenhausen pulled a "Danny Sullivan" as he motored through turn four at 2:06. The 56T Genesee 87C swapped ends, but the wily veteran avoided the hard stuff. "It gave no warning whatsoever," said Gary. (Sound familiar?) "The tires are good to a certain point and then they give up—there's no happy median."

Sammy Swindell had the engine cover bodywork to his 59 Buttera 86C blow off as he negotiated the south end at 4:39. Swindell held the car straight even though he felt the rear wheels briefly leave the ground.

Roberto Guerrero was plagued with engine smoke and could only manage 206.9 between black flags . . . Scott Brayton was back out after sitting out Thursday waiting for suspension pieces for his Amway/Autostyle 87C . . . 42 cars practiced today . . . During the yellow for Ferguson's crash, a transformer located on Georgetown Road (just across from the pit exit) blew up, knocking out power to various parts of the Speedway for over 5 hours . . . Davy Jones had a famous face on hand to draw his qualifying spot—NASCAR star (and 1980

We gave Mobil 1 and premium 10W-30 oil a stress t

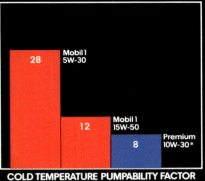

COLD TEMPERATURE PUMPABILITY FACTOR

Mobil 1 5W-30: 28
Mobil 1 15W-50: 12
Premium 10W-30*: 8

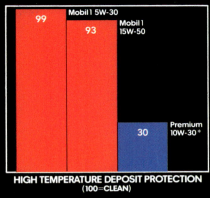

HIGH TEMPERATURE DEPOSIT PROTECTION
(100=CLEAN)

Mobil 1 5W-30: 99
Mobil 1 15W-50: 93
Premium 10W-30*: 30

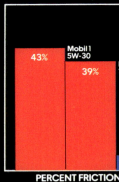

PERCENT FRICTION

Mobil 1 5W-30: 43%
Mobil 1 15W-50: 39%

The results weren't surprisin

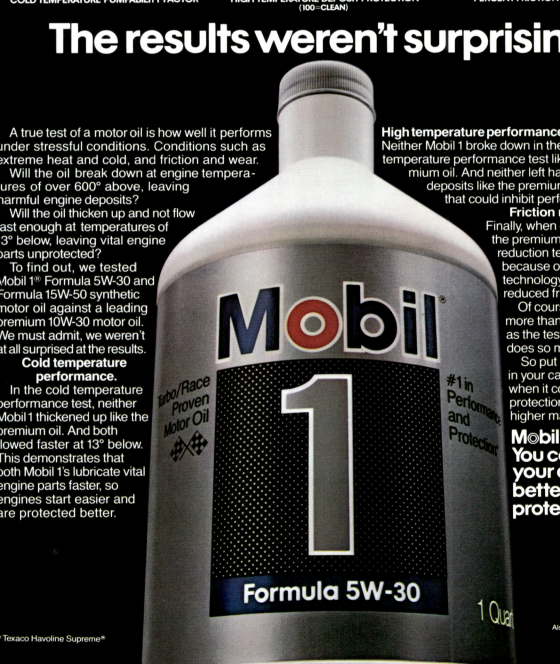

A true test of a motor oil is how well it performs under stressful conditions. Conditions such as extreme heat and cold, and friction and wear.

Will the oil break down at engine temperatures of over 600° above, leaving harmful engine deposits?

Will the oil thicken up and not flow fast enough at temperatures of 13° below, leaving vital engine parts unprotected?

To find out, we tested Mobil 1® Formula 5W-30 and Formula 15W-50 synthetic motor oil against a leading premium 10W-30 motor oil. We must admit, we weren't at all surprised at the results.

Cold temperature performance.

In the cold temperature performance test, neither Mobil 1 thickened up like the premium oil. And both flowed faster at 13° below. This demonstrates that both Mobil 1's lubricate vital engine parts faster, so engines start easier and are protected better.

High temperature performance
Neither Mobil 1 broke down in the temperature performance test lik mium oil. And neither left ha deposits like the premium that could inhibit perf

Friction r
Finally, when the premium reduction te because of technology reduced fri

Of cours more than as the test does so m

So put in your ca when it co protection higher ma

Mobil
You c
your
bette
prote

Turbo/Race Proven Motor Oil

#1 in Performance and Protection

Formula 5W-30

1 Quart

Tom Sneva slams turn one's wall HARD. (Margison)

Indy Rookie of the year) Tim Richmond . . . Danny Ongais and Dennis Firestone were released from Methodist Hospital.

Fifty-one cars drew for a time trial position. Michael Andretti claimed the 1 spot, but father Mario got stuck with 38. (There would be many in-between, however, that would no doubt pass on their attempt.) Mario knew full well that the pole wasn't a lock: "I've never felt that I've had this thing handled and I'm always concerned until the job is done." As for the possibility of a new track record being set, he said it was entirely dictated by the weather. "If the sun shines and there's no cloud cover, it's really tough because the groove draws the heat and gets really greasy. I'd take overcast and cool before I'd take 40 horsepower at this place."

Bobby Rahal drew 8 and 26; Jim Crawford got 12 and 36; Arie Luyendyk found 11 and 20; Roberto Guerrero pulled 42 and 44; Dick Simon got 14; Rick Mears's 86C drew 6; A.J. Foyt came in at 49—next to last.

Saturday, May 9
Sunny, Windy, Warm

Would someone please tell the local weatherpersons that an "ideal day" for qualifying is not bright sunshine, high winds, and oppressive heat? For the first time since 1982, the one and four-lap track records would remain intact.

Even the morning practice session, which held the promise of the much-discussed 220 MPH lap, was a big letdown. Bobby Rahal's 216.609 was his best speed of the month, but it was nearly 2 MPH behind the pace established by Mario Andretti. The

best that Mario could manage was a 215.879, the same speed turned by an improving Arie Luyendyk.

Rick Mears was the session's biggest breakthrough, working the Pennzoil March 86C/Chevy to 213.371. Michael Andretti and Dick Simon both hit 212.014, while Pancho Carter topped 210 MPH for the first time.

At 9:25, Stan Fox lost control of the 41 Kerker/Foyt 86C in turn 3, sliding into the north chute infield where he grazed the guard rail. Fox ended up in the gray stuff of turn 4, uninjured, with light damage to the car.

Kevin Cogan, Johnny Rutherford (in his

primary 21), and Randy Lewis all suffered blown engines. Roberto Guerrero not only lunched the motor in his primary 4, but the rear bodywork briefly caught fire as well. A total of 35 cars made morning practice runs.

After the traditional Pole Day ceremonies concluded—this year honoring the 50th anniversary of the end of the riding mechanics—the 18 Kraco/STP March 87C/Cosworth of Michael Andretti answered the 11:00 opening of time trials.

Andretti's first official lap was an adequate 211.263, but the next trip dropped to 209.074. Then he "almost lost it on the third lap" and rather than battle the loose handling traits, he pulled into the pits.

Ludwig Heimrath's Lola flunked tech inspection (rear wing too high) so George Snider became the second attemptee. Ziggy made two timed trips of 204.188 and 205.328 in the 84 Calumet Farm March 86C/V-6 Chevy before he likewise slowed and came in.

Through the luck of a coin flip with teammate Danny Sullivan, Rick Mears won the chance to qualify the first of Roger Penske's March 86C chassis to arrive at the Speedway. A mere 20 hours after the car first practiced, oval-meister Mears emphatically justified the banzai effort with an impressive 211.469 average in the 8TT (83) Pennzoil Z-7 Chevy.

"The track's lost a little bit of grip and our valve was a little bit low on boost from what we had this morning," said Mears. "Overall I'm happy with the run . . . It's the hardest struggle I've had in some time." He almost ran out of fuel on the last lap: "It came off of turn 4 and stumbled, and I thought, 'Boy, I hope I've got enough left to get to the finish line,' and I did."

Next out (at 11:31—the lethargy was starting to set in) came Bobby Rahal and the 1T (31) Budweiser/Truesports/Spirit of

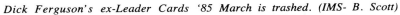

Dick Ferguson's ex-Leader Cards '85 March is trashed. (IMS- B. Scott)

30

These are the wrenches that move Mears.

Mears and the Penske mechanics. Teamed with *Snap-on* tools for championship-quality performance, race after race. On CART ovals or road courses coast to coast.

The perfect match. *Snap-on* quality and performance. And the Mears magic. Because the shortest route to winning, in the business of competition or the competition of business, is all-out performance. And *Snap-on* outperforms all the others.

With the most complete line of standard and special tools in the world. Backed by a sales and service organization second to none.

Take it from the wrenches that do their best work on the weekends. On the hot, yellow cars you're most likely to find in victory lane. They'll tell you that *Snap-on* delivers. Snap-on Tools Corporation, Kenosha, Wisconsin 53141-1410

...there is a difference

Snap-on

These instructions are pretty explicit. (IMS-D. Young)

Columbus Lola T8701/Cosworth. Avoiding a beach ball that had somehow wandered to the inner edge of the turn 4 groove, the defending champ led off with a strong 214.133, followed with laps of 213.6 and 213.0, and finished up at 212.4 for an average of 213.316.

"The car handled pretty consistently all the way through," said Rahal. "It has certainly gotten hotter and windier . . . We just sort of hung on . . . We're in and now we'll get ready for the race." And the beach ball? "I'm thinking, 'Oh, God, just don't blow across the track now.' Luckily, it stayed there."

Sandwiched between the failure of Jim Crawford's 2T and Dick Simon's 22 to pass tech inspection (their rear wings were approximately a quarter of an inch too high) came Pancho Carter's aborted attempt in the 29T (95) Hardee's March 87C/Cosworth. The Machinists Union braintrust had set 208 MPH as their bottom line, so Carter's laps of 206.167 and 207.354 were wiped off.

Gary Bettenhausen posted a first lap of 205.095 in the 56T (65) Genesee Beer Wagon March 87C/Cosworth. He then "had to get completely out of the throttle to keep from tagging the wall coming off (turn 2)" and feeling the second lap falling to an unacceptable level, he shut down.

Electrical problems that originated in morning practice cropped up again in Scott Brayton's 91T (37) Amway/Autostyle March 87C/Cosworth. Following his two warmup laps, the car "didn't seem quite right" so Brayton wisely didn't waste an attempt. Thus ended the first hour with a grand total of two qualifiers.

At 12:13, Arie Luyendyk sallied forth with the 71 LivingWell/Provimi Veal/WTTV March 87C/Cosworth. He was hoping to duplicate his 215.8 of earlier today, but after a warmup lap of only 207.1, the Big Push took him extremely close to the south chute wall (and perhaps touching it). Luyendyk came in without completing lap one and complained, "The wind spoiled it. Sand and dust were flying everywhere, which made it very unpleasant."

Rookie Jeff MacPherson came in after a weak lap of 196.451 in the 11 Team MacPherson/Galles March 87C/Honda.

Danny Sullivan made a curious run in his 3 Miller American Penske PC-16/Chevy.

He turned in a consistent, but disappointing series of 206.167, 206.171, and 206.488 and fully intended to complete the run when the crew waved him off. "Our last lap we timed at 204.9, and that would have brought us below our yardstick of a 206 average," explained Sullivan. The plan seemed to be: (a) get the PC-16 in the show, then (b) worry about the soon-to-arrive '86 March next week.

Due to cars pulling out of line during the inspection process (Emerson Fittipaldi and Rick Miaskiewicz left by choice, while the side pod of Ed Pimm's 98 was a tad too low), the track sat vacant for over 30 minutes (yawn). But since the next man out became Mario Andretti, at least it was worth the wait.

Damn the conditions, full speed ahead! First lap for the 5 Hanna Auto Wash/Newman/Haas Lola T8701/Chevy—215.874, over 2 MPH faster than Rahal's average of 215.390 MPH. Maybe it wasn't a new record, but considering our "ideal day" it was quite a feat.

Take it away, Mario! "I felt a lot of push and wind during laps 1 and 2. I had a good one and a half laps and then lost efficiency—after that it was 'skate city'. It's so slippery out there and the car was just sliding too much on both ends, really. I tried to play with the throttle, but the speed kept going down . . . This pole is important; it's a big moment, not only for me but for the team. I have a fantastic group behind me that gives me all the confidence and encouragement when I need it and they prepared the car superbly."

Little did anyone realize that not only had the entire front row been established by 1:15, but it had been accomplished with only three total qualifiers. "Leave now and avoid the rush!"

Roberto Guerrero took an exploratory round with the 4T (60) STP/True Value

This is the measurement used to determine "stagger." (Whitlow)

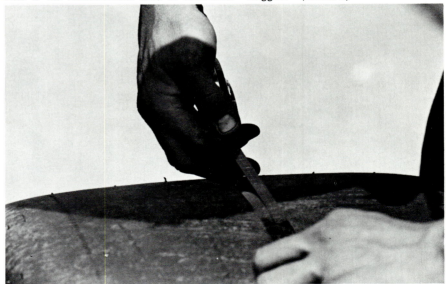

March 87C/Cosworth to "learn about the track conditions." He made one lap at 197.637 and came in. The car hadn't practiced since Monday.

Three-time winner Johnny Rutherford qualified for his 23rd Indy lineup, lending credence to his theory that "old age and treachery will win out over youth and inexperience every time." His average speed in Alex Morales's 21T Vermont American March 87C/Cosworth was a decent 208.296. "The third lap was my worst [206.8]," said Lone Star J.R. "I charged into turn 2 and the combination of the bump and the wind took my front end towards the suites. It's the nature of the March chassis that you have to have as much cushion as possible. When you go into turn 2 it's fine, but halfway through it gives up and takes off into the wall."

Josele Garza was fortunate to bring his 55 Bryant Heating and Cooling/Schaefer/ Machinists March 87C/Cosworth back to the pits unbent. He took the green flag (after a warmup lap of 199.1), then got extremely squirrely in turn 3. Somehow, Garza kept the car pointed in the proper direction and immediately headed for the safety of the pits.

Another 32 minute-long "seventh-inning stretch" (had we really only qualified 4 cars in 3 hours and 13 minutes?) resulted from continued jumbling in the tech line. Fabrizio Barbazza, Ludwig Heimrath (again), and Roberto Guerrero's 4 all dropped out of sequence for various reasons.

Finally, at 2:13, came the successful attempt by the world's oldest active Indy Car pilot, 53-year-old Dick Simon, and his 22 Soundesign Stereo '87 Lola/Cosworth. The super salesman once again reset the IMS age record with his 209.960 average arithmetic. The first two laps were 211.8 and 210.7, but his decision to utilize worn tires contributed to a 207.7 final lap. "The

This road sign from a small town near Houston mysteriously found its way into Tony Bettenhausen's garage. Reason? The procuror admires unsuccessful 1958 Floyd Patterson heavyweight title challenger Roy Harris, who was (and still is) from that locale. (Ackerman)

Several of the major sponsors had welcome retreats for hot and dusty days. (IMS-Duffy)

old set (of tires) had the best stagger, but they had 150 miles on them," Simon said. "I might have been a little better off with a new set. The oil (on the track) was more of a factor than the wind. When you've run around here as many years as I have, you're used to running in the wind."

Jim Crawford ended the qualifying period with a hairy 3-lap jaunt in the 2T (62) American Racing Series March 86C/Buick. After circuits of 206.825, 206.806, and 205.231 (reportedly grazing the wall on lap 3), the ARS crew waved off the run. They would soon come to regret their maneuver . . .

Open practice commenced at 2:49 and 23 cars made desperation runs before the 3:40 termination. Guerrero and Crawford both cranked out big numbers that were unseen by the electric eye (late lunch break, guys?). Guerrero hit 211.1, Crawford, 210.5. Carter topped 205 MPH, while Luyendyk, Fittipaldi, and Michael Andretti were all above 204. Sneva, Pimm, and Gary Bettenhausen cleared 202; Cogan, Brabham, and Brayton were around 201; Al, Jr. was stuck at 200. Johnny Parsons made an auspicious debut with the 81T KFC/Hemelgarn March 86C/ Buick; at 3:05 (and after a single hot lap of 197), he scraped the turn 2 outer wall, inflicting minor suspension and bodywork damage.

Imbued with confidence after his recent 210+ lap, Jim Crawford was eager to get the job done on his second qualifying attempt with 2T. He left the pits at 3:54; two minutes later, he was trapped in his mangled March, writhing in pain from two shattered ankles and a fractured right shin bone.

Having just taken the green flag, Crawford screamed into turn 1 (various handheld radar guns clocked him anywhere from 234 to 238 MPH!) and had the rear end immediately come around. The car made one complete spin and plastered the outer wall nearly head on. Crawford was flown to Methodist Hospital via LifeLine helicopter;

he was operated on by Dr. Terry Trammell late Saturday afternoon.

Buick demanded a veteran, big-name driver to fill the now-available seat and the early line had Al Unser, Sr. and Gordon Johncock as the leading candidates, with Johnny Parsons another possibility.

Danny Sullivan took to the track at 4:26 as the ranks began to swell behind him. This time, Sully and crew accepted a pedestrian 205.288 average that made his 3 Miller PC-16 the slowest of the six qualifiers. "Right now, I'm just happy to be in the show," said the '85 Indy winner. "Now we have some options and we can go from here. The track was about the same, but the wind was much gustier than before. I caught a really bad gust going into turn 3 on my last lap (203.6)." Danny also added, "Seeing some of the other times doesn't make us look as silly."

Roberto Guerrero duplicated his personal Pole Day of 1986 schedule—blown engine early, afternoon garage area thrash, then qualify late. Guerrero's 4 STP/True Value March 87C/Cosworth strung together a strong combination of 212.0, 211.1, 210.0, and 209.5 for a 210.680 average. "We'll take it, considering the circumstances. You have to guess a little bit on the settings for the car, and with the wind and the track conditions . . . it wasn't as perfect as I would have liked it. It wasn't the most comfortable run I've ever had."

Rich Vogler made one very slow warmup lap before parking the 81 Kentucky Fried Chicken/LivingWell/Val-Pak March 87C/ Buick on the backstretch. Faulty electrics were blamed for the stoppage, but skeptics noticed Vogler's 199 MPH afternoon practice speeds and suggested it was really a ploy to give Hemelgarn teammate Arie Luyendyk a little cooler track surface.

Luyendyk's great expectations were quelled by a rotten third lap in his 71 Provimi/LivingWell 87C. After two almost-identical clockings of 210.0, he "went into turn 2 and it seemed like somebody picked up the front end of the car and it just washed out. I had to really back out of it. I had the steering wheel turned to the left and I went straight to the wall and I just didn't touch it.'' The 204.6 hurt, but a final lap of 208.7 salvaged a 208.337 average. "We just didn't have a lot of luck today," stated Luyendyk.

A disconsolate Michael Andretti could muster only a 206.129 average in the recalcitrant 18 Kraco 87C. "As it looks, we should have taken [our early run]," said Andretti. "As luck would have it, the weather got really bad . . . windy and really hot and slippery. The car all of a sudden developed an understeer. Even with new tires it pushed right from the start. This is the slowest I've ever qualified here—I ran 207 my rookie year (1984).''

The clock read 5:07. The time had arrived for the King to do his thing. A.J. Foyt was shooting for his 30th consecutive Indy 500 starting spot. First lap for the 14 Copenhagen/Gilmore '87 Lola/Cosworth— 212.259! The crowd goes bonkers! Now, could Super Tex hold on for three more laps? With his luck the last four years, it was a legitimate concern. Hey, no problem— 210.8, 210.5, 210.0 and Mr. Foyt was back up front where he belonged.

Thirty years, A.J.? "I'm just glad I've been able to be here to see all the technology and improvements of the cars and tires, to go through all the different stages of automobile racing and still be part of it. Thirty years ago when I qualified, I was wearing a Dean Van Lines t-shirt.'' He said he experienced an "awful lot of trouble in [turn] 2. I tried to hold it there, and I figured I'd rather say I did start 30 races instead of sitting in my suite on turn 2, 'cause I was getting pretty close to gettin' up there a couple of times!''

Foyt was now stationed in the fourth starting position and it didn't take long for Carey Pittman of radio station WLSO in Spencer, Indiana to inform the free world of the "Texas Trilogy." In 1967, A.J. started 4th and won the race; ten years later, he won his 4th Indy 500 from—you guessed it— inside of the second row. Ouija boards, anyone?

Patrick Racing's backslide continued with the 5:18 ride of Emerson Fittipaldi and his 20 Marlboro March 87C/Chevy. Recall the team's performance in spring testing: 214 for Kevin Cogan and 211 for Fittipaldi. Today, Cogan was floundering at 203, while the two-time World Driving Champion from Brazil struggled to a 205.584 qualifying average, second-slowest of the eleven total checker-takers. "It's very difficult to qualify here," said Emmo. "There are so many people watching, it's the second biggest event in the world—the first one is the race. I'm very disappointed because I was looking for 210-211 . . . it was

pushing a little bit. Next week, we can work on the car on full tanks and have it really work well for the race.''

Still groping for good numbers, Josele Garza and the Machinists Union gang squandered another shot with the 55 Bryant/ Schaefer 87C. Garza stumbled through laps of 201.414 and 199.102 before the yellow bunting mercifully appeared. The next time 55 took the green flag, that would be its last chance.

Fellow Machinists Union shoe Pancho Carter experienced some sort of problem with his 29T Hardee's 87C and came in before completing his second warmup lap.

At 5:44, Ed Pimm made an aborted attempt of 202.274 and 204.174 in the 98 Mike Curb/RPH March 86C/Cosworth (which was now wearing Skoal sponsorship on its side pods).

After Gary Bettenhausen's 56T was evicted from the tech line, perennial pole threat Tom Sneva turned off the tedium with his 5:58 wave-off run in Mike Curb's 33T (73) Skoal Bandit March 87C/Cosworth. Sneva's times of 198.562 (?) and 203.064 placed a final illustrative stamp on one of the weirdest first day of qualifications ever.

The field average for the 11 qualifiers was 209.535 MPH. Our front row consisted of Mario, Rahal, and Mears (just as at 1:15). Row 2 had Foyt, Guerrero, and Simon. The third flank found Luyendyk, Rutherford, and Michael A., with Fittipaldi and Sullivan

Jim Crawford breaks from the line early in turn one . . .

. . . thumps the wall . . .

*. . . and slides down the short chute with painful leg injuries.
(sequence by Jim Adams)*

in row 4—for now. Rahal, Guerrero, Simon, and Luyendyk garnered their best-ever IMS starting spots.

Mario Andretti's run earned him not only his third Indy pole (his last came in 1967), but $75,000 in cash awards, a Starcraft custom van worth $30,000, and $2,500 worth of Master Mechanic tools. It was the first Indy pole for both a Lola chassis (the marque first appeared at the Speedway in 1965) and the Ilmor-Chevrolet engine that was brand-new last May.

Andretti mentioned that he almost gambled on pulling out of line to wait until late afternoon to make his attempt. ''There's no question we would have gone to the back of the line if 15-18 cars had already taken a qualifying run. But with the possibility of a new line forming and visualizing we might be in back of that, there were just too many things up in the air. We just decided, 'let's go and see where it takes us'.''

Sunday, May 10
Sunny, Breezy, Hot

Seven drivers, paced by rookie Ludwig Heimrath Jr., qualified on a sultry Sunday. One previous Indy winner made a triumphant surprise return, while another former champion destroyed his second car in three days.

Thirty minutes after the 10:00 start of morning practice, Tom Sneva did a virtual instant replay of his Friday wall-banging act. The 33T Skoal March 87C/Cosworth, on its first hot lap after exiting the pits, sailed beyond the turn 1 groove and bashed the concrete. ''That one acted very similar to the first one,'' said a puzzled Sneva, ''but the adjustment we made should have been helping that problem—not compounding it. [The car] just didn't turn after we got to the middle of the corner. This one didn't hit as hard, but it might have done more damage.'' With two '87 Marches now down for the count, Mike Curb decided to pull Ed Pimm's March 86C backup out of mothballs and convert it to Buick power. The car had been sitting unused all month and still wore its '86 maroon livery, plus road course wings, rain tires, and ''Mister Grocer'' associate sponsorship from the November Miami CART race.

A more fortunate Gary Bettenhausen executed his second non-contact spin since Friday in the hair-trigger 56T Genesee 87C. Gary's 11:11 incident did take him into the south chute infield and the transition from pavement to turf damaged the tunnels of his machine. ''We've got it balanced well,'' he explained, ''but we make one change and the back end decides to let go.'' Do you recall Jim Clark's comment after twice looping his Granatelli Lotus during the 1966 race—that ''STP'' meant ''Spinning Takes Practice''?

Practice speeds picked up about where

they left off Saturday afternoon. Rich Vogler set the pace at a modest 205.3; George Snider turned 204.9 and Foyt teammate Davy Jones made 204.6. Al Unser, Jr. and Gary Bettenhausen (prior to his problem) hit identical 204.4 clockings. Eighteen cars took morning excursions.

Following a slight delay, Ludwig Heimrath, Jr. rolled away at 12:12 to make his first career Indy 500 qualifying attempt. The rookie from Ontario, Canada impressed all with a consistent (laps 2 and 3 were identical) 207.591 performance in the 23 Mackenzie/Tim Horton Donuts '87 Lola/Cosworth. Heimrath was a little concerned when he took the green flag, because "the oil light came on. I checked the oil pressure gauge and it was about 20 pounds low, but I figured as long as it didn't drop below 35 pounds I'd finish the run, because the car felt really good." He said that car owner and mentor Dick Simon "keeps beating in my head consistency, consistency . . . just try and get those laps the same."

Sprint car and midget hotshoe Rich Vogler became lucky qualifier number 13 with Ron Hemelgarn's 81 Byrd's Kentucky Fried Chicken/LivingWell/Val-Pak March 87C/Buick. Rapid Rich led off with a 206.9 lap, dropped to 204.8 when "a gust of wind caught me in turn 2 and it momentarily got away from me," then brought lap 4 back up to 206.6 for a 205.887 average. "I feel that I'm solidly in the field," he said, then, realizing that he had never before qualified on the first weekend, added, "This is a new thing for me. I won't know what to do next week!"

With Geoff Brabham's 15T pulling out of the line, the track reopened for practice at 12:27 and would remain so until 4:38. At around 1:20, the announcement was given of Gordon Johncock's signing to replace the injured Jim Crawford in the ARS March/Buick. Johncock said it took him "about 30 seconds" to accept when ARS president Dick Rutherford called him with the offer.

"It's unfortunate for Jim that he got hurt, but I'm tickled to death to be back," said the '73 and '82 Indy winner. "I realized probably 4 or 5 months after I retired that I kind of made a mistake, especially after sittin' there and watchin' them on TV." Johncock hadn't driven an Indy Car since May 9, 1985. He made a brief appearance in this year's Phoenix ARS race on April 11, but said that his ARS run told him "everything's there that was there before." Al Unser, Sr. was also approached about the assignment, but he reportedly demanded more money than the Patrick/ARS/Buick organization was willing to advance.

As the afternoon progressed, some drivers were actually getting a leg up on the heat. Gary Bettenhausen switched his efforts to the year-old 56 Genesee March 86C and by 3:30 had worked up to 206.4 MPH. Scott Brayton topped that mark with his 206.9, while Derek Daly inched over 205. Pancho Carter and Geoff Brabham

Tom Sneva hits the turn one wall for a second time. (Margison)

both found 204.8, but Al Unser, Jr. fell off slightly to 203.6 MPH. Kevin Cogan sat out most of the session due to an oiling turbocharger that filled the air with smoke every time 7 was started. Phil Krueger shook down the blue and yellow 17 Intersport March 86C/Cosworth of rookie Dominic Dobson, making it the 58th different machine to practice this month. A total of 22 cars were on the track today.

Gary Bettenhausen brought practice to a halt with his 4:53 time trial attempt in the 56 Genesee Beer Wagon March 86C/Cosworth. Lap one was a solid 206.6, but a loose condition caused by a "right rear tire that got bigger and changed the stagger" dropped him to laps of 204.8, 202.6, and 203.8 for an average of 204.504. "The '86 [chassis] felt much better to me," reported the '72 near-winner. "For some reason, it's so much easier to work with, so much easier to balance. At least now we can work on a race setup and we can also work on the '87 and get it ready if we need it."

The blue, white, and hot pink 91T (37) Amway/Autostyle "Winning Spirit" March 87C/Cosworth of Scott Brayton became the third Ron Hemelgarn entry to make the grade. Starting off somewhat slowly due to a new set of tires, Brayton "reached down deep in the basement" and improved from the 204 bracket to 207.1 and 206.1 on his two laps. His 205.647 average was "more inconsistent than I wanted to be, but I feel the car is performing well. I knew [with the new tires] I was going to have to get forceful, and you don't want to do that here."

Derek Daly made one official lap of 202.844 in the 77 Scheid Tire/Superior Training/Metrolink 1411 March 87C/Buick before pulling into the pits.

At 5:13, Geoff Brabham left the line with the 15T (45) Team Valvoline March 87C/

Honda of Rick Galles and posted an up-and-down 205.503 average, becoming the 16th qualifier and the first-ever Honda to qualify at Indy. "We felt that new tires on the car would just hold out enough for 4 laps, and it nearly made it. We dropped down a bit (from 206.3 to 204.3), but I think we're still reasonable. It was a matter of just gritting your teeth and hanging on. Hopefully, I can relax now—unlike last year." (Brabham rode the bubble during the final qualifying day in '86.)

Davy Jones failed to take the green flag after a 201.5 warmup lap in A.J. Foyt's 44 UNO/New Atlantis/Copenhagen March

Teammates Arie Luyendyk and Rich Vogler share experiences from vastly different backgrounds. (deBrier)

Mario shares the pole-winning accolades with Mario Illien of Ilmor. (IMS-Swope)

86C/Cosworth.

Traditional Foyt stickman George Snider had strung together two almost-identical laps of 206.597 and 206.583 when the 84 Calumet Farm March 86C/V-6 Chevy broke loose exiting turn 2 and spun right-rear-first into the inner backstretch wall. The culprit was diagnosed as a broken wheel. "It looked like he ran across something and punctured a tire," Foyt said later. "The tire started going down and he didn't know it; then the wheel broke. It's just one of those misfortunate things." Damage was relatively light and Ziggy himself was unharmed.

After a brief clean-up period, Al Unser, Jr. made an embarrassing one-lap attempt in Doug Shierson's 30 Domino's Pizza "Hot One" March 87C/Cosworth. "We're pretty disappointed," said Little Al following his 201.423 clocking. "It's not an easy feeling being on the outside looking in." (At least the son's difficulties were keeping his free-agent father occupied. "If Al wasn't here running I don't think I'd stay here very long," said Big Al. "My patience gets short.")

A most consistent 5:44 series by Jeff MacPherson made him the second rookie (and Honda driver) to join the starting lineup. His four laps in the 11 Team Mac-Pherson/Galles March 87C/Honda varied by only .045 seconds en route to a 205.688 average. "I had the most active car I've had since I've been here," said a thrilled Mac-Pherson. "We have 2 anti-roll bars in the car; I kept adjusting them and occasionally it was pretty wild exiting turn 2. This is tremendously exciting—the pressure that's gone, I can't even begin to tell you."

Pancho Carter finished the day with a suspect 203.781 run in the ill-handling 29T Hardee's March 87C/Cosworth, making

him the slowest of the 18 total qualifiers. "We made a drastic chassis change, so we ought to be thankful we could run those type of speeds," Carter said after brushing the turn 2 wall on his final lap. "It was really a shot in the dark. The car has much, much more potential than what it showed." (With Pancho in as low man and Josele Garza's 55 burdened with two strikes, the Machinists Union team was going to have to do some fancy footwork.)

The Leader Cards 42 March 86C backup car was halfheartedly going through tech inspection as the 6:00 gun fired (the car hadn't practiced since opening day!) . . . Field average for the 18 cars was 207.951 MPH.

Monday, May 11
Sunny, Windy, Hot

The on-track IMS return of Gordon Johncock was Monday's sole newsworthy event. With the conditions a virtual clone of the weekend, only a season-low 12 machines bothered to participate.

Johncock made his grand entrance at 3:05 and by day's end had topped 190 MPH in the 2 ARS 86C/Buick. "It felt great," he said. "The car seems awful stiff on the front end, but maybe that's the way the cars have been the last couple of years. I think the faster I go, the more comfortable the car's going to feel."

Fast trip of the day was Mario Andretti's late 211.7 in his 5T backup Lola/Chevy. "The track is still quite slick and until we get a real good rain here, it's not going to get any better," opined the polesitter. Andretti was working with his backup vehicle "so we can do our race setups with this one and not take too many chances with the race car." Obviously, the Newman/Haas braintrust remembered how Mario's practice crash of May 14, 1986 forced him to give up his 5th place starting spot and move to the back of the pack.

Derek Daly's Buick paced the unqualified few with a 206.0 circuit. "We're becoming more comfortable with the tires," stated Daly. "The 206 today wasn't difficult, but I don't know what to base it against. Yesterday, we got up to 206, made two little changes, pushed it into the qualifying line and it was a disaster. Today we ran 206, made the same changes and it was a disaster again."

Dominic Dobson made his first May appearance and passed the 180 and 185 MPH rookie test phases. Dobson's ex-Kraco 17 Intersport/Jim Ward Racing '86

It was a long, hard, and mystifying month for Ian Reed and Al Unser, Jr. (Walker)

March/Cosworth was being crew-chiefed by Billy Bignotti, son of master mechanic George Bignotti.

In off-track wheeling and dealing, Andy Kenopensky, manager of the Machinists Union team, purchased a new March 87C to serve as security for either Pancho Carter or Josele Garza. Since they only entered three cars, Kenopensky needed to acquire an additional entry and found a seller in Rick Miaskiewicz. George Walther bought a March 86C from the Truesports organization to substitute for his 86C trashed by Rocky Moran on May 7. Elmer Fields was receiving a fresh March 85C tub from Pat Patrick to replace Dick Ferguson's similar machine that was wrinkled on May 8.

At 11:19, Randy Lewis became the day's first driver to practice. Eight minutes later, the left side pod-and-engine cover on the 24 March 87C ripped loose as Lewis headed down the main straightaway. The A.J. Watson-led Leader Cards crew had the car back out with replacement bodywork by 5:30 . . . Emerson Fittipaldi had just left the pits in the 20T Marlboro 87C when, at 4:45, he stopped the car in the third turn with a barely-attached left front wheel. Seems the wheel nut vacated in turn 2, and when the car was raised up off the ground, the tire slid right off.

Tuesday, May 12
Overcast, Breezy, Mild

Well, it rained overnight, but the track didn't magically turn into the yellow brick road. Danny Ongais, however, wouldn't be crossing the One Yard of Brick for the balance of the month, virtually assuring Al Unser, Sr. of a ride.

The bad news for Ongais came down at

Emerson Fittipaldi has an impish sense of humor and enjoys a good story. (Whitlow)

Gordon Johncock returns to the cockpit. (Strauser)

3:00 Tuesday afternoon. Speedway medical director Dr. Henry Bock said that tests revealed that Ongais was still recovering from the concussion received in his May 7 crash and therefore could not be cleared to drive. The announcement of Al Unser as a replacement driver was merely awaiting approval from Ted Field, Ongais's sponsor and longtime financier.

Roger Penske issued a statement saying that, "The news comes as a great disappointment not only to Danny, but also the team. Danny has logged a lot of miles in our cars this year—here, and at other tracks in preparation for this race. He fit in well with the team and everything was going so well. As soon as he is cleared, we plan to give [him] another opportunity to drive a Penske car this season." Or would Ongais rather stick with a 1987 March that Field had supposedly bought for him to run selected CART races, with Phil Casey serving as chief machanic?

The moderate late-night precipitation might have improved the racing surface a little, but the "haves" were still rockin' and the "have-nots" were still cryin'. Mario Andretti hit 212.9 in his spare 5T Newman/Haas Lola, while Bobby Rahal, Roberto Guerrero, and Rick Mears were all in the 211 bracket with their qualified mounts. Guerrero commented, "I don't think the conditions have changed, at least with our car. They're basically reasonable." A.J. Foyt and Michael Andretti (in his 18T backup) were both over 209 MPH.

Quickest of the non-qualified drivers was rookie Fabrizio Barbazza at 206.0 in the 12T Arciero Winery March 87C. "We think we found something in the car," said the '86 ARS champion. "We hope we understand the problem now. Today, we changed just little things."

Derek Daly ran 205.9 "with a half load of

fuel, trying to simulate race conditions." Al Unser, Jr. hit 205.7 and expressed guarded optimism; "We got some reaction out of the car, so that's going to give us some direction now." Ed Pimm and Kevin Cogan were also above 205 MPH, while Davy Jones was just under that number. Gordon Johncock worked up to 199.4 and said, "The car felt much more comfortable today."

Dennis Firestone was armed with releases from both Dr. Terry Trammell of Methodist Hospital and Dr. Bock of IMS clearing him to drive. As soon as Firestone could prove to USAC officials that he could adequately enter and exit his race car, he would be able to resume practice. "We'll start off tomorrow and take one step at a time," he declared.

Dominic Dobson passed his final two test phases and became the last rookie to be approved . . . by 1:00, Rick Mears was jetting to Florida to play golf with Roger Penske . . . Hemelgarn teammates Rich Vogler and Arie Luyendyk were running in close quarters at around 199 MPH . . . Sammy Swindell's 59 was back on the track wearing its original engine cover; the offending piece still wore the battle scars from its May 8 flight . . . A total of 24 cars made practice runs today.

Wednesday, May 13
Hazy and Humid

Perhaps Dennis Firestone's tennis game had been placed on indefinite hold (that is, if he indeed plays), but his Indy Car career took a strong upswing today.

Requiring assistance from crew members to get into and out of his race car, the crutch-bound Firestone still received (at 12:56) his needed clearance from USAC officials. The

The injured Dennis Firestone confers with crew chief/team driver Phil Krueger. (IMS-L. Young)

identical-to-the-original 10T (49) Raynor Motorsports '87 Lola/Cosworth made its first practice run at 2:59 and by 4:35 Firestone became the day's fastest non-qualified driver with a 206.944 clocking.

His main problem came in trying to get "full depression on the clutch pedal" when exiting the pits. "I don't have quite enough strength in my left ankle," said Dennis, "and you don't get a lot of leverage—it's strictly ankle action." The broken bones in his left foot were being held together by a stainless steel plate and six screws.

Phases two and three of Roger Penske's "Operation Backtrack" were implemented simultaneously. Danny Sullivan's 3T (58) Miller American March 86C/Chevy and the 25T (85) March 86C/Cosworth containing the long-awaited Al Unser made their initial appearances at 5:39, becoming the month's 60th and 61st different chassis to do so. While Sullivan merely warmed up his March, Big Al managed a lap of 197.5 in the yellow 86C that, for the moment, featured Hertz emblazoned along the side pods. According to team manager Derrick Walker, Unser's mount was relegated to Cosworth power due to a shortage of Chevrolet spare parts.

"I hate it for Danny's sake . . . yet somebody has to do it, so here we are," said the three-time winner about his usurping of the Ongais ride. "Now it's a matter of making the show and trying to get a race setup, and I don't have that many days. You've just got to go after it the best way you know how."

Geoff Brabham made light contact with the third turn wall at 5:28 when a wheel broke on his unqualified 15 (15) Team Valvoline 87C/Honda. Brabham had slowed down enough so that the damage to the car's right side was largely cosmetic.

Two qualified drivers paced today's 28 practicing vehicles. Michael Andretti pushed his spare 18T Kraco 87C to 211.3 and Rick Mears hit 211.0 in the Pennzoil 86C. Among those on the outside looking in, Kevin Cogan survived an early game of "chicken" with a squirrel (the south chute showdown was considered a draw) to reach 205.6 in the 7 Marlboro March 87C. Ed Pimm's year-old Mike Curb March also hit 205.6 and Fabrizio Barbazza ran 204.7 in the 12T Arciero 87C.

Gordon Johncock was only up to 200.5 in his third day with the 216 MPH 2 ARS Buick, while Sammy Swindell urged John Buttera's underpowered March 86C/Pontiac to 200.2. Numerous pit residents complained that Swindell should have been awarded the seat in 2, since he actually competed in the ARS last year and was certainly deserving of a better fate. Tony Bettenhausen inched in his 86C over 200 MPH for the first time in nearly a week.

Al Unser, Jr. reached only 199.9 when a tow-in ended his day at 3:22 . . . Dennis Firestone's replacement '87 Lola was wearing 10T, the Raynor backup '86 Lola driven by Phil Krueger was now sporting "dual T's" after its 10 . . . A white March 86C marked 35 (registration 72) was spotted in the ARS team garage early Wednesday. With "Possell" written across the top of its red rear wing, it was obviously the car originally entered for 5-race veteran Spike Gehlhausen. The C.R. Possell effort suffered from sponsorship woes, so 35 was brought in only to back up Gordon Johncock.

Thursday, May 14
Sunny, Breezy, Hot

On a day when the thermometer reached a sweltering 86 degrees, Johnny Parsons's month of May ended painfully after less than 10 total hot laps.

The red and white 81T Kentucky Fried Chicken/LivingWell March 86C/Buick had just this morning returned to action following repair work from Parsons's minor brush with the wall on May 9. After a lap of 197.6, Parsons lost control entering turn 1 at 11:59. The car did one full spin and hit the outer wall with the right front, inflicting a broken left heel and broken right ankle on the 42-year-old Parsons. Surgery was successful, and at 6:30 the 11-race-veteran was listed in good condition at Methodist Hospital.

Doug Shierson and his Domino's Pizza gang could finally afford to smile, thanks to Al Unser, Jr.'s "white-knuckle" 208.913 lap in their 30 March 87C. "I don't know what it was, but we're desperately going to try not to screw it up," said car owner Shierson. Little Al commented, "The load is off a little now. [The car] is starting to kinda feel like it was when we unloaded it at the beginning of the month." (Back when they were running 211 MPH . . .)

Head-to-head comparisons between the qualified PC-16 and the unqualified March 86C chassis began for Danny Sullivan's portion of the Penske team. "I don't really have a preference," Sully said prior to the taste tests. "I just want to be in the one that's the fastest and most comfortable to drive over the period of 500 miles." The scorecard for Thursday read: March—207.9 MPH; PC-16—198.3 MPH.

Dennis Firestone and Josele Garza turned identical 203.6 clockings; Stan Fox hit 202.9 in his first day out with the 41 Kerker 86C since his pole day morning trip through the toolies; Kevin Cogan and Randy Lewis were also above 202 MPH. In the battle of ex-Patrick Racing drivers, Sammy Swindell's 201.7 surpassed the weak 201.0 of Gordon Johncock. Reportedly, the ARS 2 had been equipped overnight with new front brake rotors due to their repeated overuse by Mr. Johncock.

The 25T March 86C/Cosworth of Al Unser, Sr. was officially re-named the Cummins Holset Turbo Special. This marked the first time that the Cummins name had been seen on an Indy entry since the pole-winning Cummins Diesel of 1952. Holset is a Cummins United Kingdom subsidiary that manufactured the turbochargers on all the Roger Penske cars. Big Al worked the car to 201.8 by day's end.

Michael Andretti continued to improve his race potential with a 209.3 in the backup 18T Kraco 87C. Mario Andretti was experimenting "incredibly with just all far-out setups" in his 5T Lola and his investigations took him to 207.2 today.

Rick Miaskiewicz took a wormy 5:23 trip off turn 2 that led the left side of his 97 Pizza Hut/RCV 86C into the backstretch inner wall, but curiously, it was the right side pod and underwing that suffered the bulk of the damage. The car was deemed repairable and Miasiewicz was unhurt.

The track debut of Pancho Carter's 29TT (46) Hardee's March 87C/Cosworth (third of identical triplets) lasted only 8 minutes, due to the left side bodywork pulling loose while at speed. After an anxious moment, Carter gathered the car up and retired for the day.

Roberto Guerrero's Vince Granatelli crew won the preliminary round of the Miller-Indy Pit Stop Championship Thursday morning, earning the fourth and final slot in the May 21 finals . . . A total of 25 cars made practice runs today . . . The Louis Schwitzer Award for innovation and engineering excellence was given to Stuart Grant, of the Goodyear Tire and Rubber Company, for the controversial radial tires.

Friday, May 15
Sunny, Breezy, Warm

The yo-yo fortunes of Raynor Motorsports took another downward turn as Dennis Firestone limped from the frying pan into the fire.

At 2:00, a malfunction in the left rear wheel caused Firestone to ram the fourth turn outer wall rear-first in a flash of flame. He was once again extracted from a damaged 10 Lola T8701 and transported to Methodist Hospital, awake and alert, with a concussion and several neck fractures, but no paralysis or further injuries to his lower extremities. Firestone had only been practicing for 42 minutes (with a best lap of 195.0) and had just gotten up to speed when the accident occurred.

Al Unser, Jr. jumped back to the forefront with a 210.231 blazer, fastest among the 34 machines utilizing the final full day of practice. Derek Daly "came back to his same basic combination" and ran 208.2 in the 77 Buick. "The radar gun had me at 226 down the front straight, and that's because I picked up another 150 revs coming off turn four," said Daly. Josele Garza stepped up with a late 207.9 in the Machinists March 87C and Fabrizio Barbazza led the remaining rookie contingent with his 207.9 from Frank Arciero's 12 March 87C.

The votes were in: The PC-16 was going back on the trailer. Danny Sullivan worked with the qualified 3 Penske/Chevy all day long and could only reach a mere 198.7 in race configuration. A long-distance 4:30 phone conversation with Roger Penske mercifully pulled the plug on the PC-16 project for this year's Indy 500. Sullivan spent the last hour of practice in his March 86C/Chevy and hit a solid 207.8 MPH.

Other drivers also used the day's somewhat "cooler" temperatures (74 degree high) to make impressive strides: Big Al Unser improved to a week-best 206.5; Pancho Carter got up to 205.9 in the 29TT Hardee's 87C; Kevin Cogan made 205.6; Davy Jones hit 205.1; Randy Lewis found his personal best of 204.4 in Ralph Wilke's 87C.

Tony Bettenhausen used some tuning tips from veteran Indy Car wrench Phil Casey to post an encouraging 203.2 in his 16 March 86C. Gordon Johncock gained his required 1 MPH for the day (199 on Tuesday, 200 on Wednesday, etc.) recording a 202.2 in the ARS Buick. Steve Chassey (200.9) and rookie Dominic Dobson (199.1) found their respective bests of the month.

Three fresh machines made first appearances on Friday, bringing the "unofficial" (but correct) total to 65. The Speedway didn't bother to count "substitute" chassis, so their tally stopped with 61. Tom Sneva finally got his hurriedly-converted 3TT (89) Skoal Bandit March 86C/Buick onto the track at 5:49 and barely had time to get into the fast groove before the 6:00 shutdown. "It was good to find out if anything was going to fall off, or fly off, which didn't happen," stated the Gas Man. "This was better than nothing—but not much." The Curb crew managed to paint the car green and white, but its rear winglets were still the original maroon.

Rocky Moran hit 195 in the dark red 76T (57) George Walther March 86C/Cosworth replacement chassis obtained from Truesports. Dick Simon shook down his third entry, the 22T (27) Mackenzie Spirit '86 Lola/Cosworth used by Davy Jones in the ROP. Scuttlebutt had Tom Bigelow in the seat of 22T before the end of the weekend.

Geoff Brabham had his crashed 15 Team Valvoline 87C back on track today . . . Engineer Tony Cicale had joined the Tom Sneva camp . . . Johnny Parsons made it through surgery with no signs of complications; Jim Crawford's progress was described as "excellent" . . . 32 cars were assured positions in the Saturday qualifying line, if they so desired.

Saturday, May 16
Sunny, Breezy, Warm

Crunch Time had arrived, and with higher temperatures predicted for Sunday, everyone who was in (or even near) the ballpark would take their best shots when time trials opened at 11:00.

Individual month-bests abounded during the cool (66 degrees at 10:00), calm, incident-free morning practice period. Al Unser, Jr.'s still-improving 210.2 wasn't his personal high speed, but Fabrizio Barbazza (209.8), Al Unser, Sr. (208.4), Gordon Johncock (206.1), Randy Lewis (206.0), and Tony Bettenhausen (205.1) all made major breakthroughs. Derek Daly also topped 209 MPH; Davy Jones, Kevin Cogan, and Danny Sullivan were above 207 MPH; Stan Fox hit 206.0, Pancho Carter found 205.7, and George Snider and Ed Pimm both cleared 204 MPH.

Tom Sneva reached 203.2 in his first hot lap session with the Skoal 86C/Buick. Josele Garza and the Machinists Union team went through a "fire drill," as Josele put it. The ex-Pancho Carter "upside-down" March 87C finally returned to track action, but it was now colored solid beige and had been renumbered 55T. Garza wanted to get the car ready "just in case" his final attempt in the primary 55 went astray; he managed 202.0 before the 10:15 shutdown. Garza ran half of a hot lap in his assigned machine, stating it felt "really, really good." A total of 21 cars took AM practice runs.

After the annual Armed Forces Day ceremonies (the highlight of which, as always, was the flyover of four F-4 fighter jets from the Hulman Field National Guard base in Terre Haute), Kevin Cogan answered the

Vince Granatelli with team manager Morris Nunn, the man who first introduced Roberto Guerrero to Indianapolis. (IMS-Dwiggins)

11:00 call to begin qualifications.

From a 207 lap in morning practice, Cogan's 7 Marlboro/Patrick Racing March 87C/Chevy deteriorated to official marks of 204.867, 204.109, and 203.486 before being waved off. "We put a little too much fuel in it and it began to push pretty bad," explained Cogan. "I was just about ready to hit the wall." His last lap would have been in the 201 range.

The hopes of short-track fans across the nation rode with the snarling 59 Center Line/Machinists/Buttera March 86C/Pontiac of two-time World of Outlaws sprint car champion Sammy Swindell. Even with the wind starting to kick up, the 31-year-old rookie from Bartlett, Tennessee drove his heart out in extracting a 201.840 average from the underpowered stock-block machine. Now, would it be fast enough to remain in the field?

"We knew if we could run 201-202, that was as good as we were going to get," said Swindell. "We had a little more push than we thought we were going to have. I'd like to see them let us come here with a little bigger motor . . . if we could get up with [the horsepower] the other guys have, I think the car would be really competitive."

Frank Arciero seems to have a knack for finding fast rookies and this year's edition, Italy's Fabrizio Barbazza, went straight to the head of his class. Barbazza (aka "The Turtle") posted a quick lap of 208.6 en route to a 208.038 average in the 12 Arciero Winery March 87C/Cosworth. "I had to run

Fabrizio Barbazza makes it. (IMS-L. Young)

a different line each lap because of a push. In the car, I didn't feel excited; I feel like the other days—no problem [with] the people. I don't feel any pressure. I talked to Teo Fabi and Mario and they tell me to take your time here."

Seven hundred miles of second-week practice paid off for Derek Daly. The Irishman-turned-Hoosier became qualifier number 21 with his 207.522 run in the 77 Scheid Tire/Superior Training/Metrolink 1411 March 87C/Buick, but there was a 5 MPH drop from lap one (209.6) to lap four (204.6). What happened, Derek? "The temperature increase, believe it or not, over this morning changed the track dramatically; whereas I had a constant push this morning, I was loose going in [to the turns] on my run. On lap 4, I got too loose in turn 2 and at that stage it wasn't worth trying to push my luck down in 3 and 4."

Tony Bettenhausen lost over 3 MPH since practice concluded and his 201.685 lap earned an immediate wave-off. The 16 March 86C/Cosworth was now devoid of its original major sponsor due to non-payment of contracted funds, so its working title became the "Bettenhausen and Associates March."

Pressure, what pressure? Josele Garza made his third and final attempt with the 55 Bryant Heating and Cooling/Schaefer/Machinists Union March 87C/Cosworth a successful one, posting a 205.692 four-lap figure. It wasn't easy, though. "The car started pushing on my second lap and I really thought we were going to drop a lot in speed [204.6 on his third lap]. Then I ran over a bird—and that's a bad sign—but somebody was watching out for me and we made it through." Phil Hedback of Bryant Heating greeted Garza with 205 silver dollars—one for each mile per hour—that he poured into his helmet.

The month-long odyssey of Al Unser, Jr. ended with another puzzling twist. Two laps in the 207 bracket were followed by two at 205.9 for a disappointing 206.752 average from the 30 Domino's Pizza "Hot One" March 87C/Cosworth. Sayeth young Al: "We went out this morning and ran 211. We parked the car in line and it was great. Now all of a sudden, it ain't great anymore, so I don't know what's wrong with it. I expected to come out with top speeds today, but I got shot down. The beginning of my second lap, I knew the car and the conditions changed. I felt it on exits of corners; it pushed and got worse and worse."

Comebacking Gordon Johncock empha-

tically responded to his critics with a stirring 207.990 performance in the 2 American Racing Series March 86C/Buick. Johncock's first three laps were above 208 MPH and he stated it "wasn't too hard to qualify that fast. I've had times here that it's been a lot shakier than it was today. I think I've probably felt more pressure here this last week than I ever have here in my life. I can imagine what people would say if I couldn't run fast enough to put it in the show, or if I stuck it in the wall. So I was just making sure that didn't happen." He also affirmed that the STP stickers on the car would be joined with his "traditional" Petty blue and day-glo red paint scheme for race day.

Closing out a hectic first hour was the make-up run of Danny Sullivan. With Roger Penske's formal withdrawal of the qualified PC-16, we were temporarily back to 23 starters, but Sullivan wasted little time in placing his 3T (58) Miller American March 86C/Chevy firmly in the show. From a 209.7 on lap 1, the '85 Indy winner ripped off three trips above 210 MPH (210.571 tops) for an average speed of 210.271, then elaborated on the decision to switch mounts. "If we could have gotten the PC-16 up to a speed that we felt was going to run in the 205 range, with a comfortable feel, during the course of the race, we would have stayed with that. But we were about 5 MPH away, so there wasn't even a question." Sullivan then warned, "We're not out of this deal yet. We've still got a chance."

Substitute driver Al Unser, Sr. culminated his eleventh-hour program with a very tidy 207.423 performance in the 25T (85) Cummins Holset Turbo Special March 86C/Cosworth, the third Roger Penske entry to make the grade. While again expressing

Indiana Senator Richard Lugar (a former mayor of Indianapolis) always comes in for Armed Forces Day at the track. (Strauser)

sympathy for original driver Danny Ongais, Big Al said his previous tenure with the Penske organization made for a smooth transition: "The crew and the team understand me, and I understand them. The car is handling very well under the circumstances of the last-minute deal, so I'm tickled to death."

At 12:12, rookie Davy Jones made a two-lap attempt that defied the laws of track physics. After a 205.381 lap in the 44 UNO/Copenhagen/Gilmore-Foyt March 86C/Cosworth, Jones had the car get "real tail-happy" while exiting turn four. It made a series of violent wiggles, the last coming within inches of the main stretch outer wall, but Davy was somehow able to keep the machine heading south and completed the second lap at 202.826. Car owner Foyt witnessed the exhibition first-hand and immediately unfurled the yellow flag.

In probably the most surprising run of the entire qualification process, Randy Lewis rode the momentum of an astounding 207.593 opening lap to post a 206.209 average in the 24 Toshiba/Altos/Leader Cards March 87C/Cosworth. Was this the same Randy Lewis who had been lectured about running too slowly in the groove earlier in the week? "You can't push a car faster than it wants to go," said the effervescent Lewis, "so I've just basically taken it fairly conservatively, taking what it wanted to give me. Then we fine-tuned it so it wanted to give me a little bit more every day. Being a 41-year-old rookie is kind of a kick . . ."

George Snider didn't even make it through both warmup laps before the balky V-6 Chevy in his 84 Calumet Farm March 86C pulled up lame. Ziggy was towed in from the backstretch respite with his precious third and final attempt still unused.

Hopefully abolishing his "retread rookie" status forever, Stan Fox took A.J. Foyt's 41 Kerker Exhaust March 86C/Coswroth through four inconsistent laps (dropping from 206 to 202 MPH) and rang up a 204.518 average. He blamed his speed decline on a loose condition: "I didn't want to chance spinning the car, so I had to ease out of the throttle. It doesn't take much here to lose 2 MPH . . . just a blip of the throttle." Fox confessed to feeling some pressure from his association with the legendary Mr. Foyt, stating, "He sets the cars up, he knows they're going to run darn good, and you want to perform or you might get the boot when you get back to the garage."

After 27th qualifier Fox completed his run, the track opened at 12:48 for a lengthy practice period (until 4:30). Ten cars had qualified in the first 90 minutes of today's time trials; by contrast, on "Pole Day" a mere 2 drivers were in the show at 12:30 and only 11 qualified all day.

The sunny, 80-degree environment cre-

There's never a shortage of photographers. (Whitlow)

Paul Newman did not make it in for the first qualifying weekend, so Mario and his personal PR man, Don Henderson, bring the team's co-owner up to date. (Whitlow)

Former teammates Kevin Cogan and Michael Andretti remain close friends. (Whitlow)

Tom Sneva's fortunes picked up when aerodynamics expert Tony Cicale came on to the team just before the final qualifying weekend. (deBrier)

ated the usual havoc for those still seeking a spot in the field. At around 3:10, Mario Andretti exhibited his mastery of the situation with an announced 215.930 lap in the backup 5T Lola/Chevy. Doubters placed the speed at a more realistic 213.7, but it was impressive, nonetheless. The 17 Intersport 86C of Dominic Dobson blew its engine on the main straightaway at 1:52, seriously fogging the area and igniting a minor blaze at its business end. Potential qualifier Kevin Cogan worked back above 207 MPH by 3:30, then Tom Sneva emulated that feat one hour later.

Wanting to give himself enough time to jump to the spare car should problems develop, Kevin Cogan took another qualifying shot at 4:34. He battled the continuing push malady in Pat Patrick's 7 Marlboro 87C and managed a 205.999 average speed. "We've had the toughest time I've ever had trying to find a good setup," said last year's Indy runner-up. "We came here in the winter time and were the fastest. We came back [in May] and couldn't do anything right."

The track returned to a practice mode from 4:40 to 5:24, with outsiders Ed Pimm, Rocky Moran, Steve Chassey, and Davy jones joined by insiders Johncock, Fittipaldi, Daly, and Mario Andretti. Phil Krueger's 202.4 in the 10TT Raynor '86 Lola was the sole personal improvement made.

Tony Bettenhausen, the "world's fastest Oldsmobile salesman," decided that 5:36 was his time to fly. He had a "thrilling ride" with his 16 March 86C (associate sponsors included Payless Markets/Babes/Q95), hopefully satisfying his 46 or so car owners. "We shot at a high 203 average mark, actually trying to be ahead of Pancho, and somehow we squeezed it through [203.892 MPH]. Unless you put your butt on the line, you won't find that extra mile an hour."

Saturday's final qualifier (and 30th total) was a relieved Tom Sneva. "This is hard on an old guy," Sneva joked after his solid 207.254 performance in Mike Curb's 33TT (89) Skoal Bandit March 86C/Buick. "We've got a good bunch of guys working on the car and they worked awfully hard all week—a lot of late hours—and it helps to make my job a little bit easier. The car felt better with every lap." He went from a 205.9 opening lap to a 207.9 closer.

The last eight minutes of the day was merely sporadic practice . . . A total of 26 cars made practice runs during the day . . . The field average was 207.363 MPH; the 30-car field average of 1986 was 210.471 (is that progress, or what?) . . . Sneva's entrance into the lineup made for a record nine former winners in one race.

AFTER 33 YEARS OF RACING AT INDY, THIS IS ALL WE HAVE TO SHOW FOR IT.

1954 1955 1956 1957 1958 1959 1960 1961 1962 1963

1964 1965 1966 1967 1968 1969 1970 1971 1973

1974 1975 1976 1977 1979 1981 1984 1985

Ever since our first Indy victory in 1954, we've found racing to be a very rewarding experience. In fact, in a relatively short time, Monroe® shocks have made the trip to Victory Lane 27 times.

And the same technology and innovation that went into all those victories also goes into our full-line of shocks. Because every time we race, we learn a little bit more about designing the best shock absorbers in the world for your car.

Of course, we also learn more about racing, too. And that's helped us to become the winningest shock absorber company ever at Indy.

Which just goes to prove another point: At Monroe, we make a lot more than great shocks.

We make history.

Monroe Auto Equipment TENNECO
Division of Tenneco Automotive

≡MONROE≡®
AMERICA RIDES MONROE

Huey Lewis spent the final afternoon in A.J. Foyt's suite and came over to trackside for Davy Jones's run. Rock fans will recognize Mario Cipollina, bass player for the News, in the background. (Dunn)

Sunday, May 17
Sunny, Breezy, Hot

Early arrivals to IMS would have noticed A.J. Foyt taking Davy Jones around the track in the Chrysler LeBaron pace car before morning practice began. By day's end, the "driver's ed" course would contribute to a stunning display of speed.

Sunday's early ink was generated by Pancho Carter and Steve Chassey. Carter, the second-slowest qualifier at the time, pushed his 29TT Hardee's 87C to a session-best 208.9 during the AM period. Team Laughrey crew chief Huey Absalom "stayed up all night" changing the setup on Chassey's 87C and Steve's great 207.6 illustrated the difference. "Yesterday, it felt like a coffin," said Chassey; "today it feels like a race car."

Phil Krueger inched upward to 203.9, while Davy Jones could only find 203.4 after his Grand Tour. Rocky Moran turned 202.2 and George Snider's 84 lost the motor after a 200.9 lap. Dominic Dobson brought out his repaired 17 March 86C (now bearing major sponsorship from L.A. Gear apparel) and

promptly oiled down the track. Seven of the 17 cars taking early runs were of the qualified persuasion.

Following a sky-diving exhibition by the Green Berets Jump Team that capped off the Armed Forces festivities, Steve Chassey eagerly exited the pits at noon with his now-tamed (or so he thought) 87 United Oil/Life of Indiana March 87C/Cosworth. Chassey's first lap—195.465?? Throw that yellow flag, Huey! "I have no idea why it changed from this morning," said a dejected Chassey, feeling the effects of being back in the Trick Bag. "All I know is the car would not turn the corners."

Machinists Union team manager Andy Kenopensky then enacted what he felt might become "the biggest mistake I've ever made" and withdrew the qualified "29T (95) Hardee's March 87C/Cosworth of Pancho Carter so he could requalify in the quicker 29TT (46) clone. The 12:09 run started strongly with laps of 207.5 and 206.0, but the final trips dropped into the 203 MPH bracket for a 205.154 average.

Carter said he wanted to get safely into the field so he could then concentrate on getting a race setup this afternoon. "It's easier to put another car in than to wait around and see if you get bumped." He said the tires started to heat up because he, "probably leaned on it a little harder than I should have," then complained of a two-inch loss of turbocharger boost during the last two laps. A bearing problem in the turbo was later diagnosed as the culprit; consequently, Carter didn't get his hoped-for race setup work.

The final chapter of Raynor Motorsports "May to Forget" was acted out by driver/mechanic Phil Krueger. The hardworking Krueger extracted a 203.920 initial circuit from the 10TT (90) '86 Lola/Cosworth (that was now carrying "4 DENNIS" on the cowling), but in doing so skimmed the north chute wall. "It must have damaged the tire or the suspension," Phil explained, "because it just didn't hold up going through [turn] one." The car broke loose and pranged the outer wall with the right front, then slid into the infield grass—briefly getting airborne—where it backed into the guard rail. Poor Krueger was uninjured, but he "felt horrible" for the seemingly-hexed team.

Open practice ruled the Speedway from 12:35 until 4:35 and the anticipated vignettes played lazily through the devastating 86-degree heat. Tom Bigelow's outside chance to drive Dick Simon's 22T year-old Lola was quashed when Simon couldn't get the car over a required 200 MPH standard soon enough for Bigelow to take a refresher test. Dick Ferguson debuted the 19T (69) L.A. Drywall March 85C/Cosworth replacement chassis of Elmer Fields (the 66th and fin-

al machine to practice) and almost immediately developed oil scavenge pump woes that sidelined him permanently before 3:00. The 97 Pizza Hut 86C of Rick Miaskiewicz returned to action at 1:30, following repairs from his May 14 wall encounter.

The 42 March 86C of Ralph Wilke was wheeled into the pits; reportedly, it would not be utilized unless a "veteran driver" needed its services (George Snider, maybe?). Snider himself took an early afternoon jaunt in Davy Jones's 44 and assured the rookie that his car felt just as uncomfortable.

Andy Kenopensky disappointed a number of people when he stated there were no plans to put Sammy Swindell in the 55T Machinists 87C/Cosworth backup car. "We continue to be hopeful that [Swindell's speed] will be sufficient to make the race." Maybe Brother Bob Tilton could rush-ship Sammy a prayer cloth . . .

Steve Chassey couldn't stand to wait any longer. At 4:47, he rolled away with much lower expectations than on his noon-time attempt, but waved-off laps of 197.754, 200.687, and 199.005 brought the 87 United/Life of Indiana 87C one stop closer to oblivion.

Rookie Rocky Moran suffered through four laps with a "soft-engined" 76T (57) George R. Walther/Trench Shoring March 86C/Cosworth, mustering a weak 199.157 figure to become the 31st qualifier. "We'd been running close to 203 this morning, and better than that last week [before his crash]. But we're down to one engine and it was going away on us. I flatfooted it all the way around and that's all there was in the car."

Ed Pimm was often deep in thought. (Whitlow)

46

The virtually devastated Raynor team receives its final blow when Phil Krueger slams the wall while qualifying. (Margison)

Another rookie, Dominic Dobson, turned his best speeds of the month while qualifying the 17 L.A. Gear/Jim Ward Racing/Intersport March 86C/Cosworth. Dobson topped out at 202.0 (his month-high had been 199.1) in posting his 201.240 average. "We got a late start

and I think I've got a total of around 400 miles this week," said the '86 CART Rookie of the Year. "I went as fast as I could—in fact, it was past comfortable. It's been a difficult month . . . but hopefully this will hold up."

Then came the run of A.J. Foyt's bud-

ding superstar, 22- year-old Davy Jones. First lap for the 44 UNO/Copenhagen/ New Atlantis March 86C/Cosworth— 207.135! Second lap, even faster at 207.4. The third lap rose to 208.7 and the final go-round was an incredible 209.176!! The average speed was 208.117, making Jones: (a) the fastest rookie in the field; (b) the 33rd member of the starting roster; and (c) Huey Lewis and the News's favorite Indy Car driver. (In town for a concert at Market Square Arena, rocker Lewis and band were hangin' out in DJ's pit.) Perhaps we should also mention: (d) highly scrutinized by various skeptics as to the legality of the run (but nothing was changed).

Comparing A.J. to another legendary figure, Indiana University basketball coach Bob "Rabbit Hunter" Knight, Jones said, "I couldn't have had a better opportunity to be here with such a great coach. He made the right adjustments and we found the speed. It couldn't have been more perfect."

Of the 9:45 track tour with Foyt, Davy stated that A.J. was showing him the "turn-in-points" of the corners and, "where you should be on the power. The hesitancy of staying off the power through the corner is what really makes the car squirrely, and that's probably what I was doing wrong." Proud mentor Foyt commented, "I'm thrilled to death for him. I was just glad to get him settled down—that was the biggest problem I was havin'."

On the heels of Jones's thrilling ride came the third and final effort by teammate George Snider. With fingers surely crossed, Snider eased the 84 Calumet Farm March 86C/V-6 Chevy to an under-achieving 203.192 mark, bouncing Rocky

INDIANAPOLIS HARLEY–DAVIDSON

Bob Schulteti and the crew at Indianapolis Harley-Davidson salute the Greatest Auto Race in the world, the Indianapolis 500. We're proud of our American heritage and equally proud to sell and service the world's greatest motorcycle. We understand and appreciate the craftmanship found at the "500" and want to extend a warm invitation to all fans to stop by and take a test ride on a new Harley.

Harley-Davidson Sales & Service, Inc.
701 S. Meridian St.
Indianapolis, IN 46225
(317) 635-7012

Celebrating Our 40th Anniversary

IF ONLY YOU COULD STICK THIS ON YOUR FOREIGN BIKE AT TRADE-IN TIME.

Harley-Davidson® motorcycles hold their value. If you haven't checked the want ads, you'd better.

You might say that Harleys cost more to begin with. In most cases you're right. And in most cases they're worth more when you want to sell.

One reason, Harleys cost more to build. Because we put more into them. There's a lot of careful hand work. A lot of meticulous assembly and constant quality control.

Here's what we mean. Take a look at any Harley-Davidson gas tank. Look at the deep, rich paint that will wax up brilliantly for years. Well that is only the half of it. If you look inside the tank, you'll see that it is painted too. Fact is, gas causes tanks to rust. Every motorcycle manufacturer knows that, but we do something about it. And we charge a little extra for it.

Across the board, we're proud to say that there are a lot of those little extras. And that's what makes up the difference in our purchase price. It also makes up a big difference at trade-in time.

So don't write-off a Harley-Davidson because it costs too much. You may end up writing-off a lot more if you don't buy one.

MOTORCYCLES. BY THE PEOPLE. FOR THE PEOPLE.

Harley-Davidson Motor Co., Inc., P.O. Box 653, Milwaukee, WI 53201
© 1983 Harley-Davidson Motor Co., Inc. All rights reserved

Steve Chassey confers with crew chief Huey Absalom. (deBrier)

Moran from the lineup. "It's been a helluva long week," said the man who had just qualified for his 23rd straight Indy 500 field. "The car wasn't too sharp, but we decided it was getting late, so we went for it." Ziggy's success gave A.J. Foyt four cars in the starting lineup.

At 5:16, Ed Pimm made his second attempt with the 98 Skoal/Curb March 86C/Cosworth, but was waved off after laps of 198.921 and 199.526.

Second-year rookie Rick Miaskiewicz made two official circuits of 198.177 and 198.794 before his crew yellow-flagged the 97 Pizza Hut/WENS/RCV March 86C/Cosworth.

With numerous tweaks having been made to his 87 March (front wings adjusted, air added to right rear tire, air removed from left rear tire), Steve Chassey made his last-gasp attempt at 5:26. The first two laps were both in the 201 bracket—Dominic Dobson still had a chance. Lap three jumped to 202.9 and Dobson was hurting. The fourth lap was 203.5, the average was 202.488, and Dobson was history.

"That was one hell of a ride," sighed Chassey. "I've never had to work so hard in my life to keep one of these things in the groove. Actually, I cut all the corners trying to keep enough room to keep the throttle on. I was all-four-wheels at one time under the yellow line . . . using Lloyd Ruby's old line." Car owner Lydia Laughrey made up for Chassey's understandable lack of enthusiasm by repeatedly screaming, "I love it!"

Now it was Sammy Swindell's turn to ride the bubble, but only Pimm and Miaskiewicz were left to duel out the final half an hour—everyone else was either qualified, broken, or not interested.

Ed Pimm was first to throw down. At 5:33, he started his sole remaining attempt in the 98 Skoal 86C with a 202.7 lap. The next three trips were all above 203 MPH and Swindell was gone, victimized by a lack of horsepower and apathy from potential rescuers.

Pimm credited his better half with the 203.284 improvement. "Earlier the car was really bad; we had old tires on it. My wife said, 'Put on new tires,' so we did. So now I'm going to listen to my wife. I held my breath for 4 laps. It pushed, then it got loose—it did a little of everything. I don't even want to see the tape because I know I look so bad."

With Swindell's departure, Chassey was now the low man that Rick Miaskiewicz had to shoot for. After tinkering until 5:50, Miaskiewicz completed a very slow, very hairy 196.192 run essentially to end time trials. There were still 5 minutes left, but no one was around to use it. Rick ignominiously parked 97 at the north pits, choosing not to be interviewed or officially photographed.

The Leader Card team tried to create a stir by sending up a bogus cry for Sammy Swindell to come drive their 42, but the car never moved toward the tech line and Swindell was apparently chilling out in the suites.

Chassey wound up the slowest qualifier, but after his two weeks of struggle, he was just glad to be in. "We've been sharp and we've been friendly," he said,

"and now I imagine we'll be friendly again."

The final field average was 207.194, as compared to last year's record average of 210.280 . . . Twenty-seven cars practiced on Sunday . . . Geoff Brabham was testing one of the ABC on-board cameras on his Team Valvoline March/Honda . . . Danny Sullivan went out for one practice session wearing Rick Mears's helmet; it seems Sullivan's helmet was experiencing radio problems, so he borrowed his teammate's hard hat while repairs were made.

Monday, May 18 to Saturday, May 23

Let's just cancel Carburetion Day from now on, OK?

For the second consecutive year, the starting lineup was altered ex post facto due to Thursday crashes. Emerson Fittipaldi wiped out the 20 Marlboro March, forcing a move to the Patrick backup car and the hated 33rd starting spot, while A.J. Foyt—of all people—tore up his Lola and required a three-day thrash to maintain his once-magical 4th place position.

The early week schedule was dominated by social functions such as the Oldtimers' Club Barbecue on Monday and the Tuesday American Dairy Association bash that honored fastest rookie Davy Jones. The IMS links were occupied with the Drivers Tournament on Monday and the CDA Celebrity Golf Tournament on Tuesday. (The Kraco and Penske teams

This looks like Rick Mears in Danny Sullivan's car but it is really Danny wearing Rick's helmet. The radio in Danny's wasn't working. (Strauser)

Racing Into Our Second Century

Proud of our past; confident in our future.

That's the Machinists Union.

Since 1888, we've stood for Justice on the Job; Security for our Families; Service to the Community.

That's why we're racing into our second century with confidence and determination.

The Machinists Union, for nearly 100 years, winners in more ways than one.

Come join us.

William W. Winpisinger
International President

Race drivers take their message to the kids and make this appearance at Northwest High School not far from the track. USAC's Donald Davidson interviews Dick Simon while Johnny Rutherford, Roberto Guerrero and Geoff Brabham await their turns. (Fleishman-Hillard)

escaped to Milwaukee to prepare for the May 31 CART event.)

Thursday's final practice period continued the month's hot and sunny pattern and it didn't take long for the fireworks to erupt.

A.J. Foyt's final race day tuneup ends with his first real wall contact in 21 years. (Rodney Margison)

A.J. Foyt was the first to foul up. He considered coming into the pits after a 205.7 lap, but decided to follow Derek Daly and Dick Simon into turn 1 to gauge his car's reaction to turbulence. Super Tex got too low—on the painted

yellow line—and lost control (at 11:34), doing a half-spin into the outer wall and heavily damaging the left side of his Copenhagen/Gilmore Lola. He climbed out of the machine, limped into the infield grass and collapsed, but the apparent injury was only a Charley horse.

A sheepish Foyt explained the scenario: "I had a meeting with my rookies (Davy Jones and Stan Fox) this morning and I told 'em there's going to be a lot of dirty air there, the track is green . . . just go out and make sure that the cars are handling half-way right, just shake 'em down. And I said, 'Don't be racin' no cars, gettin' in dirty air.' I said, 'I'll probably be the idiot that'll try that and get in trouble'—you know, jokin'—and that's exactly what happened. We haven't run this car that much and it was a little bit loose . . . just a screwup."

The car was judged repairable, but it was going to take a lot of man-hours and spare parts, many of which would come from the Truesports and Newman/Haas teams. A.J. kept up a brave face, commenting, "Well, we won't have no laps on the car before Sunday, but we kinda know where to set it . . . so I'm not really too worried." Updated Texas Trilogy trivia question: How many times had A.J. won from 4th starting position after crashing on Carb Day? Answer: absolute-

The Newman/Haas/Andretti combination keeps the momentum rolling and wins the Miller Pit Stop contest. (IMS- McQueeney)

The Patrick Team members really went through the meat-grinder this month. (Spargur)

ly zero, which is what his chances became after the accident. "Well, I just hate Carburetion Day the last 3 or 4 years," Foyt lamented. "I told [my crew] we ought to leave all the cars in the barn, and now I wish I had."

Emerson Fittipaldi's faux pas followed at 12:19. "The car was feeling a little strange in the morning," said a disgusted Emmo. "I could feel the front end was not working the normal way. We changed one set [of tires] to check if it could be anything on the tires and the second set was just scrubbing." He went through turns 1 and 2 with the Marlboro 87C still "feeling strange," headed into turn 3, "turned the steering wheel and the back end just let go." The car did one complete spin and broadsided the outer concrete, damaging the right side of the tub too severely to be fixed. The decision to switch to the 20T backup 87C was made by car owner Pat Patrick at 1:30, moving Fittipaldi from the inside of row 4 to dead last and advancing the 11th through 33rd place starters up one spot.

Mario Andretti strengthened his grip on the favorite's role by first turning the fastest speed of final practice (211.515), then winning the 11th annual Miller Indy Pit Stop Championship (and $25,000) over Bobby Rahal's Truesports team, 18.05 seconds to 23.27 seconds. Andretti's Newman/Haas participating crew members were: chief mechanic Colin Duff, Carl Dean, Graham Fuller, Don Hoevel, John Tzonanakis, and Johnny Capels, Jr. "I have every reason to feel we still have something going for us," said Mario, "but the race itself is the time when it's going to tell."

Rick Mears was second quick at

207.1, while Michael Andretti hit an early 205.8, then pulled out of his pit and bumped wheels with a cruising Tony Bettenhausen. The contact bent the right front suspension on the 18 Kraco 87C, but Michael was back out running before the 1:00 shutdown. Roberto Guerrero sustained an immediate oil leak, which prevented him from making a full hot lap, but he felt the Granatelli crew had done their "homework" setting the car up, so the problem "won't hinder us too much."

The three-day Indy Motorsports Expo at the Hoosier Dome kicked off on Thursday. Friday found the CARA

fashion Show at the Indiana Roof Ballroom, the 11th annual 500 Festival Mini-Marathon, and the nighttime Hulman Hundred Silver Crown dirt car race at the State Fairgrounds. Jeff Swindell, younger brother of Sammy, subbed for Gary Bettenhausen and came from 27th starting position to win the dirt car show; Robby Unser, son of three-time Indy champ Bobby, suffered a compound fracture of his lower right leg in a grinding crash.

Saturday's schedule included the AARBWA breakfast, the (public) Driver's Meeting, the 500 Festival Parade, and the Night Before the 500 races at

Emerson Fittipaldi's qualifier is totalled during the final practice. (John Mahoney)

Al Unser, finally in uniform, gets the inside scoop from his older brother. (Strauser)

Johnny Rutherford is a most appreciative inductee into the prestigious Hall of Fame. (deBrier)

U.S. Tobacco Co. honors A.J. Foyt's 30th year at Indianapolis with a gala reception. Former Foyt teammate Johnny Boyd, Speedway President Joe Cloutier and Foyt's long-time sponsor, Jim Gilmore, enjoy his remarks. (IMS-Spargur)

Indianapolis Raceway Park. Nick Fornoro, Jr. won the 42nd annual midget bash at IRP, while E.J. Lenzi became the first driver ever to lap the 5/8- mile oval in under 20 seconds, then captured the 60-lap Super Vee show. Bob Frey took first place in the 39th annual Little 500 sprint car marathon in Anderson.

Tony Bettenhausen inked Nationwise Auto Parts to a last- minute sponsorship deal, while the belabored Raynor team (''honored'' with the hard-luck Jigger Award by the AARBWA) came aboard Geoff Brabham's Team Valvoline March as an associate backer.

Borg-Warner's president and CEO, C.E. ''Red'' Johnson, is the only person in this shot who hasn't won the ''500''! The 1987 starting field contains a record nine winners, with no less than 18 victories between them. From left to right: Tom Sneva, Gordon Johncock, Al Unser, Mario Andretti, Johnny Rutherford, A.J. Foyt, Johnson, Danny Sullivan, Bobby Rahal and Rick Mears. (IMS-McQueeney)

Tony Bettenhausen would like to thank every one of his car owners, but it takes a while; he has about 45! (Walker)

OFFICIAL ENTRY LIST

Car No.	Driver	Car Name	Year/Chassis Engine	Entrant
1	Bobby Rahal	Budweiser/Truesports/ Spirit of Columbus	1987 Lola Cosworth	Truesports Co.
1T	Bobby Rahal	Budweiser/Truesports/ Spirit of Columbus	1987 Lola Cosworth	Truesports Co.
2	Jim Crawford		1986 March Buick	American Racing Series
2T	Jim Crawford		1986 March Buick	American Racing Series
3	Danny Sullivan	Miller American Penske Chevrolet	1987 Penske Chevrolet	Penske Racing Inc.
3T			1987 Penske Chevrolet	Penske Racing Inc.
4	Roberto Guerrero	True Value STP March	1987 March Cosworth	Vince Granatelli Racing
4T	Roberto Guerrero	True Value STP March	1987 March Cosworth	Vince Granatelli Racing
5	Mario Andretti		1987 Lola Ilmor Chev.	Newman/Haas Racing
5T	Mario Andretti		1987 Lola Ilmor Chev.	Newman/Haas Racing
7	Kevin Cogan	Marlboro Patrick Racing	1987 March Ilmor Chev.	Patrick Racing Inc.
8	Rick Mears	Pennzoil Z-7 Penske Chevrolet	1987 Penske Chevrolet	Penske Racing Inc.
8T				Penske Racing Inc.
9	Johnny Rutherford	Vermont American Special	1987 March Cosworth	Alex Morales Co. Inc.
10	Dennis Firestone	Raynor Motorsports	1987 Lola Cosworth	Raynor Motorsports
10T	Phil Krueger	Raynor Motorsports	1986 Lola Cosworth	Raynor Motorsports
11	Jeff MacPherson	Team MacPherson March/ Honda	1987 March Honda	Galles Racing
11T			1987 March Honda	Galles Racing
12	Fabrizio Barbazza	Arciero Winery	1987 March Cosworth	Arciero Racing Teams
12T	Fabrizio Barbazza	Arciero Winery	1986 March Cosworth	Arciero Racing Teams
14	A. J. Foyt, Jr.	Copenhagen-Gilmore	1987 Lola Cosworth	A. J. Foyt Enterprises
15	Geoff Brabham	Galles Racing March/ Honda	1987 March Honda	Galles Racing
15T			1987 March Honda	Galles Racing
16	Tony Bettenhausen	Call-Free March	1986 March Cosworth	Bettenhausen Racing
16T	Tony Bettenhausen	Call-Free March	1986 March Cosworth	Bettenhausen Racing
17	Dominic Dobson	Intersport March	1986 March Cosworth	Intersport Racing
18	Michael Andretti	Kraco STP March 87C	1987 March Cosworth	Kraco Enterprises Inc.
18T	Michael Andretti	Kraco STP March 87C	1986 March Cosworth	Kraco Enterprises Inc.
19	Dick Ferguson	L.A. Dry Wall Spl.	1985 March Cosworth	Elmer Fields
20	Emerson Fittipaldi	Marlboro Patrick Racing	1987 March Ilmor Chev.	Patrick Racing Inc.
21	Johnny Rutherford	Vermont American Special	1987 March Cosworth	Alex Morales Co. Inc.
22	Dick Simon	Soundesign Stereo Special	1987 Lola Cosworth	Dick Simon Racing
23	Ludwig Heimrath, Jr.	Mackenzie Spirit	1987 Lola Cosworth	Dick Simon Racing

Car No.	Driver	Car Name	Year/Chassis Engine	Entrant
24	Randy Lewis		1987 March Cosworth	Leader Cards, Inc.
25	Danny Ongais	Panavision Penske Chevrolet	1987 Penske Chevrolet	Penske Racing Inc.
25T				Penske Racing Inc.
26		Vermont American/ Morales	1986 March Cosworth	Alex Morales Co. Inc.
27			1987 Lola Cosworth	Dick Simon Racing
29	Pancho Carter	Hardee's	1987 March Cosworth	Int'l. Assoc. of Mach. & Aerospace Workers
30	Al Unser, Jr.	Domino's Pizza "Hot One"	1987 March Cosworth	Shierson Racing
30T	Al Unser, Jr.	Domino's Pizza "Hot One"	1987 March Cosworth	Shierson Racing
31		Budweiser/Truesports Spirit of Columbus	1987 Lola Cosworth	Truesports Co.
32	Rick Miaskiewicz	M-Group/J. Kattman/ R.C.V. Special	1987 Lola Cosworth	M. Group
33	Tom Sneva	Skoal Bandit	1987 March Buick	Mike Curb
33T	Tom Sneva	Skoal Bandit	1987 March Buick	Mike Curb
35	Spike Gehlhausen	J.P. Racing Team	1987 March Cosworth	C.R. Possell
40		Patrick Racing	1987 March Ilmor Chev.	Patrick Racing, Inc.
41	Stan Fox	Kerker Exhaust-A.J. Foyt Enterprises	1986 March Cosworth	A.J. Foyt Enterprises
42		Moran Electric	1986 March Cosworth	Leader Cards, Inc.
44		Copenhagen-Gilmore-Foyt	1986 March Cosworth	A.J. Foyt Enterprises
48		Jim Greer Special	1986 March Cosworth	A.J. Foyt Enterprises
51		Hemelgarn Racing, Inc.	1987 March Cosworth	Hemelgarn Racing, Inc.
55	Josele Garza	Bryant Heating & Cooling/ Schaefer Beer/Machinists Union	1987 March Cosworth	Schaefer/Machinists Union Racing Team
56	Gary Bettenhausen	Genesee Beer Wagon	1987 March Cosworth	Gohr Distr. Co., Inc.
59	Sammy Swindell	Buttera/Center Line/ Machinists Union	1986 March Pontiac	Int'l Assoc. of Mach. & Aerospace Workers
61		LivingWell Inc.-Provimi Veal-WTTV	1987 March Cosworth	Hemelgarn Racing, Inc.
65	Gary Bettenhausen	Genesee Beer Wagon	1986 March Cosworth	Brothers Racing
70		True Value STP March	1987 March Cosworth	Vince Granatelli Racing
71	Arie Luyendyk	LivingWell, Inc.-Provimi Veal-WTTV	1987 March Cosworth	Hemelgarn Racing, Inc.
76			1986 March Cosworth	George N. Walther
77	Derek Daly	Scheid Tire/Superior Training/Metro Link 1411	1987 March Buick V-6	B.C. Pace Racing
77T	Derek Daly	Scheid Tire/Superior Training/Metro Link 1411	1987 March Buick V-6	B.C. Pace Racing
80		True Value STP March	1986 March Cosworth	Vince Granatelli Racing
81	Rich Vogler	Byrd's Kentucky Fried Chicken/LivingWell/VALPAK	1987 March Buick V-6	Hemelgarn/Byrd Racing
81T	Rich Vogler	Byrd's Kentucky Fried Chicken/LivingWell/VALPAK	1986 March Buick V-6	Hemelgarn/Byrd Racing
84		Calumet Farm	1986 March Chevrolet V-6	A. J. Foyt Enterprises

Car No.	Driver	Car Name	Year/Chassis Engine	Entrant
87	Steve Chassey		1987 March Cosworth	Lydia Laughrey
87T	Steve Chassey		1986 March Cosworth	Lydia Laughrey
91	Scott Brayton	Amway/Autostyle Cars	1987 March Cosworth	Hemelgarn Racing, Inc.
91T	Scott Brayton	Amway/Autostyle Cars	1986 March Cosworth	Hemelgarn Racing, Inc.
95		Hubler Chevrolet/Mechel/ Machinists Union	1987 March Cosworth	Int'l Assoc. of Mach. & Aerospace Workers
97	Tom Bigelow	Pizza Hut/WENS	1986 March Cosworth	Sandy Racing, Inc.
98	Ed Pimm		1986 March Cosworth	Mike Curb
98T	Ed Pimm		1986 March Cosworth	Mike Curb
99	Michael Andretti	Kraco STP March 87C	1987 March Cosworth	Kraco Enterprises, Inc.
	Gordon Johncock	Gold Racing, Inc.	1987 March Cosworth	Gold Racing, Inc.

SPECIAL OLYMPICS

The Special Olympics function for the handicapped at the track is very dear to Mari Hulman George and well supported by the participants. (IMS-Binkley)

Five foot eleven-inch Johnny Rutherford is dwarfed next to this young athlete. (IMS-Binkley)

George Snider unselfishly donates some time to assist with the Special Olympics as an honorary coach. (IMS-Binkley)

THE RACE

Last-minute substitute Al Unser sails home to become a four-time winner with an upset victory.

by Donald Davidson

Front-yard parking is lucrative for the locals, despite the looks of discouragement reflected in the eyes of these youthful proprietors. (Pinkley)

It used to be quite rare for there to be any more than three or four former winners in the lineup of an Indianapolis "500", while a mere one or two were not at all uncommon. Not anymore.

Of the 33 starters in the 1987 race, no less than nine, almost a third of the entire field, had won at least once, while the winners of 18 different races, including 16 of the last 20, were represented.

Could Mario Andretti, on the pole for the first time in 20 years, finally overcome his ill fortune of almost two decades to repeat his 1969 win? He was strongly favored, but his still-new Ilmor Chevrolet powerplant posed somewhat of a question mark.

Could Bobby Rahal reverse the usual trend and become only the fifth person to win for a second consecutive year? It looked good for him, not only because he was at the wheel of a Lola (and they were apparently more stable than the new Marches this year), but because he was utilizing the well- proven Cosworth engine.

How about Rick Mears? The jump at the last minute from the Penske PC-16 to the '86 March had netted an outside front row starting position, in spite of hardly any track time, but could the Ilmor take him 500 miles?

How about Danny Sullivan, who was virtually in the same boat?

How about Al Unser, last-minute substitute for the injured Danny Ongais as the third man on the Roger Penske team, and "forced" into using a Cosworth due to a shortage of Ilmor parts?

Could this be a year for A.J. Foyt, magically rebounded after a couple of not-so-good years and poised in the very fourth spot from where he won his third "500" in 1967 and his fourth in 1977?

What of Johnny Rutherford, sitting back there in the role of a dark horse in spite of being a three-time winner?

And what were the chances of the "500" being won by a new face?

Most thought "slim", except for the very real possibility of a victory by Roberto Guerrero.

There were the usual sentimental choices, of course, but most of the experts seemed to favor either Andretti, Rahal or Guerrero. There was no weather problem this year. Race day was gorgeous.

A happy, orderly crowd filed onto the grounds, the police reporting far fewer overnight arrests than in recent years. As usual, there was no official estimate of the crowd size, although it was conceivably the largest ever, and it again drew celebrities from all walks of life, including some REAL notables who came to see rather than to be seen. The outstanding actress Meryl Streep, for instance, managed to slip in and out unannounced.

During the happy hustle-bustle of bands playing and the 33 cars being rolled out to the grid, veteran driver Emil Andres, who either started in or drove relief in every "500" held between 1936 and 1949, took a lap in a 1909 Buick once raced by Louis Chevrolet. Observing the 50th anniversary of the last occasion on which the use of a riding mechanic was mandatory in a "500", former riding mechanic Johnny Pawl (also of midget racing parts fame) rode alongside of Emil. They've known each other for something like 52 years!

A short time later came a small tractor towing the Leader Card Roadster which carried Rodger Ward to his second "500" win in 1962. Rodger was in the cockpit again on this day 25 years later, wearing a cap and smiling with a shrug of his shoulders anytime he saw a friend.

"It sounded like it was about to throw a rod and we didn't want to risk it, so we just shut it off," Rodger noted later.

As usual, the veteran drivers came out late; and it was 10:35 when A.J. Foyt appeared, dressed in a black uniform and accompanied by quite an entourage. He was being shown live on the ABC telecast of the race even as he walked to his car, and the attention caused by the group of technicians running with the cameraman helped encourage others to chase after the group.

At 10:43, Sandi Patti, a Grammy Award winner from the nearby town of Anderson, gave a beautiful rendition of "The Star Spangled Banner" and this was followed by the very moving "Taps," during which time literally thousands and thousands of people were

The gates at the old turn two tunnel are opened and in they come! (IMS-Reed)

The Purdue band is in action long before most race-goers have taken their seats. (Walker)

At the given signal, the cars of Rahal and Andretti are rolled out to begin forming the front row. (Walker)

Crew members typically watch over their mount, knowing the driver will probably wait until the last possible moment before appearing. (Walker)

seen to remove their hats.

The invocation came next, and then at 10:49, the very popular Jim Nabors jumped up onto the wall to deliver ''Back Home Again in Indiana'' as he has many times in the past.

At a signal given about halfway through the song, the ropes of not one, not two, but three tents were pulled, opening the tops and allowing thousands of brightly colored balloons to pour into the sky.

At 10:52, the widow of the late Tony Hulman, Mary Fendrich Hulman, now in her eighties, gave a strong ''Gentlemen, start your engines'' and the air was filled with glorious noise.

Two Chrysler LeBaron pace cars pulled away into the first turn at a slow speed and a third, the pace car proper, remained stationary while waiting for clearance from the tower.

Mechanics raised their arms in the air to signify that their particular cars were fired and ready to go. And the engines revved!

Finally, the pace car, driven by Carroll Shelby and carrying the USAC Registrar, Bob Cassaday, moved underway.

All 33 of the cars pulled off the line, Fittipaldi's being the last to leave.

Joseph R. Cloutier, President of the Indianapolis Motor Speedway, drove the leading pace car, his only passenger being Lee Iacocca, the head of Chrysler Corporation. Next came the car driven by Tony Hulman George and carrying Hal Sperlich and Gerry Greenwald, President and Chairman respectively of Chrysler Motors.

At the end of the second lap and the beginning of the final pace lap, the Cloutier and George cars pulled onto the pit lane, leaving the Shelby and Cassaday car alone on the track with the 33 starters.

Already a car was having difficulties. Flames were pouring from the turbocharger of the Chevrolet V-6-powered car of George Snider, and George was forced to pit before the race even began.

Quite unlike the pace laps of recent years, the lineup this time was just about perfect, with perhaps the neatest alignment of rows since the ''roadster'' days.

The pace car accelerated to about 115 MPH and roared ahead of the field on the backstretch, transferring the pacing duties to Mario Andretti. Shelby brought his LeBaron around to the pit lane far ahead of what was now a pack of 32 rather than 33.

The field, still beautifully lined up, came through turn four. Andretti began to pick up the pace, Mears staying with him, Rahal lagging slightly behind. Closer they came.

Duane Sweeney was waiting, watching, clutching his pair of green flags. Out they came - and the race was on!

SEE INDY UP CLOSE!

3rd Annual

INDY MOTORSPORTS EXPO

SPONSORED BY

PPG

MAY 26-28, 1988

Grammy winner Sandi Patti, from nearby Anderson, IN., sings the National Anthem. (IMS-D. Young)

Chrysler's head man, Lee Iacocca, on hand to ride in one of the LeBaron pace cars. (IMS-Spargur)

Front row starters Mario Andretti and Rick Mears pass the final minutes in conversation. (Whitlow)

Rahal had fallen several car lengths behind as Mears tried to beat Andretti to the turn. There was plenty of shuffling all through the pack, and one just couldn't decide where to look.

Down into the first turn they went, and there was trouble almost immediately. Josele Garza tried to go low through turn one and evidently ran into the same problem which almost spelled disaster for Danny Sullivan while taking the lead two years ago. Josele apparently lost traction on the painted yellow line and was into a spin almost before he knew it.

The tail was out and the car pirouetted towards the outer retaining wall in the short chute, miraculously being missed by cars on both sides. He almost went nose first into the left-hand side of Al Unser, but managed to miss Al before straightening out the spin. He slid in the correct direction for many yards, but was completely sideways with the tail pointing towards the outside wall. Two other cars were into slides to try to avoid him, Pancho Carter, Josele's own teammate, and ''rookie'' Stan Fox being almost sideways right behind Josele. Stan was able to get down into the infield grass to avoid a collision, but Pancho wasn't quite so lucky. Pancho was heading for the infield as well and just managed to clip Josele's left front wheel with his right rear, causing items to pop from either or both of the cars. The yellow was on 15 seconds into the race.

Pancho managed to regain control and

Emil Andres and Johnny Pawl take the 1909 Buick on a lap. (Walker)

Jim Nabors, ready to sing "Back Home Again in Indiana." (Wendt)

kept running, accompanied around to the pits by a couple of wreckers. Pancho was encountering trouble in keeping straight from some obvious suspension damage to the right rear.

Josele also kept going and made it around to the pits.

Andretti came around in the lead under yellow with Mears and Rahal right behind him. Roberto Guerrero, Dick Simon and Johnny Rutherford had each been able to get ahead of the fourth-starting A.J. Foyt, while Michael Andretti, Arie Luyendyk and Ludwig Heimrath, Jr. made up the first ten. The next ten were Rich Vogler, Jeff MacPherson, Geoff

Shelly Unser bids husband Al, Jr. a safe journey. (IMS- Binkley)

Brabham, Danny Sullivan, Scott Brayton, Fabrizio Barbazza, Gary Bettenhausen, Gordon Johncock, Derek Daly and Al Unser, Jr. Then came Tom Sneva, Davy Jones, Al Unser, Kevin Cogan, Randy Lewis, Ed Pimm, Tony Bettenhausen, Stan Fox, Emerson Fittipaldi and Steve Chassey. Pancho Carter and George Snider were both pit-bound, while Garza was about to be.

The field was held in check for the next several laps while debris from the Garza/Carter incident was picked up.

The pace car was now being driven by Don Bailey, who has performed the function during the race cautions since 1985. An exceedingly quick change of drivers was required on this occasion, since Carroll Shelby was still climbing out of the car when the yellow popped on!

The pace car came in after five laps and the green flag was given to Andretti, who immediately began to lap at better than 204 mph. Nothing much happened in the way of position changes during the opening laps, but Randy Lewis soon dropped way off and headed for the pits with only seven laps on his board.

The order at ten laps (with the average speed showing only 124.924 mph against the 202 record by Michael Andretti a year ago) was Andretti, Mears, Rahal, Guerrero, Simon, Rutherford, Foyt, Michael Andretti, Luyendyk, and Heimrath in the first ten, followed by Vogler, Sullivan, Brabham, Barbazza, Brayton, Johncock, Sneva, MacPherson, Gary Bettenhausen, Al Unser, Jr., Cogan, Daly, Jones, Al Unser, Pimm, Fox, Tony Bettenhausen, Fittipaldi and Chassey.

Pancho Carter went back into action after some repair work to his right rear suspension and the loss of ten laps.

Fittipaldi ducked in for a wing adjustment, and pretty soon Carter was back in to change plugs and the spark box.

Andretti's pace was such that he had caught and lapped Steve Chassey at 13 laps and had done the same thing to Tony Bettenhausen a lap later.

Guerrero moved up to take 3rd place away from Rahal after 15 laps and Johncock was on the move, passing Brabham for 14th.

Stan Fox went a lap down and so did Ed Pimm. As Mario came down to complete 17 laps he put one on Al Unser!

Davy Jones went under, as did Daly and Cogan. Mario seemed to be able to go anywhere he wished, lapping cars at will. He was the only person lapping consistently at over 200 and had built a ten-second lead over Mears at 20 laps. He had the average up to 153, but this fell way below the Mears 1984 record of 198.4.

The top ten at 20 laps were Andretti, Mears, Guerrero, Rahal, Simon, Rutherford, Michael Andretti, Luyendyk, Foyt and Heimrath. The second ten were Sullivan, Barbazza, Johncock, Vogler, Brabham, Sneva, Brayton, Al Unser, Jr., Gary Bettenhausen and the lapped Cogan, followed by Daly, Jones, Al Unser, Pimm, Fox, Chassey, Tony Bettenhausen and, two laps down, Fittipaldi. In the pits were Carter, Garza, Lewis, Snider and MacPherson, who would be in and out during the next several laps to check out a mysterious vibration.

Sullivan passed Heimrath and Foyt on consecutive laps to run 9th at 22 laps, as only 16 cars remained on the lead lap now.

Tony Bettenhausen, Foyt, Barbazza,

Turn one, lap one action as Josele Garza dips below the inside line between the two Unsers . . . gets sideways . . . Davy Jones clears as Big Al successfully takes evasive action . . .

and Kevin Cogan were in and out with quick stops and Johncock was in quickly for fuel.

Andretti lapped fifteenth-place Brayton at 25 laps and Guerrero passed Mears for second!

Heimrath, running 10th, went tearing in for three wheels and fuel, took off and never completed another lap. His left rear wheel came off as he was negotiating the north short chute and he spun into turn four, fortunately without contacting anything.

On came the yellow, just as some of the leaders were already making their first routine pit stops, and moments later many of the others were in too.

Andretti changed all but the front left wheel while Guerrero, who led one lap by staying out longer, took on fuel only.

Only seven cars were in the lead lap now, with Rahal, Luyendyk, Guerrero, Sullivan, Vogler and Mears the only ones not to have been lapped by Andretti. Sneva, Johncock and Barbazza completed the first ten.

Kevin Cogan, who came so close to winning the "500" in 1986, was out of this one before it was half an hour old. Engine failure was given as the reason out, while the '86 runner-up watched his car being pushed back to the garage area for the day.

Michael Andretti suddenly slowed on the mainstraight and looked as if he was going to pull off onto the first turn grass.

He made it all the way around, but his subsequent pit stop became mayhem when fire broke out. He quickly scrambled from the cockpit. He made preparations to get back in, but then it was discovered that the left rear constant velocity joint was broken, so he was done for the day anyway.

The retirements had been coming thick and fast. George Snider was declared out of it without a single lap being turned other than the pace laps. The Dick Simon entry of Ludwig Heimrath, Jr., could not continue, and the car of Randy Lewis was also being wheeled away, only eight laps on the latter.

Josele Garza returned to the track after almost a half hour of repairs, his crew deserving all kinds of credit for an outstanding "duct tape special" job!

The green was flashed to Andretti as he completed 33 laps. Luyendyk got the jump on Rahal and went to 2nd!

Poor Rich Vogler had no sooner come out of the pits in 6th than he had to go back in for a quick visit. Mears went to 6th.

A lap later Mears went to 5th as defending winner Rahal came in for a stop of almost five full minutes to check out the electrical system and replace the plugs.

The shakeup continued as only five cars now remained in the lead lap. The first ten at 35 laps were Andretti, Luyendyk, Guerrero, Sullivan and Mears in the lead lap with Sneva, Johncock, Barbazza, Rutherford and Simon a lap down. Brayton, Foyt, Al, Jr., Brabham, Pimm, Daly and Al, Sr. were the next half dozen, occupying positions 11 through 17. Rick Mears was lapped by Andretti

Machinists crew goes to work on Josele's body damage. (Whitlow)

. . .Cogan appears awfully vulnerable . . .but Josele's own teammate, Pancho Carter, unavoidably clips the left front as bits of bodywork go flying. (Sequence by Bill Ridley)

at 38 laps, just as Guerrero was regaining 2nd from Luyendyk.

The yellow popped on for the third time on the 39th lap, and this time it was to clear some debris from the track.

The average speed at 40 laps had climbed to 153.363 mph, but was far below Mario's own record of 192.724 set in 1984.

The complete rundown at 100 miles had Andretti, Guerrero, Luyendyk, and Sullivan in the leader's lap, followed by Mears, Sneva, Rutherford, Johncock, Simon and Brayton as the top ten, one lap down. Next came Little Al, Big Al, Foyt, Brabham, Pimm, Daly, and Barbazza, also one lap down. Two laps behind were Gary Bettenhausen, Vogler,

Fox, and Chassey. Three laps down were Fittipaldi and Tony Bettenhausen, followed by Davy Jones and Rahal at six laps down. Jeff MacPherson had logged in 27 laps, Pancho Carter 22 and Garza a mere seven. He was back in the pits again and ranking 32nd, according to the number of laps completed!

Davy Jones, the fastest "rookie" in the field as well as the youngest driver this year at only 22, was also going to the sidelines at this point with what was mysteriously described as "a hole in the engine".

The twenty-seven survivors (actually 26 plus the pit stop-plagued Garza) came around for the green on Andretti's 42nd lap. Johncock had just stopped quickly

for fuel, but dropped himself from the first ten as Little Al came in at the bottom of it.

Andretti continued to dominate. He picked up the pace again with several laps at 202 and then moved up into the 203/204 range with the lapped Tom Sneva as the only other person routinely at over 200. Mario's lead over Guerrero and Luyendyk of five seconds and seven seconds respectively at 43 laps went to 14 and 15 seconds by lap 50. Mario's 50th lap was turned at 204.2 with nobody else over 200 on that lap, his average coming up to over 156 but still 30 mph down on his own 1984 record.

The top ten at the one quarter distance were Andretti, Guerrero, Luyendyk, Sul-

Randy Lewis is an early casualty. (Strauser)

MacPherson spends much of the first half hour heading for the pits. (deBrier)

65

Heimrath sheds a left rear and digs into infield grass . . . slides out behind Geoff Brabham . . . and pirouettes around . . . while the wreckers are rolling before he has stopped. (sequence by Arnie deBrier)

livan, Sneva, Mears, Rutherford, Brayton, Little Al and Simon. Then came Big Al, Brabham, Barbazza, Pimm, Daly, Johncock and Foyt.

The Al Unsers, father and son, each made up a position on the 51st lap, Little Al moving around Brayton for 8th and Big Al entering the top ten for the first time at the expense of Simon.

Mario's pace backed off to under 200, but he still maintained his 15-second lead over Guerrero. At 56 laps he lapped Daly and Foyt for the second time.

Josele Garza reentered the race after another round of body patchwork to complete his eighth lap just as Mario was turning his 56th!

The next round of pit stops was approaching and Sneva was the first of the leading ten to come in. Luyendyk was next, with Brayton, Rutherford and Mears all in for quick stops. Al Unser, Jr. stalled as he was leaving and ended up losing more than a minute. A small fire erupted but was quickly extinguished.

Guerrero came in as he was completing his 60th lap, Mario staying out until the next time around. Roberto took fuel only in 20 seconds but was to give up 2nd place to Danny Sullivan, who had not yet stopped.

Andretti, whose pit was north of the start/finish line, was given fuel and three fresh wheels in under 18 seconds. He was gearing up down the pit lane just as Sullivan came by on the track to take the lead. Andretti went chasing after him, but then the yellow light came on! More debris was reported on the track.

The pace car picked up Sullivan, who continued to stay on the track until his 64th lap, when he came in for a 16-second stop for fuel. Andretti was returned to the lead with Guerrero in second place, while Sullivan kept himself in 3rd as the only other person in the lead lap. Sneva's excellent stop had elevated him to 4th, one lap plus a few yards out of the lead.

It was Brayton directly behind the pace car ahead of Gary Bettenhausen, Vogler, Barbazza and then Andretti, followed by Brabham, Garza, Sneva and then Guerrero.

It took Mario just a couple of laps to thread his way through the slower cars in front of him once the green returned, and he was plain sailing by the 70th lap. Guerrero did not have as easy a time of it, however, and was obliged to run behind Brayton and Sneva for several laps.

The order at 70 laps was Andretti, Guerrero and Sullivan in the lead lap, followed by Sneva, Big Al, Mears, Luyendyk, and Rutherford one lap behind, and Brayton, Barbazza, Brabham, Simon, Foyt, Daly and Pimm two laps behind.

Rahal was back in the pits for his third

66

Mario simply dominates the race. (IMS-Sparks)

lengthy stop of the day, the engine cover removed yet again while attempts were being made to cure an electrical disorder.

Once again it was Sneva who was the only person to be lapping at over 200 other than Andretti. Guerrero was still racing Brayton and losing a second lap to Andretti.

Steve Chassey's run looked as if it was over just after Andretti had completed his 70th lap. Smoke was pouring from the exhaust on Chassey's car as he brought it through turn four below the yellow line.

A few moments later, Geoff Brabham came in, explaining that the oil light was on and that he didn't wish to blow the engine. It later turned out that an electrical glitch was causing the light to burn when there was really no problem at all. He had therefore given up 11th place and retired with a car that had nothing wrong with it!

There was quite a procession to the garage area as the cars of Chassey and Brabham were taken there within a few moments of each other. There were still more. Pancho Carter's crew diagnosed a broken valve on his machine, and so he was done.

Rahal wasn't the only former winner with an electrical problem, as Rick Mears gave up 6th place to head pitward. Mears

would stay for better than five minutes, during which time Rahal's crew would be forced to give up. The car of the defending winner was withdrawn and pushed away.

Andretti had an eight-second lead over Guerrero at 80 laps, and no sooner had they completed the 200-mile mark than the yellow came on for the fifth time. Danny Sullivan, running 3rd, had spun through turn four and kept going without hitting anything. The yellow was thrown nevertheless, requiring that the pace car procedure be followed through.

This was great timing for the leaders, who both ducked in next time around. Guerrero was given credit for leading the 81st lap, inasmuch as he had to cross the start/finish line in order to reach his pit, while Andretti did not. Mario's outstanding crew had all four wheels changed and a supply of fuel all completed in under 18 seconds. Roberto's car evidently had a faulty air jack in the rear and it was necessary to use a jack stand. The stop took 27 seconds, which was rather immaterial because of the yellow flag situation but would have been costly under green.

Sullivan was in for a tire check and a change on three corners. Not only did he protect 3rd place, the pack-up situation

allowed him to close up not far behind Andretti and Guerrero! He was nine cars behind Mario in the single file line.

The withdrawal of so many cars was encouraging for those in the back who were still running. Meanwhile, two other winners were having their troubles. Rick Mears made a 4 1/2 minute stop to try to cure yet another electrical malady and Gordon Johncock was having his spark plugs changed.

Mears went back out for one more lap on the track and then returned to retire after a consultation with his crew. His car was rolled back from his far south pit to Gasoline Alley and the car of Gordon Johncock was taken there also. There were now 21 cars running.

Only minutes before, every one of the record nine former winners had still been in contention. Not only had three of them just dropped out in short order, a fourth was now pit-side. Three-time winner Johnny Rutherford was also having electrical problems, but Johnny Capels and the crew were replacing the distributor rotor and the spark box. Rutherford would be detained for almost 20 minutes.

Andretti had only Dick Simon ahead of him behind the pace car as the green was waved on Mario's 84th lap. Guerrero had only the lapped car of Tony Bettenhausen

JOIN OUR TEAM
"SAY _NO_ TO DRUGS"

A. J. FOYT
USAC, CART, NASCAR, IMSA

GREG SACKS
NASCAR

MICHAEL ANDRETTI
USAC, CART, IMSA

NEIL BONNETT
NASCAR

GEOFF BRABHAM
USAC, CART, IMSA

CALE YARBOROUGH
NASCAR

TERRY LABONTE
NASCAR

BOBBY RAHAL
USAC, CART, IMSA

Find out how **you** can join the team to help make America "drug-free." Call the National Federation of Parents for Drug-Free Youth at 1-800-55**4-KIDS**.

Team
VALVOLINE.
SAY _NO_ TO DRUGS

87-VMO-053-4
Printed in U.S.A.

Michael Andretti hops out as fire erupts. (IMS-Hunter)

between him and Andretti.

Off went Andretti again. His 86th lap was almost 204. Laps of 202 and 203 were quite common for him at this stage, while not one other competitor was over 200. Guerrero had fallen to a 7 1/2-second deficit at 90 laps.

Andretti's average for 90 laps was up to 160.676 mph, but quite a bit under Rahal's 174 mph record from last year because of the yellows.

Guerrero, of course, was 2nd and Sullivan was 28 seconds behind in 3rd. Al Unser was now in 4th, ahead of Sneva, with Luyendyk hanging in there with both of them one lap behind. Dick Simon was back up to 7th, two laps down, as

were Barbazza, Brayton, Foyt, and Pimm, who ranked through 11th. Daly, Fittipaldi, Little Al and Gary Bettenhausen were next, 87 laps on their boards. Then it was Vogler and Fox, 86 laps, and Tony Bettenhausen, 84. The other three still in it were Rutherford, who was pit-side with 79 laps, and the delayed MacPherson with 76, plus Garza, who now had 41 laps completed. Mac-Pherson was showing as 21st and Garza 27th, still with a lap total that was less than several people who had dropped out.

Andretti began to stretch his lead at will again, building approximately one second per lap to his advantage over Guerrero. The only other runner regularly in the 200 range during this segment of

green was Dick Simon, who was a couple of laps behind in 7th. On the other hand, Danny Sullivan, who had been only seven seconds out of the lead under caution, was running below 190 to Andretti's 202's and losing between three and four seconds per lap for some reason. Andretti lapped Sullivan on the 94th lap, an indication right there that Danny was running well off the pace. The only change among the positions, however, was that Foyt passed Brayton for 9th on the leader's 93rd lap.

Dick Simon's good fortune for the day was put on temporary hold as he was slowing down on the course. He had run out of fuel and was attempting to make it around to his pit. He came up short, so the yellow was displayed while the Simon car was towed in.

This was most timely for all of the front runners, who were due at this time anyway.

Once again Guerrero and Andretti came in together, and once again Andretti forfeited the race lead to Guerrero by being pitted north of the start/finish line. Andretti took on fuel and three wheels in 18 seconds, while Guerrero took fuel only in 14. But Andretti went roaring down the pit lane and was able to get around Guerrero before lining up behind the pace car.

Luyendyk had gained the most advantage during the latest round of spots by coming out ahead of Al Unser and Sneva for 4th place.

It was Stan Fox lined up directly behind the pace car ahead of MacPherson and Vogler, then Andretti and Guerrero right together. Tony Bettenhausen came next, followed by the 3rd and 4th-placed cars of Sullivan and Luyendyk together, the lapped car of Gary Bettenhausen, and the 5th and 6th- placed cars of Al Unser

Chris Mears charts her husband's progress. (IMS-Binkley)

Rookie Fox prepares to be lapped by defending winner Rahal. (Walker)

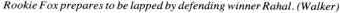

Critical fuel consumption leads crew members to perform this maneuver routinely after each stop. (IMS-L. Young)

and Sneva, who were in the same lap with Sullivan and Luyendyk. Next came 7th-placed Barbazza, two laps down, and then eight other hardy souls who were still hanging in there.

The Dick Simon car was pushed down the pit lane to its pit and soon was back in action with a full load of fuel.

The green returned as Andretti was completing his 101st lap.

Johnny Rutherford returned to the track after a 20-minute delay to change the spark box, but he did only one slow lap before coming back in. This time the heat shield was changed, another five-minute job.

As fate would have it, Simon got out and up to speed directly in front of Andretti and Guerrero. Mario got around but Roberto did not. Mario built another five seconds by his 110th lap as Simon and Guerrero circulated together for lap after lap at right under 200.

Ed Pimm, who had just gone to 9th place, had to come in and begin a series of long stops for the problem of the day, electrics.

Josele Garza was on his seventh stop of the day, this time to change a radiator.

Johnny Rutherford's second long stop was now completed just as Andretti completed 110 laps.

The order was: Andretti by five seconds over Guerrero, followed by Sullivan, Al Unser, Luyendyk and Sneva,

each a lap down and with Sneva falling further behind with an engine that had developed a decided bark to it. Barbazza, Foyt and Brayton were 7th, 8th and 9th, two laps behind. Al Unser, Jr., Fittipaldi and Daly were three laps behind, Vogler and Gary Bettenhausen four laps behind, followed by Pimm and Fox, five laps behind. Simon and Tony Bettenhausen each had 103 laps in, MacPherson, 95, Rutherford 81 and Garza, pit-side and actually 26th on the board, 51 laps in.

Not only had Sneva dropped off the pace, Luyendyk was losing some ground as well. Andretti lapped both of them for the second time in short order.

Guerrero finally found a way around Simon in traffic on his 118th lap and was now seven seconds behind.

Andretti had the average at 120 laps up to 164.227, which was about eight miles per hour shy of Rahal's 1986 record but picking up. Sullivan and Al Unser were right together for 3rd and 4th, but about a lap and a half behind Andretti. Luyendyk and Sneva were still 5th and 6th but losing ground now to Fabrizio Barbazza, who was by far the strongest of the ''rookies''. Brayton and Foyt were 8th and 9th, three laps down, with Al Unser, Jr., Fittipaldi, Daly, and Gary Bettenhausen each four laps in arrears.

The car of Rich Vogler was pushed away, the victim of a broken rocker arm. Many people were disappointed when A.J. Foyt drifted in to retire from his 30th consecutive Indianapolis ''500''. He was running 9th when he pulled in. Nineteen cars were left.

Garza came back in, his total pit stop time for the day so far amounting to almost one hour!

Luyendyk's ''drop-off'' rate was now greater than Sneva's, but Barbazza was now right on the tails of both of them. Sneva took 5th from Luyendyk on Andretti's 123rd lap and then Barbazza passed both of them the next time around!

Ed Pimm went back onto the track just after Andretti had completed 125 laps, a

Smoke signals the end for Davy Jones. (Strauser)

ten-minute stop to change the spark box merely preceding an even longer one to change the battery.

Al Unser stopped for fuel and wheels on all four corners during Andretti's 126th lap and went down a second lap but never lost 4th place. Some real drama was about to unfold.

Andretti went by for the 127th time and Guerrero peeled off into the pits. Roberto received fuel and three wheels in 20 seconds.

Guerrero went scampering back into the race, but Andretti did not stop on the next lap.

Mario waited until the 129th before coming in for fuel and three wheels, also in 20 seconds. Guerrero flashed by the line 22 seconds after Andretti had crossed the line on his way back into the race, but Roberto was obviously slicing away at that disadvantage, since he was at speed on the track and Mario was still getting underway.

Simon loses valuable time by running out of fuel. (Whitlow)

Tony Bettenhausen loses a right front wheel . . .   . . . and it is hit head-on by Guerrero. (Sequence by John Mahoney)

Guerrero was tearing through the north short chute with his sights set on the whereabouts of Andretti up ahead of him. Instantly, there was an object in his way. The right front wheel from Tony Bettenhausen's car had come adrift and while Tony was moving to the apron to bring the car on in, the wheel was still rolling at speed in the groove. Guerrero had no alternative but to smash headlong into the errant wheel. It popped the nose cone from the front of the car and ran up over the windshield just inches from Guerrero's head. It could have spelled disaster for Guerrero. Instead, it spelled disaster for somebody else.

Guerrero immediately pulled down to the inside of turn four and headed at speed for his pit, minus the nose cone. The infamous wheel had been struck so hard by Guerrero's 200 mile per hour head-on hit that it had been projected straight up in the air to a considerable height. It then arced and began its descent on the wrong side of the seemingly more than adequate protective fence. It headed down for the back of an uncovered grandstand on the outside of the track and came within inches of clearing it entirely. As fate would have it, one luckless spectator in the very top row, 41-year-old Lyle Kurtenbach of Rothschild, Wisconsin, was struck as it went over and for the first time in 49 years, a spectator was to lose his life as a result of something that occurred on the track.

Arie Luyendyk was out of the race. Slowing somewhat but still running 8th, he came in for his sixth stop and hit a wheel that was sitting ready to be placed on his car. A crewman was also struck, but he escaped with nothing more than a "sore body", also known as "race track

rheumatism". The striking of the wheel had damaged the right front suspension to the extent that the car had to be withdrawn.

Guerrero lost over a lap in having his car checked over and fitted with a spare nose cone, which had thoughtfully been placed pit-side in readiness.

There was concern that Guerrero's handling might now be hampered as Sullivan moved up into 2nd place.

Danny immediately ducked in for a stop, which now returned 2nd to Guerrero and placed Andretti alone in the lead lap.

Sullivan actually dropped to 4th, just behind Al Unser, as he returned to the track. Barbazza, 5th, was exactly three laps behind Andretti, being next in line behind Mario in the procession following the pace car. Scott Brayton was elevated to 6th, also three laps behind. Tom Sneva was in the first ten, but dropped out of it due to a three-minute stop to tighten a loose turbocharger hose. Moving up to

complete the first ten were Al Unser, Jr., Fittipaldi, Daly and Gary Bettenhausen. The green came out for Mario's 134th lap.

Suddenly, Al Unser was in the picture. Not only was he 3rd, he was right behind Guerrero.

Andretti moved back into the 200 mph range and the only person to match him was Guerrero. Al began to fade, but just a fraction each lap.

Fittipaldi came down the inside of the mainstraight and pulled his 8th-place runner off into the first turn infield grass. Daly and Gary Bettenhausen went to 8th and 9th while the delayed Sneva claimed 10th the next time around.

No sooner had Daly taken 8th than he drifted into his pit. Up they moved again with Gary Bettenhausen to 8th, Sneva to 9th and Simon to 10th. It had become very much a race of survival and more of an endurance contest than anything. The only people who really hadn't encountered any problems thus far were Andret-

Steve Chassey is through for the day. (deBrier)

Today's Full-Size Car

A luxury car without room just isn't luxurious. But everything you expect from a luxury car, along with comfortable room, is still available in one high quality vehicle... a Starcraft van. As shown below, a full-size Starcraft lets you take along family, friends, and all their gear.

With Starcraft you get style and tasteful elegance. You also get all the features found in today's luxury cars, as well as features not found on **any** car. In fact, a world class Starcraft with all options costs thousands less than some luxury automobiles.

In addition to comfort, luxury, and room, you also get Starcraft's reputation for quality that dates back to 1903. Our total committment to quality also assures you of prompt turnaround on parts, service, and warranty claims. That's why there are more Starcrafts on the road than any other brand.

Find out what first class travel was always meant to be. For more information, write for our free full-color 34-page catalog. Starcraft vans are available on GMC, Chevrolet, and Ford chassis.

**Starcraft
2703 College Avenue
Goshen, IN 46526**

Starcraft vans have earned a reputation for quality and luxury throughout the Indy Car Circuit. Only Starcraft has been selected as the supplier of V.I.P. vehicles for this year's Indianapolis 500. Starcraft is also the Official Van of the Michigan International Speedway, the Pocono 500, and the Championship Drivers Association. For the best van made today, there's only one choice... Starcraft.

STARCRAFT

Quality and Integrity Since 1903

Guerrero heads for his pit minus the nose cone. (deBrier)

for three wheels and fuel in 19 seconds, but a fantastic 16-second stop only for fuel had Al Unser out in 2nd place!

Ed Pimm's crew finally had to give up on their car during this caution period for Sneva's accident so that car left the pit area with 109 laps to its credit and reduced the field to just 14.

The Sneva cleanup process required eleven minutes and took Andretti to his 158th lap. He maintained his one-lap advantage over Unser, Guerrero and Sullivan, while the only people between him and a clear track were Garza and Fox. He disposed of them without difficulty and ran his 160th lap at over 200.

Mario's 161.8 mph average was ten miles per hour under the Rick Mears record of 1986, but he was still enjoying that full lap lead over any challenger.

It was Al Unser, Guerrero and Sullivan with 159 laps, Barbazza, 157, Brayton, 156, Al Unser, Jr., 155 and Gary Bettenhausen, 154 making up the first eight, followed by Simon at 152 and Stan Fox now up into the top ten with 151. Tony Bettenhausen had 150, MacPherson, 141, Rutherford, 130 and Garza, 88 for the balance of the runners. MacPherson was showing as 13th and Rutherford as 16th, inasmuch as the retired trio of Sneva, Daly and Fittipaldi had lap counts of 143, 133 and 131 respectively. Garza was now up to 21st! More drama.

Fabrizio Barbazza came from behind to pass Tony Bettenhausen, Dick Simon and Gary Bettenhausen over a period of several laps, and no sooner had he lapped Gary than he darn near took out all four of them!

He spun through turn four, ended up straight and kept going, while Gary moved to the inside of the main straight and slowed a little to regain composure. A sideplate had broken from the rear wing of Barbazza's car to cause an unexpected change in handling.

The yellow was called for and subsequently appeared for the ninth time as smoke from Barbazza's tires dissipated across turn four.

ti, Al Unser and Barbazza, everyone else having had some encounter or another.

Mario had a lap plus a dozen or so seconds over Guerrero and Unser at his 140th lap. Sullivan had faded somewhat and was another 14 seconds behind them. Barbazza was three laps behind in 5th with Brayton 6th. Then it was Al, Jr., 136 laps, Gary Bettenhausen, 135, Sneva, 134, and Simon, 133 for the top ten. Eleventh at this point was Daly, who was in the pits, followed by Fox, who was still running with 132 laps. Tony Bettenhausen had 131 laps, MacPherson, 123, Rutherford, 111, Pimm (in the pits), 107 and Garza, 72. Josele was running 23rd, although only 17 cars remained in the race. Technically, Fittipaldi still ranked 13th, Luyendyk, 15th, Foyt 17th and Vogler 19th, although all four were out of the race and would be pushed down in the standings as survivors completed greater distances.

Another who would go no further was Daly, sidelined by undisclosed engine problems.

It was Mario by a lap plus 13 seconds when the yellow was thrown for the eighth time on the 150th lap.

Tom Sneva had contacted the outer wall exiting turn two while running 9th.

Tom climbed out uninjured but was obviously through for the day with extensive damage down the right side of the car.

The timing was again outstanding for Mario. In he went for three wheels, a shot of fuel and was on his way in under 18 seconds.

Guerrero was in the next time around

Sneva creams the turn two concrete. (Eakins)

Little people need big people.

Little people like this need big people like you to help them grow up right. They need a grownup for a friend...somebody to pal around with, and look up to, and trust. ☐ That's the reason for Big Brothers and Big Sisters. We're here to put you together with a kid who really needs you. ☐ Think about helping. Look up Big Brothers/Big Sisters in your white pages and give us a call. We'll send you complete information. **BIG BROTHERS/BIG SISTERS OF AMERICA** 🅑
National Headquarters, 230 North 13th Street, Philadelphia, Pennsylvania 19107

Barbazza has a magnificent day. (IMS-W. Young)

Barbazza stopped for a complete set of tires during this yellow and while he lost a little time on the track, he never lost a position. In fact, he GAINED one! Moments earlier, Danny Sullivan had lost power and drifted to a stop out on the course.

There were no stops among the leaders during this brief yellow, as those below Sullivan would subsequently pick up a spot.

The green came out for the completion of Mario's 166th lap and Guerrero got the jump on Unser!

This time Guerrero and Unser stayed hooked up with Andretti while Rutherford was right with them, although spotting them some 30 laps. The quartet broke from the others and circulated at better than 200.

At 170 laps it was Mario at 161.261 mph (the record being 170.097 mph by Mears from last year) by a lap plus a few feet over Guerrero and Unser. Barbazza had 167 laps in for 4th while Brayton had 166 in for 5th. Then it was Al Unser, Jr. at 165 and Gary Bettenhausen at 164 for 6th and 7th. Dick Simon had 162 for 8th and Stan Fox was running 9th with 161. Tony Bettenhausen had moved into 10th with 160 and the now-pitted Sullivan was 11th. MacPherson had 151 laps in for 12th, while Rutherford and Garza showed 140 and 98 respectively. Danny Sullivan's car was pushed past the start/finish line on its way back to its pit, Danny still showing in 11th place.

Once again, Al Unser had fallen behind by several seconds, but Guerrero was now matching Andretti lap for lap, just a few yards plus one lap behind. Rutherford had also fallen behind a little.

Al Unser then zipped in under green and made a remarkable fuel stop for only

11 seconds! He shouldn't have to stop again and he now stood an excellent opportunity of returning to the lead lap when Mario's imminent stop came.

One hundred and seventy-five laps and the leaders were at 202.

One hundred and seventy-six laps and they were again at 202.

One hundred and seventy-seven laps AND MARIO WAS SLOWING DOWN!

Over to the inside, down the straight next to the inner wall, and the crowd ovation was phenomenal! Guerrero was around and into the lead lap.

Onto the backstretch and Mario was still on the inside, Guerrero streaking away from him.

Guerrero streaked over the line, still not in the lead but hurtling towards it.

Mario was still making his way around. He'd make it to the pits. Down into the lane he came, and screaming by went Guerrero into the lead!

Mario's trouble-free run was now ruined. He had led 170 of the 177 laps just completed, giving up only to Sullivan for four laps during pit stops and three others to Guerrero, perhaps only because of pit placement. Had Mario been pitted south of the start/finish line, he might have led 173 of the 177 laps up until this point.

It was electrical. The electronic fuel-metering device was malfunctioning. The spark box was changed and the wastegate was changed.

Guerrero now had a lead of 42 seconds over Al Unser, but there was another stop due for Roberto.

Still more drama among the top ten. Scott Brayton, up to a fine 5th place for the last several laps, was knocked out of it with an engine failure. Sullivan was out of it now!

Guerrero was up to 203, and as he completed his 180th lap he lapped Unser! Roberto still had that final stop to go, but he was flying now and apparently heading for the checker. Andretti was still pit-side.

The amazing Barbazza went to 3rd but almost three laps down to Guerrero.

Coming around for the start of his 183rd lap, and Guerrero was heading in for his stop.

The tires? They were fine. Just a quick shot of fuel to last for the final 18 laps. Away he went . . . AND HE STALLED! The crowd went crazy. HE STALLED AGAIN! THERE WENT AL UNSER INTO THE LEAD LAP!

Frantically, the crew pushed the car, breaking into a desperate run.

The engine caught and the car rumbled

MARIO SLOWS! (deBrier)

Andretti crew members search for the problem. (D. Young)

out of the pits, while Al Unser was covering ground at the rate of a football field for every second on the clock.

Out of turn four came Unser, down the straight, over the line and into the lead. Through turns one and two. There was Guerrero. Down the backstretch and before Roberto could reach his maximum, he was pipped by the amazing Al, to be pushed a lap down.

Down to complete the 185th lap, and it was Al with a lap plus three seconds over Roberto, who was still cursing his overheated clutch.

Third again was Barbazza, while the retirement of Brayton and the plight of Andretti advanced Little Al from 6th to 5th to 4th and Gary Bettenhausen from 7th to 5th.

Mario came out of the pits to take just one slow lap and return for another change of spark box. Guerrero went to work on Al.

He clipped two seconds on the 186th lap and another second on the 187th.

Interestingly enough, Al, Jr. had been in front of both of them for a couple of laps and there was more than a little speculation that Little Al may try the same thing he did to Tom Sneva in an effort to assist his father near the end of the 1983 race. He didn't, however. Roberto blew by Al on the 190th lap to regain the lap. Out went Mario again for another lap. Barbazza made a quick stop for fuel and remained in 3rd.

Little Al was four laps behind in 4th, trailed by Gary Bettenhausen, 185 laps, Simon, 183, Fox, 182, and Andretti 179. MacPherson was up to 9th, in spite of having only 172 laps, and 10th was Tony Bettenhausen, who was sitting at his pit. Rutherford had 161 laps, Garza, 119 and that was it!

Guerrero was barely one second inside of the lap with Al Unser when the most incredible thing happened for Roberto. The yellow came on again.

Mario Andretti had been unsuccessful in completing another lap and was now stopped out on the track.

The knowledgeable crowd went wild again. They fully understood the ramifications. Out came the pace car.

The pace car allowed the speeding cars to catch up with it and then attempted to pull in front of Al Unser, who had closed up behind Guerrero. They were close together, so the pace car was obligated to pull in front of Roberto instead. Only after they had checked their speeds and were in single file was Roberto legally waved around the pace car and permitted to make up the lap and join on the back of the pack.

Andretti was out of the race now and so was Tony Bettenhausen. There were ten cars on the track.

Al Unser was directly behind the pace car at 195 laps and ready for the final blast to the finish. Next came Rutherford, some 29 laps behind! Then it was Simon, seven laps down and running 6th, Little Al, four laps down and 4th, and Garza still running with plenty of duct tape and 124 laps. Third-placed Barbazza was next in line with 193 laps on his board. Then followed Gary Bettenhausen, five laps behind in 5th, after whom was Guerrero. MacPherson, 9th with 177 laps and Fox, 7th with 187 completed the procession of battle-worn warriors.

The green came out and Guerrero immediately disposed of Bettenhausen and Barbazza.

He took care of Garza on the 197th lap and Little Al on the 198th, but that was as close as he could get.

Al completed his 198th lap at 200 with Rutherford right on his tail. Guerrero was stuck behind Simon! The gap was four seconds with two laps to go. The white flag was out for Al and another 200 mph lap heaped another half a second on the Guerrero disadvantage.

Out of the final turn and it was plain sailing for Al Unser. Right fist clenched behind his neck and elbow pushed into the air, he took the victory salute and thrust himself onto the plateau of A.J. Foyt with a fourth win in the Indianapolis ''500''.

Rutherford was right behind him with enough laps in to take 11th, salvaging at least something of what might conceivably have been a fourth victory for him as well.

It was Dick Simon over the line for 6th, his first finish ever in the top 12 on his 16th attempt, yet dealing with bewilderment at what might have happened had he not lost several laps by running

Another fast stop for Al Unser. (IMS-Hunter)

out of fuel.

Right behind Simon came Roberto Guerrero, just 4 1/2 seconds short and bobbing his head down in the cockpit momentarily at the checker as a muffled expletive was no doubt being annunciated.

Little Al came in for 4th after a long, long month, but with what turned out to be his highest finish here thus far.

Gary Bettenhausen, some problems along the way, survived for 5th and crossed the line just behind Josele Garza, who through the persistence of his crew was around at the finish instead of being eliminated on the opening lap. He was scored with 129 laps.

Then it was Stan Fox in the only surviving Foyt entry, completing 192 laps for 7th, and then the amazing Fabrizio Barbazza, backing off wisely on the final couple of laps to protect his fine 3rd place.

Jeff MacPherson, who lost nearly seven minutes during three stops in the first 23 laps and who never really got going, kept the Honda engine running in his car and was rewarded with 182 laps and an eighth-place finish in his first "500" start.

It was interesting to note the look on the face of Roger Penske during the usual pandemonium of Victory Circle. As the scissor-type mechanism elevated the entire platform bearing the winning car and crew skyward, his expression could perhaps best be described as incredulous.

Penske, who had just broken the long-standing record of the late Lou Moore by becoming the first entrant ever to win the "500" for a sixth time, obviously had believed throughout the winter and spring that he could win again. Perhaps he had

Consternation is on Katy Guerrero's face as Roberto stalls. (Whitlow)

not envisioned it quite in the manner it materialized!

The vast expense of developing the PC-16 chassis had certainly gone for naught—for the time being at least. By the same token, none of the Ilmor Chevrolet engines from the company he partially owned had been able to win, while the one which HAD performed (and in fact had completely DOMINATED for the first 88% of the race) was fielded by a team other than his own, which had done all of the initial testing and developing over the last year.

Rick Mears and Danny Sullivan, the two regulars of the Penske effort, had both been sidelined and could do nothing in the closing stages other than cheer on their on-again, off-again, on-again, off-again, on-again teammate.

Al Unser wasn't even assigned to a car

until three days before the final qualifying weekend. He was on the verge of leaving for home when he hired on with Penske merely as a replacement for the injured Danny Ongais, filling a vacancy the team wouldn't even have bothered to fill with anyone else. They used an old Cosworth engine because they were too low on available Ilmor Chevrolet parts and they bolted it into a March chassis that was not only a full year old, it had begun the month as a show car in the lobby of a Pennsylvania hotel!

But Al Unser was beaming up there. He'd certainly take it!

Five days short of his 48th birthday, Al was now a winner of the "500" for a record-tying fourth time, registering a finish within the first four for an unbe-

Al Unser is interviewed over the public address system after his lap of honor. (Walker)

Crew haul the Guerrero car back for a refire. (Whitlow)

81

Happy crew as Unser takes the lead. (Whitlow)

lievable tenth different year.

And there was one other statistic which linked an accomplishment by Al Unser all the way back to the very beginning of "500" history. The great Ralph DePalma had led some laps during the very first "500" in 1911 and then had paced the field for an incredible 196 laps in 1912, only to break down just a lap and a quar-

ter from the finish while still leading. No driver had led more laps than he had for the first two races combined. DePalma then led for great chunks in several subsequent races and was far and away at the head of the all-time list after the 1921 race with 613 total laps led.

Half a century after DePalma's final leading lap, however, the names of A.J.

Foyt and Al Unser had begun to creep ever closer, and Unser entered the 1987 race only 19 laps shy of finally overhauling DePalma's 66-year-old record.

Al had, just minutes earlier, assumed the lead on the 183rd lap and held it to the finish. He had led for 18 laps.

He hadn't broken DePalma's record. Incredibly enough, he had tied it!

Scott Brayton makes it to 5th before dropping out late. (deBrier)

Barbazza is thrilled with 3rd place. (Strauser)

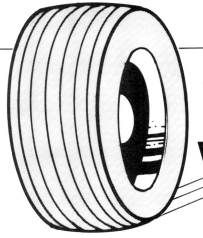
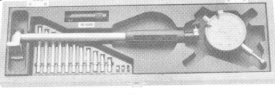

Everybody here is named Al Unser! (IMS-Scott)

USAC GOLD CROWN CHAMPIONSHIP BOX SCORE
1987 INDIANAPOLIS 500-MILE RACE
Indianapolis Motor Speedway - Indianapolis, Indiana
2.5-Mile Paved Oval
May 24, 1987 - 500 Miles
Total Purse - $4,490,375
Race Organizer - Joseph R. Cloutier

FIN. POS.	ST. POS.	DRIVER	CAR NAME/ NUMBER	MONEY WON	LAPS COMP.	RUNNING/ REASON OUT
1	20	Al Unser	Cummins Holset Turbo Spl.(25)	$526,763	200	Running
2	5	Roberto Guerrero	True Value STP March (4)	$305,013	200	Running
3	17	Fabrizio Barbazza	Arciero Winery (12)	$204,663	198	Running
4	22	Al Unser, Jr.	Domino's Pizza "Hot One" (30)	$142,963	196	Running
5	15	Gary Bettenhausen	Gohr Racing/Genesee Beer Wagon (56)	$132,213	195	Running
6	6	Dick Simon	Soundesign Stereo Spl. (22)	$131,813	193	Running
7	26	Stan Fox	Kerker Exhaust-Skoal Classic (41)	$111,263	192	Running
8	12	Jeff MacPherson	Team MacPherson March Honda (11)	$117,313	182	Running
9	1	Mario Andretti	Hanna Auto Wash Newman/Haas (5)	$368,063	180	Ignition
10	27	Tony Bettenhausen	Nationwise/Payless Mkt. (16)	$105,838	171	Engine
11	8	Johnny Rutherford	Vt. American Car (21)	$104,313	171	Running
12	13	Scott Brayton	Amway/Autostyle/Livingwell (91)	$103,063	167*	Engine
13	16	Danny Sullivan	Miller American Spl. (3)	$120,713	160	Engine
14	21	Tom Sneva	Skoal Bandit (33)	$103,313	143	Accident
15	19	Derek Daly	Scheid/Superior Trg./Metro (77)	$100,763	133	Engine
16	33	Emerson Fittipaldi	Marlboro Patrick Racing (20)	$ 98,263	131	Lost Power
17	25	Josele Garza	Bryant/Schaefer/Mach. Union (55)	$103,350	129	Running
18	7	Arie Luyendyk	Livingwell/Provimi Veal/WTTV (71)	$ 97,113	125	Suspension
19	4	A.J. Foyt, Jr.	Copenhagen-Gilmore (14)	$102,963	117	Oil Seal
20	11	Rich Vogler	Ky. Fried Chicken/Livingwell/Valpak (81)	$ 98,263	109	Rocker Arm
21	30	Ed Pimm	Skoal Classic (98)	$ 95,513	109	Lost Boost
22	18	Gordon Johncock	STP Oil Treatment Spl. (2)	$ 94,913	76	Valve
23	3	Rick Mears	Pennzoil Z-7 Spl. (8)	$112,463	75	Coil Wire
24	14	Geoff Brabham	Team Valvoline March Honda (15)	$ 92,963	71	Oil Pressure
25	32	Steve Chassey	United Oil/Life of Ind. (87)	$ 97,913	68	Engine
26	2	Bobby Rahal	Budweiser/True Sports/Spirit of Col. (1)	$123,013	57	Ignition
27	29	Pancho Carter	Hardee's March (29)	$ 93,263	45	Valve
28	28	Davy Jones	Skoal Long Cut/Gilmore/UNO (44)	$115,463	34	Engine
29	9	Michael Andretti	Kraco STP March (18)	$ 91,113	28	CV Joint
30	10	Ludwig Heimrath, Jr.	Mackenzie/Horton Donuts (23)	$111,513	25	Spun, Lost Wheel
31	24	Kevin Cogan	Marlboro Patrick Racing (7)	$ 90,763	21	Oil Pump
32	23	Randy Lewis	Toshiba/Altos/Leader Cards (24)	$ 90,763	8	Gearbox
33	31	George Snider	Calumet/Copenhagen (84)	$ 92,713	0	Fuel Leak

AVERAGE SPEED: 162.175 mph.
TIME: 3:04:59.147
FAST QUALIFIER: Mario Andretti (#5) - 215.390 ,mph (4-Lap Average Speed - 2:47.139 (4-Lap Time).
LAP LEADERS: Laps 1-27 Mario Andretti, Lap 28 Guerrero, Laps 29-60 Mario Andretti, Laps 61-64 Sullivan, Laps 65-80 Mario Andretti, Lap 81 Guerrero, Laps 82-96 Mario Andretti, Lap 97 Guerrero, Laps 98-177 Mario Andretti, Laps 178-182 Guerrero, Laps 183-200 Al Unser.
YELLOW FLAGS: Laps 1-5 Garza-Carter contact in turn 1; Laps 27-33 Heimrath spun, lost wheel in turn 4; Laps 39-42 Debris on track; Laps 62-67 Debris on track; Laps 81-84 Sullivan spun in turn 4; Laps 96-101 Simon out of fuel; Laps 131-134 T. Bettenhausen lost wheel in turn 3; Laps 150-158 Sneva hit wall in turn 3; Laps 162-166 Barbazza spun in turn 4; Laps 192-196 Mario Andretti stalled in turn 4.
*Penalized 2 laps for yellow flag rules violations.

Three-time pole position winners Johnny Rutherford and Mario Andretti attend the Front Row party at Jonathon's Pub, with massive cake and iced Borg-Warner trophy created by Jose Mula (center). (Yohler/Tiffany Studio)

MISCELLANEOUS NOTES
by David Scoggan

Just as the "official" IMS tally of 61 cars on the track differed from the actual 66-car total (due to non-acknowledgment of replacement chassis), a few additional machines showed up in the garage area that were not observed or recorded by the Speedway. Scott Brayton allegedly had another Amway/Autostyle March 87C arrive late, but I certainly couldn't find it; there was, however, a 71 March 86C painted in Provimi/LivingWell livery that was used for a taping session with long-time local TV ghoul "Sammy Terry" of Channel 4's "Nightmare Theater." The Vince Granatelli team brought in a 4 STP/True Value 86C for an early-month STP commercial shoot (now being shown frequently on your tube—it has the head-on shot of Guerrero lighting up the tires). Buried deep in the Team Laughrey gar-

age was their dark maroon 86C show car that was featured—along with driver/model Steve Chassey—on local Pizza Hut billboards and flyers. Kraco Racing again had a third partially-assembled March 87C chassis at Michael Andretti's disposal (more likely being prepared for Milwaukee). The 35 C.R. Possell 86C was brought in to back up Gordon John-cock after Possell's own venture ran short of money.

* * * * *

Looks like Oldsmobile's Aerotech closed-course speed record dream may re-appear yet this summer. Following an encouraging initial track test in which designated lab rat A.J. Foyt lapped the 5-mile GM proving ground circle in Mesa, Arizona at 218.4 MPH last November 16, the streamlined creation has since de-

veloped unnerving mechanical gremlins. (And how would you like to face the possibility of exploding a Quad 4 turbo-motor at, oh, say . . . . 260 MPH?! Thanks, but no thanks.)

* * * * *

A hot winter '86 rumor had Danny Sullivan joining the Marlboro McLaren F1 organization as number two driver to World Champion Alain Prost, but Sullivan denied any contact with Ron Dennis and team, so it was all wishful thinking on some one's part . . . . It's official, Al Unser, Sr. will drive the Porsche Indy Car in its late '87 competitive debut. Plans are for team manager Al Holbert to handle the early testing chores in Germany; then Unser will step in once the Quaker State-sponsored machine arrives stateside. The selection of next year's

Much of the responsibility for the month falls upon the shoulders of Chief Steward Tom Binford, Superintendent of the Grounds Charlie Thompson, and Director, Advertising Sales and Promotions Bill Donaldson. (deBrier)

driver(s) remains to be made . . . . Was this the first May on record that lost absolutely zero running time to rainfall? . . . . May 3 was a bad day for flying race cars. Pancho Carter performed his aerial act at IMS and Bobby Allison's NASCAR Winston Cup Buick stock car got airborne and ripped out 120 feet of mainstretch fencing at Alabama International Motor Speedway in Talladega, nearly going rear-end-first into the grandstand. No one was critically injured, but just imagine an IndyCar at fence level

Qualifiers face IMS Chief Photographer Ron McQueeney with a battery all his own. (Strauser)

(Lord help us) . . . . The 500 Oldtimers' Club Barbecue on May 18 saw four new additions to their Speedway Hall of Fame. Three-time winner Johnny Rutherford was joined by posthumous nominees Jack McGrath, Art Sparks, and Earl Gilmore . . . . Ex-Galles chauffeur Roberto Moreno was a low-profile Carb Day visitor. The diminutive Brazilian, 19th place finisher in the '86 Indy 500, has spent this year racing a works Ralt-Honda in the European F3000 series . . . . Any truth to the rumor that Bill Neely's next book will be titled "Stroker Al"? . . . . Gordon Johncock on the real reason for his comeback: "I don't have to race, but it's the easiest and quickest way for me to make money."

* * * * *

Another candidate for the "strangest yellow light" award came at 12:50 on Carb Day, when Tom Sneva's Skoal Bandit ventured onto the track with a notebook lying on his rear wing . . . . Coors was absent as a major sponsor for the first time since 1983. Fleeing the Rick Galles team, the "Colorado Kool-Aid" brewey has concentrated more heavily on NASCAR (Bill Elliott), WoO sprints (Steve Kinser), and NHRA/IHRA drag racing (Tom McEwen and Dan Pastorini) . . . . The two safest bets of the month were (a) Mario Andretti winning the pole, and (b) George Snider becoming the first driver out of the race. I'm surprised Chevrolet doesn't either start a full-scale testing program with the V-6 turbo stock-block powerplant or tell A.J. to leave the thing in Houston, because as it stands right now the whole "project" is something of a joke . . . . Super Vee standout and '86 ROP participant Steve

Bren may have a deal cooking with Mike Curb for an upcoming Indy Car drive.

* * * * *

Did anyone else hear the unintentionally hysterical Pennzoil post-race radio spot featuring winner Al Unser? Possibly the shortest running commercial in broadcast history. (Where's Rick Shaffer when you need him?) . . . . Most popular non-obscene T-shirt design had to be those bearing the likeness of the ubiquitous Spuds MacKenzie, the Bud Light "party animal" . . . . The dissolution of Carl Haas's ex-Beatrice FORCE F1 effort not only brought Tyler Alexander back into the Indy Car fold, it also returned Teddy Mayer, Alexander's running mate during Team McLaren's IMS glory years (highlighted by Johnny Rutherford's victories in '74 and '76). Mayer came aboard Roger Penske's staff to run the race car construction shop in Poole, England . . . . Ted Field's Interscope Productions was the driving force behind the Bette Midler/Shelley Long flick "Outrageous Fortune" . . . . CART may schedule a non-points race in Brazil sometime this century.

* * * * *

Gary Bettenhausen was the 1987 recipient of the Jimmy Clark Award. The sportsmanship prize is now sponsored by Kroger . . . . Howdy Holmes was ground-bound for the second successive May. The '79 Rookie of the Year reportedly had a substantial sum of money burning a hole in his pocket but couldn't make connections with a suitable ride . . . . Reports from overseas indicate that '83 polesitter Teo Fabi wants to take

Bobby Rahal talks over the tire situation with Goodyear's Director of Racing, Leo Mehl. (deBrier)

another crack at the Speedway . . . . Lola Cars designated their short-track and road-course 1987 chassis as a T8700, while the superspeedway version was labeled a T8701.

* * * * *

Bobby Rahal, Al Unser, Jr., and Geoff Brabham carried the ABC on-board cameras on Race Day; why hasn't anyone tried pointing the camera at the rear of the car, so we can observe approaching vehicles? How about it, copycats? . . . . Hardee's, the fast-food restaurant chain, was going to donate $100,000 to the Special Olympics if their driver, Pancho Carter, won the 500, but stablemate Josele Garza cancelled that out with his obtuse first-lap maneuver. Strangely enough, Garza was quoted in a Machinists Union press release as stating, "The key to the start when you're as far back as I am is to keep your nose clean." (Pass the Kleenex, Josele?) Both Carter's 29 and Garza's 55 were repaired (although Garza's deteriorating left side pod tape job was decidedly suspect), allowing Garza to raise money for the downtown Indianapolis Soldiers and Sailors Monument restoration project, thanks to the efforts of Phil Hedback of Bryant Heating and Cooling.

* * * * *

This year marked the first time that A.J. Foyt qualified a Lola chassis at Indy. He first brought a Lola to IMS in 1965, but opted for an updated '64 Lotus and graciously put then-struggling rookie Al Unser in the Lola. In 1985, A.J. tested a Lola T900 in March, then brought the car back to the Speedway in May, but almost immediately sold it to

Sign painters identify the 33 individual pits for race day. (IMS-Duffy)

Derek Daly's Kapsreiter Bier team and stuck with his fleet of Marches . . . . Dick Simon has truly become the "Father Flanagan" of Indy Car racing. Last year, he gave Chip Robinson and West Coast Formula Atlantic star Tom Phillips their initial CART rides. For 1987, Simon hired Ludwig Heimrath, Jr. to be his full-time driver and took Montana road-racer John Richards under his wing for starts at the Meadowlands, Cleveland, and Toronto. The next benefactor should be Wally Dallenbach, Jr., who is scheduled to run a Simon entry at Elkhart Lake on August 30; can Willy T.

Ribbs be far behind?

* * * * *

New Ferrari F1 designer John Barnard (late of Team McLaren and brainchild of the awesome Chaparral 2K Indy Car) has pushed the completed "prancing horse" Indy Car even further onto the back burner. Can it really be true that the machine is an exact copy of the March 85C that Truesports took to Italy for exploratory testing? . . . . Stan Fox was sitting in his March 86C, ready to go out for practice, when car owner A.J. Foyt made a wing adjustment. "I mentioned that it felt like he was taking too much

Channel 8's Dick Rae interviews lady car owner Lydia Laughrey. (deBrier)

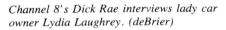

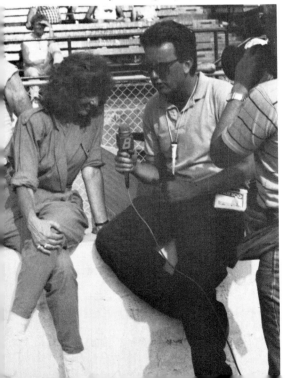

Two of the nicest people in racing are Bill and Skip Mears, parents of drivers Rick and Roger. (IMS-Seidman)

Jim Crawford arrives for qualifications sans moustache. (Whitlow)

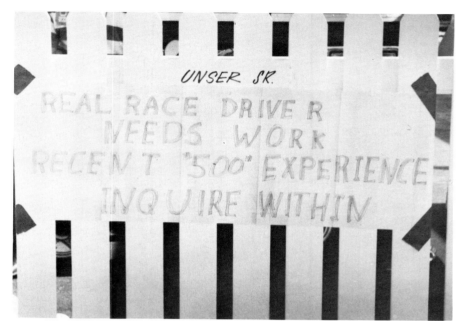

This sign appeared outside of Al Unser's motorhome soon after the race. (IMS-D. Young)

UNSER SR.

REAL RACE DRIVER
NEEDS WORK
RECENT "500" EXPERIENCE
INQUIRE WITHIN

[downforce] out,'' said Fox. ''A.J. said, 'I'm working on the car—you're driving it!''' . . . . Potential new entrants for the 1988 season abound (dependent largely on sponsorship, of course). Longtime IMSA owner Phil Conte has abandoned his March/Buick project and hopes to switch to CART. Fellow IMSA-ites Bob Akin and Rob Dyson may combine forces for a CART effort (for Price Cobb?). Genoa Racing of Italy could jump from European Formula 3000 into Indy Cars, with Corrado Fabi perhaps figuring into the equation.

* * * * *

The Interscope 87C lives! Danny Ongais tested the all-black, Phil Casey-wrenched 1987 March/Cosworth of Ted Field at the Speedway in late June. The chassis is the 200th Indy Car produced by March Engineering . . . . Is Danny Sullivan just too cool or what? not only did he appear as himself in the May 7 (taped) episode of the ABC daytime soap

NASCAR star Tim Richmond returns to his old stomping ground. He led the race and was Rookie of the Year here in 1980. (IMS-D. Young)

Pancho catches a nap. (IMS-Spargur)

Chief starter Duane Sweeney doesn't miss a thing. (Strauser)

They can dream, can't they? (IMS-Dwiggins)

"All My Children," but he gets paid big bucks by Bausch & Lomb every time a photograph is published of him wearing their Ray-Ban shades . . . . Al Unser, Jr. wants to "play around" with Kenny Bernstein's 270-MPH Budweiser King Buick LeSabre nitro Funny Car whenever KB can set up an appointment. "I want to feel that horsepower," said Little Al, and with around 3,000 ponies on tap he would definitely get a handful . . . . Ex-drag racer and current hot rodder John Buttera won the inaugural Clint Brawner Mechanical Excellence Award for the flawless workmanship on his 59 Center Line/Machinists stock- block Pontiac- powered March 86C.

* * * * *

What do you do with a low-mileage '87 March when your one-race program is concluded? If you're Noblesville, Indi- ana resident Derek Daly, you put it on the cover of "Wheels and Deals," a loc- al used car advertising magazine. While

A moment of relaxation for Guerrero. (Wendt)

Truesports crew chief Steve Horne compares Lola observations with A.J. Foyt. (deBrier)

Popular Tom Bigelow almost ran a third Dick Simon car. ESPN's Gary Lee checks the story. (Bonwell)

the 77 Pace Electronics 87C went on the market, Daly signed on to replace the injured Dennis Firestone in the Raynor Lola for the duration of the season . . . .

Howdy Holmes (with new bride, Carole) was without a car to drive for the second consecutive year. (Wendt)

A graphic indication of Life with My PC-16 for Rick Mears came on May 8 (its last day of service) when Mears and machine were bombarded with pigeon droppings while touring the track at under 205 MPH. "I figured we ought to do something if a pigeon was able to catch us," quipped Mears of his hurried switch to a 1986 March.

* * * * *

If you thought the regular ABC race broadcast was suspect, you should have seen the satellite version of same— complete with inane chatter during the commercial breaks. (I've got an idea . . . . no, no, never mind.") . . . . Will active suspension (as found on the Lotus 99T Formula One car) be banned before it reaches the Indy Car series? . . . . One of the up-and-coming young motorsports artists is Gordon Cox, of Greenwood, Indiana. Mr. Cox, AKA "T. Master," currently has two stunning pencil-and-watercolor works—one of Rick Mears and one of Bobby Rahal—that are available in local galleries and well worth the investment . . . . The IMS press room has been officially dedicated as the Al Bloemker Media Center. Bloemker had been the Speedway public relations director from 1946 until his retirement this year.

* * * * *

After crashing heavily in May of '85 and '86, Herm Johnson's only IMS ride for 1987 was his bicycle. The two- time Indy starter is hoping to get back into Indy Cars after spending the winter months ice racing in the Frozen North

. . . . The vaunted Goodyear radials have been shelved for the August 2 Marlboro 500 at Michigan International Speedway ("Dogleg City") and all competitors will run bias-ply tires. (Better late than never, huh?) . . . . If no big-buck Indy Car owner has the common sense to hire Sammy Swindell following his solid May performance (he never put a wheel wrong in his grossly underpowered machine, while more experienced drivers were tasting concrete all around him), then there's definitely no hope left for sprint car drivers (if there ever was any hope).

* * * * *

Here is the heritage of Roger Penske's three March 86C chassis (and it's not exactly as explained in a team press release): Al Unser's winning mount, 86C-22, was Rick Mears's Indy pole-winning/record-setting car of last year; it also won the Meadowlands race for Danny Sullivan and took Mears to the Michigan 500 pole at over 223 MPH. Danny Sullivan's ride, 86C-37, was driven by Danny Ongais in the 1986 Indy 500, then bought by Penske after Sullivan's original 86C was wiped out in a skirmish with Michael Andretti at Portland. The Rick Mears machine, 86C-41, did not run in the '86 Indy 500 and only competed in one race—the fall Michigan 250—but did set the closed-course speed record of 233.934 at MIS in November.

* * * * *

It was again my pleasure to serve as trackside Motorsports Analyst for WFBQ, the top-rated radio station in Indianapolis. For the second consecutive year, Jay Baker's "Dick's Picks" sports show (found at the conclusion of Bob Kevoian and Tom Griswold's morning shift on Q95) emanated from the IMS confines, and the fequent broadcasts from outside Tony Bettenhausen's garage always attracted a large crowd. The talents of Robin Miller and Rick Shaffer of the IndianapolisStar and Leader Cards crewman Bob "Reverend Moon" Eastman built through the month until Carb Day's climax—the live, unrehearsed, acapella performance of the Shaffer-penned "Indy Car Shuffle" rap song featuring "Mario," "A.J.," "Big and Little Al," "Emmo," "Sam Posey," etc. (It had to happen!) . . . . If and when sponsorship money is obtained, John Andretti could make his Indy Car debut before this season concludes. Andretti, son of Mario's twin brother Aldo, hopes to take over the Laughrey Racing 87C driven in the 500 by Steve Chassey.

* * * * *

Addendum to the back-breaking final pit stop of Roberto Guerrero: Supposedly, a certain Granatelli crew member with IMSA experience would have had the foresight to recognize the clutch problem and would have dumped water under the rear wheels so Guerrero could drop down off the air jacks with the car in gear and the rear tires spinning. The problem? Said crewman had been sent off to fetch 1-year-old Marco Guerrero for the Victory Lane celebration! . . . . Yes, that's the former Herb and Rose Wysard 34 blue and white March 83C used by Kevin Cogan in the Aqua Velva TV blurb. ("Have a nice day at work, Kevin.") Cogan can also be found in print ads for Playboy Fashions, a deal substantial enough to warrant being written on the sides of his helmet . . . . Professional golfer Greg Norman was an interested spectator at the 500. "I guess I'm just a frustrated race driver," said the Great White Shark.

* * * * *

Emerson Fittipaldi needed to shake down his re-assembled 20T backup Marlboro March 87C prior to "Gentlemen, Start Your Engines," so the Patrick team borrowed the Columbus, Indiana airport belonging to Jack Rhoades, Indy 500 entrnt from 1979 to 1983. Emmo warmed up the machine at 6:00 a.m. (!) on the day before the race . . . . And let's stop jumbling the grid because of Carb Day crashes. Why move the Unlucky Ones to the last row if they have virtually identical cars to substitute? Heck, they can wipe out half the field at the beginning of a Formula One race, but everyone just rolls out their "T" car and assumes their rightful position. Starting an untested, repaired car from its original spot seems a riskier proposition than doing the same with an undamaged replacement chassis, so why penalize them further? . . . . A.J. Foyt has a new black-and-gold Kenworth tractor- trailer rig. The transporter is adorned with twin murals of Foyt's Indy Car, NASCAR Olds stock car, and IMSA Porsche 962 . . . . Canadian Scott Goodyear, graduate of the Formula Atlantic wars, is competing in the '87 CART road races for Dick Hammond's Gohr/Genesee group.

* * * * *

Fans seated on the outside of the main straightaway on Sunday, May 17 were entertained by the afternoon antics of a persistent chipmunk. The little critter would periodically emerge from a drain hole in the inside wall and scamper down the track to another drain hole, then reverse the procedure . . . . Every May, a member of the local print media leads people to believe there is an acute driver shortage. Listen, the only thing we're short of is car owners (and the only thing they're short of is money). Why should drivers like Steve Kinser, Pete Halsmer, Jan Lammers, Tom Gloy, Roger Mears, Scott Pruett, etc. leave their heavy involvement in whatever series to walk the IMS pits in vain because (a) they don't have $1 million in their pockets and/or (b) there aren't any decent cars left anyway? Holy highball, this ain't like the old "hat in hand" days . . . . (I'd question many of the current crop of Super Vee drivers' ability to advance—a lot of them have absolutely no idea what a yellow light means!)

* * * * *

Billy Vukovich III, terror of the West Coast supermodified ranks, was at the Speedway for a few days and got a ride in the pace car on May 14. The 23-year-old Vukovich was offered the Elmer Fields March 85C before Dick Ferguson assumed the seat. Warren Mockler, USAC sprint and midget shoe from Westfield, Indiana, also considered a proposal from the Fields operation, but couldn't make connections either. Two-time 500 veteran (1961 and '64) and Fields team manager Norm Hall is battling cancer, but said his involvement with the effort was "great therapy. I've stopped worrying about myself and instead I'm worrying about all the problems with the car." . . . . Roger Penske's 8T (28) Pennzoil/Miller PC-15 spare car showed up in the second qualifying day 6:00 p.m. lineup with Interscope/Panavision markings and a 25T affixed, but the yellow creation never practiced in that configuration.

* * * * *

The articulate Bobby Rahal is becom-

Is Danny Sullivan cool or what? (Whitlow)

Rapidly changing handling characteristics had Johnny Capels and Johnny Rutherford completely baffled on practice days. (Wendt)

ing quite an on-screen presence. Following a fall '86 gig on NBC's "Late Night with David Letterman" show (Dave loves those Indy Cars!), Rahal has shot a slick Valvoline TV ad with Truesports boss Steve Horne ("Rahal's Rule"), and appears with former Notre Dame football coach Ara Parseghian in a pair of light-hearted point/counterpoint spots for Plasti-kote paints . . . . Angelo Pizzo, writer of the movie "Hoosiers" (his paean to Indiana's love of basketball), is currently working on a screenplay about a father/son Indy Car team . . . . The May 25 issue of Time magazine reported the engagement of American Airlines captain Warren Levine and Janet Guthrie, the first (and still only) woman to compete in the Indy 500 . . . . Add still another name to the list of second generation drivers starting to make progress on the Road to the Brickyard. P.J. Jones, son of 1963 Indy winner Rufus Parnell ("Parnelli") Jones, is doing quite well in California midget competition. How about a match race between P.J., Andy Hurtubise, and Roger McCluskey, Jr.?

* * * * *

According to Fischer Engineering worker Scott "Slick" Gauger, three of the four (total) Buick-propelled drivers in the race severely damaged their equipment by overrevving their respective engines while exiting the pits, tagging the valves . . . . Michael Chandler was at the track trolling for a ride. The 29-year-old Chandler, Speedway starter from 1981-83, has been absent from Indy Car competition since receiving serious head injuries in a May 11, 1984 turn three IMS crash . . . . To the hierarchy of Channels 6, 8, and 13 in Indianapolis: We race fans would love to watch (and tape) all three of your race-evening highlight programs, but we can't do so if they're all on at the same time! This applies to qualification shows, also. Instead of 100 of the interested viewers watching each station, you guys only got about a third of the audience you could have obtained . . . . Speaking of local video coverage, WISH/Channel 8 broadcasts absolutely the finest time trial and race wrap-ups. Their chronological, "you are there" format is far superior to the "talking heads" style found elsewhere. Now if we could just get a late-night, daily practice show . . . . Of course, if the suggested plan to implement pool TV footage and/or pool radio reports comes to pass, all the Speedway coverage would look and sound alike, anyway. Beware of creeping track communism!

* * * * *

After setting quick time on Monday, May 4, Dennis Firestone made the statement that: "Over the past 6 years, I think the only way I could have won a race was if lightning had struck the other 32 cars." The next day, Firestone's Raynor

Lola zapped the fourth turn wall and their month began to unravel . . . . While it was George Walther's son, Jeff, who was the impetus for the family's IMS return, the more well-known Walther son, David "Salt" Walther, ran afoul of the law last winter. The once brash and flamboyant 7-time Indy starter was busted for trying to illegally obtain the painkiller Dilaudid (one of Elvis's favorites), then later attempted to cash a worthless $300 check at an Ohio grocery store.

* * * * *

When Dick Simon (age 53) was again awarded the $1,000 oldest starter prize from Cornelius Printing, he called A.J. Foyt (age 52) to the Driver's Meeting podium to exhibit proof of his claim—his birth certificate. Foyt countered by saying he "protested" in 1986 because he "had this won until Carburetion Day" (when Dennis Firestone's crash put first alternate Simon into the field). Then A.J. glanced at the document and joked, "Yeah, he's a lot older!" . . . . The "Thanks, Mr. B." printed on the nose of Foyt's Lola was a reference to U.S. Tobacco (Copenhagen) chief executive officer Louis Bantle and their gala bash thrown in honor of A.J.'s 30th Indy start.

* * * * *

Bill and Skip Mears (two of the nicest individuals on the planet) desire film or video of their son Rick's furious chasing down of Gordon Johncock in the '82 500. They have footage of when Rick finally caught up to Johncock, but it was in getting there that Rick feels he performed some of his personal best . . . . Two former 500 drivers suffered incapacitating injuries just prior to the track's opening. A motorcycle mishap gave Champion Spark Plug rep Jerry Grant a badly broken leg and '62 Rookie of the Year Jim McElreath incurred a broken vertebra while competing in a Modified race. The kicker to the McElreath story is the rumor that the 59-year-old Texan was planning to bring a Cosworth engine to the Speedway and use it to barter for a ride!

* * * * *

The World of Outlaws traveling band of winged sprint car racers stopped at the Indiana State Fairgrounds on Saturday, May 9. Californian Jimmy Sills won the "Pole Night" 25-lap feature over Steve Kinser and Sammy Swindell, while Swindell blazed around the one-mile oval at a track record 132.3 MPH in qualifying . . . . Last year, the Goodyear blimp had to fend off the one-day challenge posed by a McDonald's airship; this May a Fuji Film zeppelin made a brief appearance over the IMS grounds . . . . Wary of prying eyes and gossip, Chevrolet demanded that Pat Patrick move his engine operation from Indianapolis to Texas. Patrick's motor building crew, led by Louis "Butch" Meyer III,

relocated in the Midland shops of VDS . . . . The long-forgotten Primus chassis (remember Chris Kneifel?) was displayed at the Motorsports Expo in Scott Brayton's pink, blue and white Amway/Autostyle livery . . . . Want to see an American-made Indy Car battling the British Marches, Lolas, and Penskes? Well, so would David Bruns, designer of the Swift DB-4 Formula Atlantic car that won pole position in its first start (Watkins Glen, July 5). Formerly involved in the Lindsey Hopkins Lightning chassis project, Bruns says that if proper financial backing were secured, a swift Indy Car would be rolling.

* * * * *

There was serious talk this spring among the IMS brass of modifying the time trial procedure to ensure more "action" on each of the four scheduled days. The plan was to take only the fastest nine qualifiers from each of the first three days, then six on the final day, forcing everyone slower than 9th quick to continually re-qualify. If they really want action, try this: Lock the front row in on Day One (so the fans that have to drive back to Bug Tussle can say, "I saw the Pole Run.") Then allow everyone else to make one complete 4-lap attempt every day (and pay them for it—it's the ultimate incentive) and take each driver's fastest overall series. This way, positions 4-33 wouldn't be established until 6:00 on Day Four. Could you imagine, say, Michael Andretti setting a new track record on a cool, cloudy third day of trials, moving from 10th starting spot to fourth? Talk about sustaining interest—sponsor exposure— increasing attendance! And you wouldn't have any fluke qualifiers; this would definitely weed them out. No more Chet Fillips sneaking in at 24 MPH off the pole pace! It would even lessen the effect of inclement weather, because there would be no reason to wait until the last minute to qualify when you would always upgrade your speed. Oh well, it's just a thought . . . .

* * * * *

Love Fabrizio's T-shirt! (Wendt)

OFFICIAL SPEEDWAY RECORDS

AS OF JUNE 1, 1987

LAPS	MILES	TIME	MILES PER HOUR	DRIVER	CAR NAME	

QUALIFYING RECORDS

LAPS	MILES	TIME	MILES PER HOUR	DRIVER	CAR NAME	
1	2½	41.364	217.581	Rick Mears	Pennzoil Z-7 Special	1986
4	10	2:46.030	216.828	Rick Mears	Pennzoil Z-7 Special	1986

RACE RECORDS

LAPS	MILES	TIME	MILES PER HOUR	DRIVER	CAR NAME	
1	2½	44.348	202.940	Michael Andretti	Kraco-STP-Lean Machine	1986
2	5	1:27.958	204.643	Michael Andretti	Kraco-STP-Lean Machine	1986
4	10	2:56.008	204.536	Michael Andretti	Kraco-STP-Lean Machine	1986
10	25	7:24.755	202.359	Michael Andretti	Kraco-STP-Lean machine	1986
20	50	15:07.170	198.419	Rick Mears	Pennzoil Z-7 Special	1984
30	75	23:23.652	192.355	Mario Andretti	Newman/Haas Budweiser Lola	1984
40	100	31:07.957	192.724	Mario Andretti	Newman/Haas Budweiser Lola	1984
50	125	40:10.838	186.657	Mario Andretti	Newman/Haas Budweiser Lola	1984
60	150	50:57.29	176.627	A.J. Foyt, Jr.	Gilmore Racing Team	1974
70	175	1:01:21.770	171.113	Rick Mears	Pennzoil Z-7 Special	1986
80	200	1:09:30.659	172.635	Michael Andretti	Kraco-STP-Lean Machine	1986
90	225	1:17:31.599	174.134	Bobby Rahal	Budweiser Truesports March	1986
100	250	1:25:06.356	176.251	Bobby Rahal	Budweiser Truesports March	1986
110	275	1:36:38.480	170.734	Bobby Rahal	Budweiser Truesports March	1986
120	300	1:44:14.431	172.678	Bobby Rahal	Budweiser Truesports March	1986
130	325	1:51:55.526	174.223	Bobby Rahal	Budweiser Truesports March	1986
140	350	2:03:53.758	169.497	Rick Mears	Pennzoil Z-7 Special	1986
150	375	2:12:04.258	170.363	Rick Mears	Pennzoil Z-7 Special	1986
160	400	2:19:39.163	171.855	Rick Mears	Pennzoil Z-7 Special	1986
170	425	2:29:54.870	170.097	Rick Mears	Pennzoil Z-7 Special	1986
180	450	2:37:31.192	171.407	Rick Mears	Pennzoil Z-7 Special	1986
190	475	2:45:08.397	172.581	Kevin Cogan	7-Eleven	1986
200	500	2:55:43.480	170.722	Bobby Rahal	Budweiser Truesports March	1986

Total Prize Money Each Year of the Tony Hulman Regime

Year	Amount	Year	Amount	Year	Amount
1946	$115,450	1959	$338,100	1973	$1,006,105
1947	137,425	1960	369,150	1974	1,015,686
1948	171,075	1961	400,000	1975	1,001,321
1949	179,050	1962	426,162	1976	1,037,776
1950	201,135	1963	494,030	1977	1,116,807
1951	207,650	1964	506,575	1978	1,145,225
1952	230,100	1965	628,399	1979	1,271,954
1953	246,300	1966	691,808	1980	1,503,225
1954	269,375	1967	734,634	1981	1,605,375
1955	270,400	1968	721,269	1982	2,067,475
1956	282,052	1969	805,127	1983	2,411,450
1957	300,252	1970	1,000,002	1984	2,795,899
1958	305,217	1971	1,001,604	1985	3,271,025
		1972	1,011,845	1986	4,001,450

PIT STOP REPORT

1st Place—AL UNSER SR.   CUMMINS HOLSET TURBO SPECIAL

25	1	28	Fuel-R.R.-L.F.-L.R. Tires-Engine Stalled-Installed New Wicker Bill On Rear Wing	18
	2	30	Worked On Rear Wing	22
	3	63	Fuel-R.F.-R.R.-L.F.-L.R. Tires	23
	4	80	Fuel Only	14
	5	97	Fuel-R.F.-R.R.-L.R. Tires	20
	6	123	Fuel-R.F.-R.R.-L.F.-L.R. Tires	17
	7	150	Fuel Only	16
	8	173	Fuel Only	11

TOTAL TIME:141

2nd Place—ROBERTO GUERRERO   TRUE VALUE/ STP MARCH

4	1	29	Fuel Only	18.3
	2	60	Fuel-Worked On Rear Air Jack	20.6
	3	81	Fuel-R.F.-R.R.-L.F. Tires-Used Jack Stand On Rear	26.9
	4	97	Fuel-Adjust Front Wing-Worked On Rear Air Jack	14.3
	5	127	Fuel-R.F.-L.F.-L.R. Tires	19.9
	6	130	Replaced Nose Cone Lost From Hitting Wheel From Car No. 16-Adjust Front Wing	52.5
	7	151	Fuel-R.F.-R.R.-L.F. Tires	19.2
	8	182	Fuel Only-Engine Stalled-Two Times-Push Started Six Men Over Wall	68.6

TOTAL TIME:240.3

3rd Place—FABRIZIO BARBAZZA   ARCIERO WINERY

12	1	20	Fuel-Adjust Front Wings	18.3
	2	39	Fuel-R.F.-R.R.-L.R. Tires	12
	3	61	Fuel Only	13.2
	4	70	Fuel Only	11
	5	94	Fuel-R.F.-R.R. Tires	30
	6	126	Fuel-L.F. Tire	22.6
	7	148	Fuel-R.F.-R.R. Tires-Removed Portion Of Left Rear Wing End Plate	31.2
	8	160	Fuel-R.F.-R.R.-L.F.-L.R. Tires-Removed Rest Of Rear Wing End Plate	26
	9	189	Fuel Only	19.6

TOTAL TIME:183.9

4th Place—AL UNSER JR.   DOMINO'S PIZZA "HOT ONE"

30	(1)		Fuel Topped Off Before Lining Up For Start	
	2	26	Fuel-R.F.-R.R. Tires	17
	3	58	Fuel-R.F.-R.R. Tires-Engine Stalled	18
	4	58	Restarted Engine	60
	5	80	Fuel-R.F.-R.R. Tires	16
	6	96	Fuel Only	12
	7	125	Fuel-R.F.-R.R.-L.R. Tires	19
	8	147	Fuel-R.F.-R.R. Tires	15
	9	158	Fuel-R.F.-R.R.-L.R. Tires	13
	10	180	Fuel Only	9

TOTAL TIME:179

5th Place—GARY BETTENHAUSEN   GOHR RACING/ GENESEE BEER WAGON

56	1	26	Fuel-R.F.-R.R. Tires-Jacks Would Not Work-Engine Stalled-Restarted	58
	2	56	Fuel Only-Air Jacks Not Working	29
	3	78	R.F.-R.R.-L.R. Tires-No Fuel-Hose Too Short	24
	4	79	Fuel Only	14
	5	94	Fuel Only	11
	6	120	Fuel Only	17
	7	128	Fuel Only-Engine Stalled-Restarted	67
	8	146	Fuel-R.F.-R.R. Tires	23
	9	175	Fuel-R.F.-R.R. Tires	36

TOTAL TIME:279

6th Place—DICK SIMON   SOUNDESIGN STEREO SPECIAL

22	1	26	Fuel-R.F.-R.R.-L.F.-L.R. Tires-Removed Plate Fuel Inlet	26
	2	58	Fuel-R.R.-L.R. Tires-Adjust Front Wing-Tires Unattended	23
	3	94	Fuel-R.R.-L.R.-Tires-Adjust Front Wing	46
	4	122	Fuel-R.F.-R.R.-L.R. Tires	22
	5	143	Fuel-R.F.-R.R.-L.R. Tires	18
	6	176	Fuel Only	16

TOTAL TIME:151

7th Place—STAN FOX   KERKER EXHAUST-SKOAL CLASSIC

41	1	25	Fuel Only-Six Men Over Wall	27.5
	2	52	Fuel-R.F.-R.R.-L.R. Tires-Six Men Over Wall	27.6
	3	76	Fuel Only	15.7
	4	106	Fuel-L.F. Tire-Dead Engine-Restarted	28
	5	121	Fuel-R.F.-R.R.-L.R. Tires	22
	6	153	Fuel Only-Engine Dead-Restarted	19
	7	185	Fuel Only	7

TOTAL TIME:146.8

8th Place-JEFF MACPHERSON   TEAM MACPHERSON MARCH HONDA

11	1	14	Fuel-Adjust Front Wing-Check Steering & Rear Vibration	98
	2	18	R.F.-R.R.-L.F.-L.R. Tires-Checked Front And Rear Suspension	141
	3	22	Checked Front and Rear Suspension	166
	4	27	Fuel-Adjust Front Wing	63
	5	58	Fuel-R.F.-R.R.-L.R. Tires	19
	6	68	Fuel-R.F. Tire	20
	7	100	Fuel-R.F.-R.R.-L.F.-L.R. Tires-Adjust Rear Suspension	38
	8	115	Fuel-R.F.-R.R.-L.R. Tires-Adjust Rear Suspension	30
	9	140	Fuel-R.F.-R.R.-L.R. Tires	23
	10	175	Fuel Only	8

TOTAL TIME:606

9th Place—MARIO ANDRETTI   HANNA AUTO WASH-NEWMAN/HAAS

5	1	28	Fuel-R.F.-R.R.-L.R. Tires	17.3
	2	61	Fuel-R.F.-R.R.-L.R. Tires	17.8
	3	81	Fuel-R.F.-R.R.-L.F.-L.R. Tires	17.7
	4	97	Fuel-R.F.-R.R.-L.R. Tires	18
	5	129	Fuel-R.F.-R.R.-L.R. Tires	20.2
	6	151	Fuel-R.F.-R.R.-L.R. Tires	17.4
	7	178	Fuel-R.F.-R.R.-L.R. Tires-Changed Wastegate & Spark Box	334
	8	179	Changed Spark Box	122
		180	Out Of Race-Engine Problems	

TOTAL TIME:564.4

10th Place—TONY BETTENHAUSEN   NATIONWISE AUTO PARTS/ PAYLESS MARKETS

16	1	20	Fuel-R.F.-R.R.-L.R. Tires-Adjust Front Wings	30
	2	27	Fuel-Adjust Front Wings-Adjust RR. Spring	21
	3	56	Fuel-Adjust Front Wings	21
	4	75	Fuel-R.R.-L.R. Tires	23
	5	91	Fuel-L.F. Tire	17
	6	122	Fuel-R.F. Tire-R.F. Wheel Not On Car When Entering Pits	35
	7	142	Fuel-R.R.-L.R. Tires	30
	8	170	Fuel Only	18
		171	Out Of Race-Engine Failure	

TOTAL TIME:195

11th Place—JOHNNY RUTHERFORD   VERMONT AMERICAN

21	1	26	Fuel-R.F.-R.R.-L.R. Tires	20
	2	58	Fuel-R.F.-R.R.-L.R. Tires	23
	3	79	Fuel-Replaced Distributor Rotor And Spark Box	1135
	4	80	Replaced Heat Shield	311
	5	102	Fuel Only	21
	6	121	Fuel-R.F.-R.R.-L.F.-L.R. Tires	18
	7	153	Fuel Only	20
		171	Running At End Of Race	

TOTAL TIME:1548

12th Place—SCOTT BRAYTON   AMWAY/AUTOSTYLE CARS/ LIVINGWELL

91	1	28	Fuel-R.F.-R.R. Tires-Visual Inspection Under Car	18
	2	59	Fuel-R.F.-R.R.-L.F. Tires-Clean Out Radiators	20
	3	81	Fuel Only-Checked Tires	14
	4	97	Fuel-R.F.-R.R.-L.F. Tires-Adjust Left Front Wing	23
	5	129	Fuel-R.F.-R.R.-L.R. Tires-Adjust Right Front Wing	21
	6	148	Fuel-R.F.-R.R. Tires-Adjust Right Front Wing	20
		169	Out Of Race-Engine Failure	

TOTAL TIME:116

13th Place—DANNY SULLIVAN   MILLER AMERICAN SPECIAL

3	1	29	Fuel-R.F.-R.R.-L.R. Tires	20
	2	65	Fuel Only	16
	3	82	Fuel-R.F.-R.R.-L.R. Tires	21
	4	84	Fuel-Removed R.R. Wheel To Check For Problem	16
	5	98	Fuel-Adjust R.F. Wing-Greased R.R. CV Joint	10
	6	132	Fuel-R.F.-R.R.-L.R. Tires-Pit Radio Fell On Car And Ended Up On Race Track	20
	7	151	Fuel-R.F.-R.R.-L.R. Tires	13
		160	Out Of Race-Engine Failure	

TOTAL TIME:116

14th Place—TOM SNEVA   SKOAL BANDIT

33	1	27	Fuel-R.F.-R.R.-L.R. Tires	24
	2	56	Fuel-R.F.-R.R. Tires	20
	3	81	Fuel Only	18
	4	97	Fuel-R.F.-R.R.-L.R. Tires	18
	5	125	Fuel Only	22
	6	129	Adjusted Log Hose To Turbo-Loose At Intake Side	210
		144	Out Of Race-Hit Wall Turn Two	

TOTAL TIME:312

15th Place—DEREK DALY   SCHIED TIRE/SUPERIOR TRAINING/METRO LINK

77	1	27	Fuel-R.F.-R.R.-L.F. Tires	39
	2	57	Fuel-R.F.-R.R.-L.F. Tires	29
	3	78	Fuel-R.F.-R.R.-L.F. Tires-Adjust Front Wings	41
	4	95	Fuel-R.F.-R.R.-L.R. Tires	19
	5	125	Fuel-R.F.-R.R.-L.F.-L.R. Tires	30
	6	133	Out Of Race-Engine Problems	

TOTAL TIME:158

16th Place—EMERSON FITTIPALDI   MARLBORO PATRICK RACING

20	1	12	Fuel-R.F.-R.R.-L.R. Tires-Adjust Both Front Wings	20
	2	26	Fuel-R.F.-R.R.-L.R. Tires	16
	3	61	Fuel-R.F.-R.R.-L.R. Tires	18
	4	79	Fuel Only	11
	5	95	Fuel-R.F.-R.R.-L.R. Tires	16
	6	119	Fuel-R.F.-R.R.-L.R. Tires	21
		131	Out Of Race-Engine Problems	

TOTAL TIME:102

17th Place—JOSELE GARZA   BRYANT HEATING & COOLING/SCHAEFER/MACHINIST UNION

55	1	1	L.F. Tire And Total Wheel Assembly Replaced Because Of Accident In First Turn	1635
	2	8	Repaired Vent Damage Left Side	896
	3	11	Fuel Only	13
	4	21	Repair Left Side Damage	14
	5	34	Fuel Only	11
	6	50	Fuel-R.F.-R.R.-L.R.-Tires-Repair Vent Damage	110
	7	53	Replace Radiator And Repair Vent Damage	803
	8	77	Fuel-Repair Left Side Vent	33
	9	79	Added More Tape To Left Side Vent	81
	10	106	Fuel-R.F.-R.R.-L.R. Tires	17
		129	Running When Checkered Flag Fell	

TOTAL TIME:3613

18th Place—ARIE LUYENDYK   LIVINGWELL/PROVIMI VEAL/WTTV

71	1	28	Fuel Only	17.5
	2	59	Fuel-R.F.-R.R.-L.R. Tires	23.5
	3	62	Fuel Only	8.5
	4	80	Fuel Only	11.5
	5	96	Fuel-Adjust Rear Wing	12
	6	125	Fuel-R.F.-R.R.-L.R. Tires-Hit Wheel Entering Pit Ran Over Air Hose-Knocked Crewman Down	47
		125	Out Of Race-Damaged R.F. Suspension	

TOTAL TIME:120

19th Place—A.J. FOYT, JR.   COPENHAGEN-GILMORE

14	1	24	Fuel Only	16
	2	39	Fuel-R.F.-R.R.-L.R. Tires	20
	3	62	Fuel Only	15
	4	80	Fuel-R.F.-R.R.-L.R. Tires	18
	5	97	Fuel Only	13
	6	117	Fuel-Out Of Race-Engine Problems	112

TOTAL TIME:194

20th Place—RICH VOGLER   KENTUCKY FRIED CHICKEN/LIVINGWELL/VALPAK

81	1	29	Fuel-R.F.-R.R.-L.R. Tires	29
	2	32	Fuel System Problems-Checked L.R. Wheel	21
	3	58	Fuel-R.F.-R.R.-L.R. Tires-Cleaned Radiators	21
	4	80	Fuel-R.F.-R.R.-L.F. Tires-Air Jack Problems Socket Hung Up On L.F. Wheel	58
	5	108	Fuel-R.F.-R.R.-L.R. Tires-Adjust Front Wings	22
		109	Out Of Race-Broken Rockerarm In Engine	

TOTAL TIME:151

21st Place—ED PIMM   SKOAL CLASSIC

98	1	28	Fuel-R.F.-R.R.-L.R. Tires	32
	2	59	Fuel Only	22
	3	81	Fuel-R.F.-R.R.-L.R. Tires	25
	4	97	Fuel-Adjust Front Wings	21
	5	103	Fuel-Engine Problems Shut Off-Restarted	79
	6	106	Engine Off-Changed Spark Plugs & Spark Box	663
	7	108	Engine Off-Replaced Battery For Ignition System	917
		109	Out Of Race-No Boost-Engine Problems	

TOTAL TIME:1759

22nd Place—GORDON JOHNCOCK   STP OIL TREATMENT SPECIAL

2	1	22	Fuel Only	18
	2	40	Fuel Only	25
	3	62	Fuel-R.F.-R.R.-L.R. Tires	24
	4	78	Fuel-Replaced Spark Box	
		78	Out Of Race-Engine Problems	

TOTAL TIME: 67

23rd Place—RICK MEARS   PENNZOIL Z-7 SPECIAL

8	1	26	Fuel-R.F.-R.R.-L.R. Tires	19
	2	58	Fuel-R.F.-R.R.-L.R. Tires	17
	3	73	Fuel-Electrical Problems	264
	4	75	Out Of Race-Broken Coil Wire	

TOTAL TIME:300

24th Place—GEOFF BRABHAM   TEAM VALVOLINE MARCH HONDA

15	1	28	Fuel-R.F.-R.R.-L.R. Tires-Adjust Front Wings	22.5
	2	60	Fuel-R.F.-R.R.-L.R. Tires	16.5
	3	74	Fuel-Out Of Race No Oil Pressure	69

TOTAL TIME:108

25th Place—STEVE CHASSEY   UNITED OIL/LIFE OF INDIANA

87	1	28	Fuel-R.F.-R.R. Tires	21
	2	61	Fuel Only	19
	3	68	Out Of Race-Engine Failure	

TOTAL TIME: 40

26th Place—BOBBY RAHAL   BUDWEISER/TRUESPORTS/SPIRIT OF COLUMBUS

1	1	28	Fuel-R.F.-R.R.-L.R. Tires-Adjust Rear Wing	19
	2	34	Fuel-Replace Spark Plugs	285
	3	49	Fuel-Drill Holes In Spark Box Cover-Crimped Plug Wires-Adjust Front And Rear Wings	121
		57	Out Of Race-Ignition Problems	

TOTAL TIME:425

27th Place—PANCHO CARTER   HARDEE'S MARCH

29	1	1	R.F.-R.R.-L.F.-L.R. Tires-Involved In First Lap Contact-Worked On R.R. Suspension	599
	2	4	Fuel-Change Plugs And Spark Box	260
	3	22	Fuel-Engine Problems	750
	4	43	Fuel-R.F.-R.R.-L.R. Tires	25
		44	Out Of Race-Broken Valve In Engine	

TOTAL TIME:1634

28th Place—DAVY JONES   SKOAL LONG CUT CLASSIC/GILMORE/UNO

| 44 | 1 | 24 | Fuel-R.F.-R.R.-L.R. Tires | 20 |
| | | 34 | Out Of Race-Engine Failure | |

TOTAL TIME: 20

29th Place—MICHAEL ANDRETTI   KRACO/STP MARCH

| 18 | 1 | 27 | Fuel-R.F.-R.R.-L.R. Tires-Fuel Fire In Pit Out Of Race L.R. C.V. Joint Broke | |

30th Place—LUDWIG HEIMRATH JR.   MACKENZIE-TIM HORTON DONUTS

| 23 | 1 | 25 | Fuel-R.F.-R.R.-L.R. Tires-Adjust Front Wing | 25 |
| | | 26 | Out Of Race-Lost Wheel-Spun Out | |

TOTAL TIME: 25

31st Place—KEVIN COGAN   MARLBORO PATRICK RACING

| 7 | 1 | 20 | Fuel-R.F.-R.R.-L.R. Tires | 20 |
| | | 21 | Out Of Race-Engine Failure | |

TOTAL TIME: 20

32nd Place—RANDY LEWIS   TOSHIBA/ALTOS/LEADER CARD

| 24 | 1 | 8 | Out Of Race-Gear Box Failure | |

33rd Place—GEORGE SNIDER   CALUMET FARM/COPENHAGEN

| 84 | 1 | 1 | Out Of Race-Fire In Engine Compartment | |

LAP FIGURES AND PRIZES

PRELIMINARY LAP FIGURES

LAP NO.	CAR NO.	LAP TIME	SPEED
1	5	1:09.133	130.184
2	5	2:59.515	100.270
4	5	6:43.718	89.171

FASTEST LEADING LAP

LAP NO.	CAR NO.	LAP TIME	SPEED
7	5	43.927	204.885

FASTEST LAP OF RACE

LAP NO.	CAR NO.	LAP TIME	SPEED
57	4	43.900	205.011

LAP PRIZE LIST - FIRST PLACE

TOOK LEAD ON LAP	NO. OF LAPS LED	CAR NO.	CAR NAME	DRIVER	EARNINGS
1	27	5	Hanna Auto Wash Newman/Haas	Mario Andretti	$12,150.00
28	1	4	True Value STP March	Roberto Guerrero	450.00
29	32	5	Hanna Auto Wash Newman/Haas	Mario Andretti	14,400.00
61	4	3	Miller American Special	Danny Sullivan	1,800.00
65	16	5	Hanna Auto Wash Newman/Haas	Mario Andretti	7,200.00
81	1	4	True Value STP March	Roberto Guerrero	450.00
82	15	5	Hanna Auto Wash Newman/Haas	Mario Andretti	6,750.00
97	1	4	True Value STP March	Roberto Guerrero	450.00
98	80	5	Hanna Auto Wash Newman/Haas	Mario Andretti	36,000.00
178	5	4	True Value STP March	Roberto Guerrero	2,250.00
183	18	25	Cummins Holset Turbo Special	Al Unser, Sr.	8,100.00
					$90,000.00

LAP PRIZE LIST - SUMMARY

CAR	CAR NAME	DRIVER		LAPS	EARNINGS
5	Hanna Auto Wash Newman/Haas	Mario Andretti	1st	170	$76,500.00
25	Cummins Holset Turbo Special	Al Unser, Sr.	1st	18	8,100.00
4	True Value STP March	Roberto Guerrero	1st	8	3,600.00
3	Miller American Special	Danny Sullivan	1st	4	1,800.00

COMPLETE PRIZE FUND FOR THE 1987 INDIANAPOLIS 500 MILE RACE

Indianapolis Motor Speedway Corporation $3,510,000.00   (1)

Citizens Speedway Committee (Lap Prizes) 90,000.00

Citizens Speedway Committee (Parade) 10,000.00

Designated Awards 880,375.00   (2)

$4,490,375.00   (3)

(1) New all-time record: Previous record $3,058,550.00

(2) New all-time record: Previous record   842,900.00

(3) New all-time record: Previous record   4,001,450.00

DESIGNATED PRIZES

Accusplit/Jim Ellis Enterprises	$ 5,000	Indiana National Bank	$ 7,500
American Dairy Association	5,000	Indiana Oxygen Company	5,000
Ameritech	5,000	International Games	60,000
AmeriTrust	10,000	Kay Jewelers	5,000
Amoco Oil Company	10,000	Loctite Corporation	6,000
Bank One	10,000	Machinists Union	6,000
Bear Automotive Service Equip Co.	5,700	Mallory Ignition	5,000
Beatrice Meats, Inc.	10,000	Merchants National Bank	5,000
Bell Helmets	6,000	Miller Brewing Company	50,000
Borg-Warner Automotive, Inc.	6,000	Misc.	3,350
Borg-Warner Corporation	10,000	Mobil Oil Corporation	5,000
Budweiser/Starcraft Dodge Trucks	25,000	Monroe Auto Equipment	11,700
Call-Free Incorporated	5,000	National Automobile Dealers Assoc.	10,000
Canon, U.S.A.	5,000	PPG Industries, Inc.	165,000
Champion Spark Plug Company	5,000	Pennzoil Company	10,000
Clint Brawner Mechanic Excellence	5,000	Philip Morris, USA	75,000
Composite Systems, Inc.	5,000	Premier Industrial Corp.	6,000
Cornelius Printing Company	5,000	Preston Safeway, Div. Allied Comp.	5,000
Cotter & Company	7,500	Raybestos Brake Systems, Inc.	20,000
Domino's Pizza, Inc.	6,000	Robert Bosch Corporation	60,500
Earl's Performance Products	6,750	Rockwell International	5,275
Eastman Kodak Company	7,500	Sears Roebuck & Company	31,500
First Brand - STP Oil Treatment	15,000	Simpson Sports	7,100
First Brand - STP Racing	5,000	Snap-On Tools	5,000
Fischer Engineering	5,000	Speed-Pro by Sealed Power	5,000
GT&T Racing Products	5,000	St. Pius X, Knights of Columbus 3433	5,000
GTE Telecommunications	30,000	Stant Incorporated	5,000
General Foods Corporation	5,000	Stewart-Warner Corporation	5,000
Goodyear Tire & Rubber Company	5,000	The Kingsford Products, Co.	25,000
Herff Jones, Div., of Carnation Co.	5,000	Uniden	5,000
IMS	5,000	Valvoline Oil Company	5,000
Ideal Div., Parker Hannifin Corp.	5,000	Vandervell America	5,000

TOTAL DESIGNATED PRIZES $880,375

Merchandise won by race participants included:

Chrysler LeBaron Convertible

Starcraft/Dodge Van ($30,000 value)

Herff Jones "Champion of Champions" ring ($5,000 value)

Goodyear "Car Owner's" ring ($3,300 value)

Tony Foyt Award, Rolex watch ($8,000 value)

Tool sets from Snap-On Tools and Master Mechanic Tools

PPG "Starter's" rings ($500 value each)

Kay Jewelers/Longines watch ($550 value)

Trophies were presented to race participants by the following companies:

Amoco Oil Company	GTE Telecommunications	Merchants National Bank
Bank One Indianapolis	Indiana National Bank	Miller Brewing Company
Borg-Warner Corporation	Indiana Oxygen Company	National Automobile Dealers Association
Budweiser	Loctite	Premier/DA Lubricant Company
Sid Collins Memorial Fund	Machinists Union	Sears Craftsman
Cornelius Printing Company	Marlboro	Stewart-Warner Corporation
	Master Mechanic Tools	

Qualified Cars In The Starting Field

#5 MARIO ANDRETTI HANNA AUTO WASH NEWMAN/HAAS LOLA USAC Reg. No. 5 Qual: 5/9 @ 13:09 2:47.139 215.390 41.691 215.874 41.605 216.320 41.860 215.002 41.983 214.372	**#1 BOBBY RAHAL** BUDWEISER/TRUESPORTS/SPIRIT OF COL. USAC Reg. No. 31 Qual: 5/9 @ 11:31 2:48.764 213.316 42.030 214.133 42.133 213.609 42.239 213.073 42.362 212.455	**#8 RICK MEARS** PENNZOIL Z-7 SPECIAL USAC Reg. No. 83 Qual: 5/9 @ 11:19 2:59.230 211.467 42.484 211.844 42.465 211.939 42.624 211.149 42.666 210.941
#14 A.J. FOYT, JR. COPENHAGEN-GILMORE USAC Reg. No 14 Qual: 5/9 @ 17:07 2:50.669 210.935 42.401 212.259 42.688 210.832 42.743 210.561 42.837 210.099	**#4 ROBERTO GUERRERO** TRUE VALUE STP MARCH USAC Reg. No. 4 Qual: 5/9 @ 16:33 2:50.875 210.680 42.448 212.024 42.629 211.124 42.857 210.001 42.941 209.590	**#22 DICK SIMON** SOUNDESIGN STEREO USAC Reg. No. 22 Qual: 5/9 @ 14:13 2:51.461 209.960 42.490 211.815 42.696 210.793 42.950 209.546 43.325 207.732
#71 ARIE LUYENDYK LIVINGWELL, Inc./PROVINI VEAL/WTTV USAC Reg. No.71 Qual: 5/9 @ 16:52 2:52.797 208.337 42.844 210.064 42.846 210.055 43.985 204.615 43.122 208.710	**#21 JOHNNY RUTHERFORD** VERMONT AMERICAN CAR USAC Reg. No. 9 Qual: 5/9 @ 13:28 2:52.831 208.296 43.012 209.244 43.160 208.526 43.505 206.873 43.154 208.555	**#18 MICHAEL ANDRETTI** KRACO STP MARCH USAC Reg. No. 18 Qual: 5/9 @ 16:58 2:54.648 206.129 43.534 206.735 43.424 207.259 43.780 205.573 43.910 204.965
#23 LUDWIG HEIMRATH, JR MACKENZIE/TIM HORTON DONUTS USAC Reg. No. 23 Qual: 5/10 @ 12:12 2:53.418 207.591 43.287 207.915 43.432 207.220 43.432 207.220 43.267 208.011	**#81 RICH VOGLER** KY FRIED CHICKEN/LIVINGWELL/VALPAK USAC Reg. No. 81 Qual: 5/10 @ 12:17 2:54.863 205.887 43.489 206.949 43.945 204.801 43.869 205.156 43.550 206.659	**#11 JEFF MACPHERSON** TEAM MACPHERSON MARCH HONDA USAC Reg. No. 11 Qual: 5/10 @ 17:44 2:55.022 205.688 43.784 205.555 43.750 205.714 43.739 205.766 43.749 205.719
#91 SCOTT BRAYTON AMWAY/AUTOSTYLE/LIVINGWELL USAC Reg. No. 37 Qual: 5/10 @ 17:02 2:55.057 205.647 43.933 204.857 44.026 204.425 43.450 207.135 43.648 206.195	**#15 GEOFF BRABHAM** TEAM VALVOLINE MARCH HONDA USAC Reg. No. 45 Qual: 5/10 @ 17:13 2:55.180 205.503 43.840 205.293 43.610 206.375 43.689 206.002 44.041 204.355	**#56 GARY BETTENHAUSEN** GOHR RACING/GENESEE BEER WAGON USAC Reg. No. 56 Qual: 5/10 @ 16:53 2:56.036 204.504 43.549 206.664 43.924 204.899 44.418 202.621 44.415 203.874
#3 DANNY SULLIVAN MILLER AMERICAN SPECIAL USAC Reg. No. 58 Qual: 5/16 @ 11:56 2:51.208 210.271 42.917 209.707 42.768 210.438 42.741 210.571 42.782 210.369	**#12 FABRIZIO BARBAZZA** ARCIERO WINERY USAC Reg. No. 12 Qual: 5/16 @ 11:11 2:53.045 208.038 43.374 207.498 43.214 208.266 43.133 208.657 43.324 207.737	**#2 GORDON JOHNCOCK** STP OIL TREATMENT SPECIAL USAC Reg. No. 2 Qual: 5/16 @ 11:48 2:53.085 207.990 43.192 208.372 43.192 208.372 43.135 208.647 43.566 206.583
#77 DEREK DALY SCHEID TIRE/SUPERIOR TRNG/METROLINK USAC Reg. No. 77 Qual: 5/16 @ 11:16 2:53.476 207.522 42.926 209.663 43.138 208.633 43.432 207.220 43.980 204.638	**#25 AL UNSER, SR.** CUMMINS HOLSET TURBO SPECIAL USAC Reg. No. 85 Qual: 5/16 @ 12:02 2:53.558 207.423 43.278 207.958 43.208 208.295 43.367 207.531 43.705 205.926	**#33 TOM SNEVA** SKOAL BANDIT USAC Reg. No. 89 Qual: 5/16 @ 17:45 2:53.700 207.254 43.690 205.997 43.390 207.241 43.344 207.641 43.276 207.967
#30 AL UNSER JR. DOMINO'S PIZZA "HOT ONE" USAC Reg. No. 30 Qual: 5/16 @ 11:34 2:54.122 206.752 43.425 207.254 43.289 207.905 43.699 205.954 43.709 205.907	**#24 RANDY LEWIS** TOSHIBA/ALTOS/LEADER CARDS USAC Reg. No. 24 Qual: 5/16 @ 12:18 2:54.580 206.209 43.354 207.593 43.745 205.738 43.691 205.992 43.790 205.526	**#7 KEVIN COGAN** MARLBORO PATRICK RACING USAC Reg. No. 7 Qual: 5/16 @ 16:34 2:54.758 205.999 43.757 205.681 43.604 206.403 43.750 205.714 43.647 206.200
#55 JOSELE GARZA BRYANT HTG@CLG/SCHAEFER/MACH UNION USAC Reg. No. 55 Qual: 5/16 @ 11:27 2:55.019 205.692 43.561 206.607 43.785 205.550 43.970 204.685 43.703 205.936	**#41 STAN FOX** KERKER EXHAUST-SKOAL CLASSIC USAC Reg. No. 41 Qual: 5/16 @ 12:30 2:56.024 204.518 43.792 205.517 43.584 206.498 44.144 203.878 44.504 202.229	**#16 TONY BETTENHAUSEN** NATIONWISE AUTO PARTS/PAY LESS MKTS USAC Reg. No. 16 Qual: 5/16 @ 17:36 2:56.564 203.892 44.267 203.312 44.308 203.666 44.017 204.466 44.090 204.128
#44 DAVY JONES SKOAL CLASSIC/GILMORE/UNO USAC Reg. No. 44 Qual: 5/17 @ 17:05 2:52.900 208.117 43.450 207.135 43.383 207.455 43.121 208.715 43.026 209.176	**#29 PANCHO CARTER** HARDEE'S USAC Reg. No. 46 Qual: 5/17 @ 12:09 2:55.478 205.154 43.367 207.531 43.672 206.082 44.250 203.390 44.189 203.671	**#98 ED PIMM** SKOAL USAC Reg. No. 22 Qual: 5/9 @ 14:13 2:57.092 203.284 44.391 202.744 44.146 203.869 44.298 203.169 44.257 203.358
#84 GEORGE SNIDER CALUMET FARM/COPENHAGEN USAC Reg. No. 84 Qual: 5/17 @ 17:11 2:57.172 203.192 43.938 204.834 44.133 203.929 44.566 201.948 44.535 202.088	**#87 STEVE CHASSEY** UNITED OIL/LIFE OF INDIANA USAC Reg. No. 87 Qual: 5/17 @ 17:26 2:57.788 202.488 44.569 201.934 44.649 201.572 44.344 202.959 44.226 203.500	**#20 EMERSON FITTIPALDI** MARLBORO PATRICK RACING USAC Reg. No. 20 Qual: 5/9 @ 17:18 2:55.111 205.584 43.616 206.346 43.690 205.997 43.971 204.680 43.834 205.320

The average speed of the 33 cars that started
the race in 1986 was 210.280 MPH.
(2.142 MPH faster)

The average speed of the 33 cars that started
the race in 1987 was 207.194 MPH.
(3.086 MPH slower)

QUALIFIED CARS NOT IN THE STARTING FIELD

#59 SAMMY SWINDELL
BUTTERA/CENTER LINE/MACH UNION
USAC Reg. No. 59
Qual: 5/16 @ 11:06
Bumped from field by Car No. 98
2:58.359 201.840
44.712 201.288
44.568 201.939
44.490 202.293
44.589 201.844

#17 DOMINIC DOBSON
INTERSPORT MARCH
USAC Reg. No. 17
Qual: 5/17 @ 16:59
Bumped from field by Car No. 87
2:58.891 201.240
44.896 200.463
44.543 202.052
44.792 200.929
44.660 201.523

#76 ROCKY MORAN
GEORGE N.WALTHER
USAC Reg. No. 57
Qual: 5/17 @ 16:54
Bumped from field by Car No. 84
3:00.762 199.157
45.253 198.882
44.990 200.044
45.084 199.627
45.435 198.085

#97 RICK MIASKIEWICZ
PIZZA HUT/WENS/R.C.V.
USAC Reg. No. 97
Qual: 5/17 @ 17:50
Not Fast Enough
3:03.494 196.192
45.686 196.997
45.641 197.191
45.878 196.172
46.289 194.431

QUALIFIED CARS WITHDRAWN FROM THE STARTING FIELD

#3 DANNY SULLIVAN
MILLER AMERICAN PENSKE CHEV.
USAC Reg. No. 3
Qual: 5/9 @ 16:26
Withdrawn on 5/16 at 11:54
2:55.363 205.288
43.773 205.606
43.514 205.830
43.886 205.077
43.190 205.666

(Sullivan subsequently qualified Car 3 - USAC No. 58)

#29 PANCHO CARTER
HARDEE'S
USAC Reg. No. 95
Qual: 5/10 @ 12:05
Withdrawn on 5/17 at 12:05
2:56.660 203.781
44.205 203.597
44.218 203.537
44.002 204.536
44.235 203.459

(Carter subsequently qualified Car 29 - USAC No. 46)

CHANGES IN THE STARTING FIELD SUBSEQUENT TO CLOSE OF QUALIFYING

#20 EMERSON FITTIPALDI - Damaged in practice. Entry
moved to rear of starting
field due to car substitution.

The USAC serial number is a unique identification, assigned to each car prior
to the start of practice. If the number painted on the car is different from
the assigned USAC serial number, the car must display a "T" during practice
and qualification. At the close of qualification, each car in the starting
field must have a unique program number painted on the car for identification
on race day.

MARIO ANDRETTI, Nazareth, Pennsylvania

Indianapolis 500 Record (Passed Driver's Test 1965)

Year	Car	Qual.	S	F	Laps	Speed or Reason Out
1965	Dean Van Lines	158.849	4	3	200	149.121
1966	Dean Van Lines	165.899	1	18	27	Engine
1967	Dean Van Lines	168.982	1	30	58	Lost Wheel
1968	Overseas Natl. Airways	167.691	4	33	2	Piston
1968	*Overseas Natl. Airways			28	10	Piston
	*(Rel. L. Dickson)					
1969	STP Oil Treatment	169.851	2	1	200	156.867
1970	STP Oil Treatment	168.209	8	6	199	Flagged
1971	STP Oil Treatment	172.612	9	30	11	Accident
1972	Viceroy	187.167	5	8	194	Out of Fuel
1973	Viceroy	195.059	6	30	4	Piston
1974	Viceroy	186.027	5	31	2	Piston
1975	Viceroy	186.480	21	28	49	Accident
1976	CAM2 Motor Oil	189.404	19	8	101	Running
1977	CAM2 Motor Oil	193.351	6	26	47	Broken Header
1978	Gould Charge	194.647	33	12	185	Flagged
1980	Essex	191.012	2	20	71	Engine
1981	STP Oil Treatment	193.040	32	2	200	Running
1982	STP Oil Treatment	203.172	4	31	0	Accident
1983	Budweiser Lola	199.404	11	23	79	Accident
1984	Budweiser Lola	207.467	6	17	153	Broken Nose Cone
1985	Beatrice Lola	211.576	4	2	200	Running
1986	Newman/Haas Lola	212.300	30	32	19	Handling
1987	Hanna Auto Wash	215.390	1	9	180	Ignition

MICHAEL ANDRETTI, Nazareth, Pennsylvania

Indianapolis 500 Record (Passed Driver's Test 1984)

Year	Car	Qual.	S	F	Laps	Speed or Reason Out
1984	Electrolux Kraco	207.805	4	5	198	Running
1985	Electrolux Kraco	208.185	15	8	197	Running
1986	Kraco/STP/Lean Machine	214.522	3	6	199	Running
1987	Kraco/STP	206.129	9	29	28	CV Joint

FABRIZIO BARBAZZA, Monza, Italy

Indianapolis 500 Record (Passed Driver's Test 1987)

Year	Car	Qual.	S	F	Laps	Speed or Reason Out
1987	Arciero Winery	208.038	17	3	198	Running

GARY BETTENHAUSEN, Monrovia, Indiana

Indianapolis 500 Record (Passed Driver's Test 1968)

Year	Car	Qual.	S	F	Laps	Speed or Reason Out
1968	Thermo King Auto Air Cond.	163.562	22	24	43	Oil Cooler
1969	Thermo King Auto Air Cond.	167.777	9	26	35	Burned Piston
1970	Thermo King Auto Air Cond.	166.451	20	26	55	Dropped Valve
1971	Thermo King	171.233	13	10	178	Flagged
1972	Sunoco McLaren	188.877	4	14	182	Ignition
1973	Sunoco-DX McLaren	195.599	5	5	130	Red Flag
1974	Score	184.492	11	32	2	Broken Valve
1975	Thermo King	182.611	19	15	158	Wrecked
1976	Thermo King	181.791	8	28	52	Waste Gate Flange
1977	Agajanian-Evil Knievel	186.596	21	16	138	Clutch Failure
1978	Oberdorfer	187.324	31	16	147	Engine
1980	Armstrong Mould, Inc.	182.463	32	3	200	142.485
1981	Hopkins	190.870	11	26	69	Broken Rod
1982	Kraco	195.673	30	12	158	Engine
1986	Vita Fresh/Timex	209.756	29	11	193	Running
1987	"Genesee Beer	204.504	15	5	195	Running

TONY BETTENHAUSEN, Speedway, Indiana

Indianapolis 500 Record (Passed Driver's Test 1980)

Year	Car	Qual.	S	F	Laps	Speed or Reason Out
1981	Provimi Veal	187.013	16	7	195	Flagged
1982	Provimi Veal	195.429	27	26	37	Accident
1983	Provimi Veal	199.893	9	17	152	Half Shaft
1984	Provimi Racing	202.813	17	26	86	Piston
1985	Skoal Bandit	204.824	29	29	31	Wheel Bearing
1986	Bettenhausen Racing	208.933	18	28	77	Valve Spring
1987	Nationwise/Payless	203.892	27	10	171	Engine

GEOFF BRABHAM, Noblesville, Indiana

Indianapolis 500 Record (Passed Driver's Test 1981)

Year	Car	Qual.	S	F	Laps	Speed or Reason Out
1981	Psachie-Garza Esso	187.990	15	5	197	Flagged
1982	Pentax Super	198.906	20	28	12	Engine
1983	UNO British Sterling	198.618	26	4	199	Running
1984	Kraco Car Stereo	204.931	8	33	1	Fuel Line
1985	Coors Light Silver Bullet	210.074	9	19	131	Engine
1986	Valvoline Spirit	207.082	20	12	193	Running
1987	Team Valvoline	205.503	14	24	71	Oil Pressure

SCOTT BRAYTON, Coldwater, Michigan

Indianapolis 500 Record (Passed Driver's Test 1981)

Year	Car	Qual.	S	F	Laps	Speed or Reason Out
1981	Forsythe Industries	187.774	29	16	173	Engine
1983	SME Cement	196.713	29	9	195	Running
1984	Buick Dealers of America	203.637	26	18	150	Transmission
1985	Hardee's #37	212.354	2	30	20	Turbocharger
1986	Hardee's Living Well	208.079	23	30	69	Engine
1987	Amwawy/Autostyle	205.647	13	12	167	Engine

DUANE (Pancho) CARTER JR., Brownsburg, Indiana

Indianapolis 500 Record (Passed Driver's Test 1974)

Year	Car	Qual.	S	F	Laps	Speed or Reason Out
1974	Cobre Firestone	180.605	21	7	191	Flagged
1975	Cobre Tire	183.449	18	4	169	Running
1976	Jorgensen	184.824	6	5	101	Running
1977	Jorgensen	192.452	8	15	156	Blown Engine
1978	Budweiser Lightning	196.829	21	24	92	Header
1979	Alex XLNT Foods	185.806	17	20	129	Wheel Bearing
1980	Alex XLNT Foods	186.480	8	6	199	Running
1981	Alex XLNT Foods	191.022	10	28	63	Lost Comp.
1982	Alex Foods	198.950	10	3	199	Running
1983	Alex Foods Pinata	198.237	14	7	197	Running
1984	American Dream Racing	201.820	21	19	141	Engine
1985	Valvoline Buick Hawk	212.583	1	33	7	Oil Pump
1986	Coors Light Silver Bullet	209.635	14	16	179	R. F. Bearing
1987	Hardee's	205.154	29	27	45	Valve

STEVE CHASSEY, Carmel, Indiana

Indianapolis 500 Record (Passed Driver's Test 1981)

Year	Car	Qual.	S	F	Laps	Speed or Reason Out
1983	Genesee/Sizzler	195.108	19	11	192	Running
1987	United Oil/Life of Indiana	202.488	32	25	68	Engine

KEVIN COGAN, Redondo Beach, California

Indianapolis 500 Record (Passed Driver's Test 1981)

Year	Car	Qual.	S	F	Laps	Speed or Reason Out
1981	Jerry O'Connell Racing	189.444	12	4	197	Flagged
1982	The Norton Spirit	204.082	2	30	0	Accident
1983	Master Mech./Caesar's Palace	201.528	22	5	198	Running
1984	Dubonnet-Curb Records	203.622	27	20	137	Wheel Froze
1985	Kraco/Wolff Sun	206.368	32	11	192	Running
1986	7-Eleven	211.922	6	2	200	Running
1987	Marlboro/Patrick	205.999	24	31	21	Oil Pump

DEREK DALY, Dublin, Ireland

Indianapolis 500 Record (Passed Driver's Test 1983)

Year	Car	Qual.	S	F	Laps	Speed or Reason Out
1983	Wysard Motor Company	187.658	28	19	126	Engine
1984	Provimi Veal Racing	202.443	29	27	76	Handling
1985	Kapsreiter Bier	207.548	31	12	190	Running
1987	Sheid/Superior/Metro	207.522	19	15	133	Engine

EMERSON FITTIPALDI, Sao Paulo, Brazil

Indianapolis 500 Record (Passed Driver's Test 1984)

Year	Car	Qual.	S	F	Laps	Speed or Reason Out
1984	W.I.T. Promotions	201.078	23	32	37	Oil Pressure
1985	7-Eleven	211.322	5	13	189	Engine
1986	Marlboro	210.237	11	7	199	Running
1987	Marlboro/Patrick	205.584	33	16	131	Lost Power

Year	Car	Qual.	S	F	Laps	Speed or Reason Out

STAN FOX, Janesville, Wisconsin

Indianapolis 500 Record (Passed Driver's Test 1984)

Year	Car	Qual.	S	F	Laps	Speed or Reason Out
1987	Kerker Exhaust/Skoal Classic	204.518	26	7	192	Running

A. J. FOYT, Houston, Texas

Indianapolis 500 Record (Passed Driver's Test 1958)

Year	Car	Qual.	S	F	Laps	Speed or Reason Out
1958	Dean Van Lines	143.130	12	16	148	Spun Out
1959	Dean Van Lines	142.648	17	10	200	133.297
1960	Bowes Seal Fast	143.466	16	25	90	Clutch
1961	Bowes Seal Fast	145.907	7	1	200	139.130
1962	Bowes Seal Fast	149.074	5	23	69	Accident
1962	*Sarkes Tarzian		17		20	Starter
	*Rel E. George 127-146					
1963	Sheraton-Thompson	150.615	8	3	200	142.210
1964	Sheraton-Thompson	154.672	5	1	200	147.350
1965	Sheraton-Thompson	161.233	1	15	115	Gearbox
1966	Sheraton-Thompson	161.355	18	26	0	Accident
1967	Sheraton-Thompson	166.289	4	1	200	151.207
1968	Sheraton-Thompson	166.821	8	20	86	Engine
1969	Sheraton-Thompson	170.568	1	8	181	Flagged
1970	Sheraton-Thomp ITT	170.004	3	10	195	Transmission
1971	ITT-Thompson	174.317	6	3	200	156.069
1972	ITT-Thompson	188.996	17	25	60	Engine
1973	*Gilmore Racing	188.927	23	25	37	Conn. Rod
	*Rel George Snider		12		101	Gearbox
1974	Gilmore Racing	191.632	1	15	142	Gearbox
1975	Gilmore Racing	193.976	1	3	174	Running
1976	Gilmore Racing	185.261	5	2	102	Running
1977	Gilmore Racing	194.563	4	1	200	161.331
1978	Gilmore Racing	200.122	20	7	191	Flagged
1979	Gilmore Racing	189.613	6	2	200	Running
1980	Gilmore Racing	185.500	12	14	173	Valve
1981	Gilmore Racing	196.078	3	13	191	Flagged
1982	Valvoline/Gilmore	203.332	3	19	95	Transmission
1983	Valvoline/Gilmore	199.557	24	31	24	Shift Link
1984	Gilmore/Foyt Racing	203.806	12	6	197	Running
1985	Copenhagen/Gilmore	205.782	21	28	63	Engine
1986	Copenhagen/Gilmore	213.212	21	24	135	Brakes/Accident
1987	Copenhagen/Gilmore	210.935	4	19	117	Oil Seal

JOSELE GARZA, Mexico City, Mexico

Indianapolis 500 Record (Passed Driver's Test 1981)

Year	Car	Qual.	S	F	Laps	Speed or Reason Out
1981	Psachie Garza Esso	195.101	6	23	138	Accident
1982	Schlitz Gusto	194.500	33	29	1	Engine
1983	Machinists Union Silhouette	195.671	18	25	64	Oil Leak
1984	Schaefer/Machinists	200.615	24	10	193	Running
1985	Schaefer/Machinists	206.677	18	31	16	Engine
1986	Schaefer/Machinists	208.938	17	18	167	Running
1987	Bryant/Schaefer	205.692	25	17	129	Running

ROBERTO GUERRERO, Medellin, Columbia

Indianapolis 500 Record (Passed Driver's Test 1984)

Year	Car	Qual.	S	F	Laps	Speed or Reason Out
1984	Master Mechanic Tools	205.717	7	2	198	Running
1985	Mast. Mech./Emer. Elec	208.062	16	3	200	Running
1986	True Value/Emer. Elec	211.576	8	4	200	Running
1987	True Value/STP	210.680	5	2	200	Running

LUDWIG HEIMRATH, JR., Toronto, Ontario, Canada

Indianapolis 500 Record (Passed Driver's Test 1987)

Year	Car	Qual.	S	F	Laps	Speed or Reason Out
1987	MacKenzie/Horton	207.591	10	30	25	Lost Wheel, Spun

GORDON JOHNCOCK, Pima, Arizona

Indianapolis 500 Record (Passed Driver's Test 1965)

Year	Car	Qual.	S	F	Laps	Speed or Reason Out
1965	Weinberger Homes	155.012	14	5	200	146.417
1966	Weinberger Homes	161.059	6	4	200	143.084
1967	Gilmore Broadcasting	166.559	3	12	188	Spun Out
1968	Gilmore Broadcasting	166.775	9	27	37	Gerbox

Year	Car	Qual.	S	F	Laps	Speed or Reason Out
1969	Gilmore Broadcasting	168.626	5	19	137	Piston
1970	Gilmore Broadcasting	167.015	17	28	45	Engine
1971	Norris Industries	171.388	12	29	11	Accident
1972	Gulf McLaren	188.511	26	20	113	Valve
1973	STP Double Oil Filter	192.555	11	1	133	159.036
1974	STP Double Oil Filter	186.750	4	4	198	Flagged
1975	Sinmast	191.652	2	31	11	Ignition
1976	Sinmast	188.531	2	3	102	Running
1977	STP Double Oil Filter	193.517	5	11	184	Valve Spring
1978	N. American Van Lines	195.833	6	3	199	Penalized 1 lap
1979	N. American Van Lines	189.753	5	6	197	Running
1980	N. American Van Lines	186.075	17	4	200	Running
1981	STP Oil Treatment	195.429	4	9	194	Engine
1982	STP Oil Treatment	201.884	5	1	200	Running
1983	STP Oil Treatment	199.748	10	14	163	Engine
1984	STP Oil Treatment	207.545	5	25	103	Accident
1987	STP Oil Treatment	207.990	18	22	76	Valve

DAVY JONES, Syracuse, New York

Indianapolis 500 Record (Passed Driver's Test 1987)

Year	Car	Qual.	S	F	Laps	Speed or Reason Out
1987	Skoal/Gilmore/UNO	208.117	28	28	34	Engine

RANDY LEWIS, Hillsborough, California

Indianapolis 500 Record (Passed Driver's Test 1987)

Year	Car	Qual.	S	F	Laps	Speed or Reason Out
1987	Toshiba/Altos	206.209	23	32	8	Gear Box

ARIE LUYENDYK, Rosmalen, Holland

Indianapolis 500 Record (Passed Driver's Test 1985)

Year	Car	Qual.	S	F	Laps	Speed or Reason Out
1985	Dutch Treats/Sport Mag./Scot Lad/CNN	206.004	20	7	198	Running
1986	MCI Race for Life	207.811	19	15	188	Accident
1987	Living-Well/Provimi	208.337	7	18	125	Suspension

JEFF MacPHERSON, Rancho Santa Margarita, California

Indianapolis 500 Record (Passed Driver's Test 1987)

Year	Car	Qual.	S	F	Laps	Speed or Reason Out
1987	Team MacPherson	205.688	12	8	182	Running

RICK MEARS, Bakersfield, California

Indianapolis 500 Record (Passed Driver's Test 1977)

Year	Car	Qual.	S	F	Laps	Speed or Reason Out
1978	CAM2 Motor Oil	200.078	3	23	103	Engine
1979	Gould Charge	193.736	1	1	200	158.899
1980	Gould Charge	187.490	6	5	199	Running
1981	Gould Charge	194.018	22	30	58	Car Fire in Pits
1982	The Gould Charge	207.004	1	2	200	Running
1983	Pennzoil Penske	204.301	3	3	200	Running
1984	Pennzoil Z-7	207.844	3	1	20	163.612
1985	Pennzoil Z-7	209.796	10	21	123	Engine
1986	Pennzoil Z-7	216.828	1	3	200	Running
1987	Pennzoil Z-7	211.467	3	23	75	Coil Wire

ED PIMM, Dublin, Ohio

Indianapolis 500 Record (Passed Driver's Test 1984)

Year	Car	Qual.	S	F	Laps	Speed or Reason Out
1985	Skoal Bandit	205.724	22	9	196	Running
1986	Skoal/Pace/Curb	210.874	10	17	168	Electrical
1987	Skoal Classic	203.284	30	21	109	Lost Boost

BOBBY RAHAL, Columbus, Ohio

Indianapolis 500 Record (Passed Driver's Test 1982)

Year	Car	Qual.	S	F	Laps	Speed or Reason Out
1982	Red Roof Inns	194.700	17	11	174	Engine
1983	Red Roof Inns	202.005	6	20	110	Radiator
1984	7-Eleven/Red Roof Inns	202.230	18	7	197	Running
1985	Budweiser Truesports	211.818	3	27	85	Engine
1986	Budweiser Truesports	213.550	4	1	200	170.722
1987	Budweiser Truesports	213.316	2	26	57	Ignition

Year	Car	Qual.	S	F	Laps	Speed or Reason Out

JOHNNY RUTHERFORD, Ft. Worth, Texas

Indianapolis 500 Record (Passed Driver's Test 1963)

Year	Car	Qual.	S	F	Laps	Speed or Reason Out
1963	U.S. Equipment Co.	148.063	26	29	43	Transmission
1964	Bardahl	151.400	15	27	2	Accident
1965	Racing Associates	156.291	11	31	15	Rear End
1967	Weinberger Homes	162.859	19	25	103	Accident
1968	City of Seattle	163.830	21	18	125	Fuel Tank
1969	Patrick Petroleum	166.628	17	29	24	Oil Leak
1970	Patrick Petroleum	170.213	2	18	135	Brkn. Header
1971	Patrick Petroleum	171.151	24	18	128	Flagged
1972	Patrick Petroleum	183.234	8	27	55	Conn. Rod
1973	Gulf McLaren	198.413	1	9	124	Flagged
1974	McLaren	190.446	25	1	200	158.589
1975	Gatorade	185.998	7	2	174	Running
1976	Hy-Gain	188.957	1	1	102	148.725
1977	First Natl. City T.C.	197.325	17	33	12	Bent Valves
1978	First Natl. City T.C.	197.098	4	13	180	Flagged
1979	Budweiser	188.137	8	18	168	Running
1980	Pennzoil Chaparral	192.256	1	1	200	142.862
1981	Pennzoil Chaparral	195.387	4	32	25	Fuel Pump
1982	Pennzoil Chaparral	197.066	12	8	187	Engine
1984	Gilmore/Greer/Foyt	202.062	30	22	116	Engine
1985	Vt. Am./Alex Foods	208.254	30	6	199	Running
1986	Vt. Amer/Pinata	210.220	12	8	198	Running
1987	Vermont American	208.296	8	11	171	Running

DICK SIMON, Salt Lake City, Utah

Indianapolis 500 Record (Passed Driver's Test 1970)

Year	Car	Qual.	S	F	Laps	Speed or Reason Out
1970	Bryant Heating-Cooling	165.548	31	14	168	Flagged
1971	TraveLodge		33*	14*	151	Flagged
	*Qualified by J. Mahler					
1972	TraveLodge	180.424	23	13	186	Flagged
1973	TraveLodge	191.276	27	14	100	Piston
1974	TraveLodge	184.502	10	33	1	Valve
1975	Bruce Cogel Ford	181.892	30	21	133	Running
1976	Bryant Heating	182.343	16	32	1	Rod
1977	Bryant Heating	185.615	30	31	24	Overheating
1978	La Machine	192.967	10	19	139	Wheel Bearing
1979	SANYO	185.071	20	26	57	Clutch
1980	Vt. Amer./Silhouette/					
	Regal 8	182.788	29	22	58	Lost Wheel
1983	Vermont American	192.993	10	15	161	Running
1984	Break Free	201.834	20	23	112	In Pits
1985	Break Free	208.536	14	26	87	Engine
1986	Duracell Coppertop	204.978	33	14	189	Running
1987	Soundesign Stereo	209.960	6	6	193	Running

TOM SNEVA, Spokane, Washington

Indianapolis 500 Record (Passed Driver's Test 1973)

Year	Car	Qual.	S	F	Laps	Speed or Reason Out
1974	Raymond Companies	185.147	8	20	94	Ring. Pinion
1975	Norton Spirit	190.094	4	22	125	Accident
1976	Norton Spirit	186.355	3	6	101	Running
1977	Norton Spirit	198.884	1	2	200	160.918
1978	Norton Spirit	202.156	1	2	200	161.244
1979	Sugaripe Prune	192.998	2	15	188	Accident
1980	Bon Jour Jeans	185.290	33	2	200	Running
1981	Blue Poly	200.691	20	25	96	Clutch
1982	Texaco Star	201.027	7	4	197	Engine
1983	Texaco Star	203.687	4	1	200	162.117
1984	Texaco Star	210.029	1	16	168	Left CV Joint
1985	Skoal Bandit	208.927	13	20	124	Accident
1986	Skoal Bandit	211.878	7	33	0	Accident
1987	Skoal Bandit	207.254	21	14	143	Accident

GEORGE SNIDER, Bakersfield, California

Indianapolis 500 Record (Passed Driver's Test 1965)

Year	Car	Qual.	S	F	Laps	Speed or Reason Out
1965	Gerhardt	154.825	16	21	64	Rear End
1966	Sheraton-Thompson	162.521	3	19	22	Accident
1967	Wagner-Lockhead	164.256	10	26	99	Spun Out
1968	Vel's Parnelli Jones	162.264	29	31	9	Valve
1969	Sheraton-Thompson	166,914	15	16	152	Flagged

Year	Car	Qual.	S	F	Laps	Speed or Reason Out
1970	Sheraton Thomp ITT	167.660	10	20	105	Suspension
1971	G. C. Murphy	171.600	21	33	6	Stalled
1972	ITT-Thompson	181.855	21	11	190	Flagged
1973	Gilmore Racing	190.355	30	12	101	Gearbox
1974	Gilmore Racing	183.993	13	28	7	Valve
1975	Lodestar	182.918	24	8	165	Running
1976	Hubler Chevrolet	181.141	27	13	98	Running
1977	Simon Assoc./					
	Greenwood Center	188.976	13	24	65	Valve
1978	Gilmore Racing/					
	Citicorp	192.627	23	8	191	Flagged
1979	Spirit of Neb./					
	KBHL-FM	185.319	35	33	7	Valve
1980	Gilmore Racing	185.385	21	15	169	Engine
1982	Cobre Tire	195.493	26	21	87	Transmission
1983	Calumet Farm	198.544	13	32	22	Ignition
1984	Calumet Farm Racing	201.860	31	11	193	Running
1985	A.J. Foyt Chevrolet	205.465	28	32	14	Engine
1986	Calumet/Copenhagen/					
	Gilmore	209.025	31	26	110	Ignition
1987	Calumet/Copenhagen	203.192	31	33	0	Fuel Leak

DANNY SULLIVAN, Louisville, Kentucky

Indianapolis 500 Record (Passed Driver's Test 1982)

Year	Car	Qual.	S	F	Laps	Speed or Reason Out
1982	Forsythe-Brown Racing	196.242	13	14	148	Accident
1984	Domino's Pizza "Hot One"	203.567	28	29	57	Broken Wheel
1985	Miller Amer.	210.298	8	1	200	152.982
1986	Miller Amer.	215.382	2	9	197	Running
1987	Miller American	210.271	16	13	160	Engine

AL UNSER, SR., Albuquerque, New Mexico

Indianapolis 500 Record (Passed Driver's Test 1965)

Year	Car	Qual.	S	F	Laps	Speed or Reason Out
1965	Sheraton-Thompson	154.440	32	9	196	Flagged
1966	STP Oil Treatment	162.272	23	12	161	Accident
1967	Retzloff Chemical	164.594	9	2	198	Flagged
1968	Retzloff Chemical	167.069	6	26	40	Accident
1970	Johnny Lightning 500	170.221	1	1	200	155.749
1971	Johnny Lightning 500	174.622	5	1	200	157.735
1972	Viceroy	183.617	19	2	200	160.192
1973	Viceroy	194.879	8	20	75	Piston
1974	Viceroy	183.889	26	18	131	Valve
1975	Viceroy	185.452	11	16	157	Conn. Rod
1976	American Racing	186.258	4	7	101	Running
1977	American Racing	195.950	3	3	199	Flagged
1978	First Natl. City T.C.	196.474	5	1	200	161.363
1979	Pennzoil	192.503	3	22	104	Tranmission Seal
1980	Longhorn Racing	186.442	9	27	23	Cylinder
1981	Valvoline Longhorn	192.719	9	17	166	Flagged
1982	Longhorn Racing	195.567	16	5	197	Engine
1983	Hertz Penske	201.954	7	2	200	Running
1984	Miller High Life	204.441	10	3	198	Running
1985	Hertz Special	210.523	7	4	200	Running
1986	Hertz Penske/Chev.	212.295	5	22	149	Vibration
1987	Cummins Holset Turbo	207.423	20	1	200	162.175

AL UNSER, JR., Albuquerque, New Mexico

Indianapolis 500 Record (Passed Driver's Test 1983)

Year	Car	Qual.	S	F	Laps	Speed or Reason Out
1983	Coors Light Silver Bullet	202.146	5	10	192	Out of Fuel
1984	Coors Light Silver Bullet	203.404	15	21	131	Water Pump
1985	Domino's Pizza "Hot One"	209.215	11	25	92	Running
1986	Domino's Pizza "Hot One"	211.533	9	5	199	Running
1987	Domino's Pizza "Hot One"	206.752	22	4	196	Running

RICH VOGLER, Glen Ellyn, Illinois

Indianapolis 500 Record (Passed Driver's Test 1980)

Year	Car	Qual.	S	F	Laps	Speed or Reason Out
1985	Ky. Fried Chicken	205.653	33	23	120	Accident
1986	Ky. Fried Chicken/Vt. Am.	208.089	27	25	132	Accident
1987	Ky. Fried Chicken/Living Well/Valpak	205.887	11	20	109	Rocker Arm

OFFICIAL TEN LAP STANDINGS

LAP NO. 10

CAR NO.	POSITION	ELAPSED TIME HR MN SECOND	AVERAGE SPEED
5	1	12 00.437	124.924
8	2	12 03.446	124.405
1	3	12 03.834	124.338
4	4	12 04.649	124.198
22	5	12 06.311	123.914
21	6	12 07.658	123.684
14	7	12 10.100	123.271
18	8	12 10.184	123.257
71	9	12 11.531	123.030
23	10	12 15.320	122.396
81	11	12 16.329	122.228
3	12	12 16.708	122.165
15	13	12 18.558	121.859
12	14	12 18.993	121.787
91	15	12 19.717	121.668
2	16	12 20.136	121.599
33	17	12 21.190	121.426
11	18	12 22.579	121.199
56	19	12 26.167	120.616
30	20	12 26.838	120.508
7	21	12 31.497	119.761
77	22	12 32.608	119.584
44	23	12 32.728	119.565
25	24	12 33.086	119.508
98	25	12 33.207	119.489
41	26	12 34.984	119.208
16	27	12 37.129	118.870
20	28	12 37.246	118.852
87	29	12 38.289	118.688
29	30	25 56.725	57.814
55	31	54 11.814	27.677

LAP NO. 20

CAR NO.	POSITION	ELAPSED TIME HR MN SECOND	AVERAGE SPEED
5	1	19 34.781	153.220
8	2	19 45.004	151.898
4	3	19 45.364	151.852
1	4	19 47.941	151.523
22	5	19 56.821	150.398
21	6	19 57.523	150.310
18	7	19 58.883	150.140
71	8	19 59.247	150.094
14	9	19 59.295	150.088
23	10	20 00.055	149.993
3	11	20 02.128	149.734
12	12	20 03.575	149.554
2	13	20 04.129	149.486
81	14	20 04.716	149.413
15	15	20 06.303	149.216
33	16	20 08.118	148.992
91	17	20 13.645	148.314
30	18	20 17.505	147.843
56	19	20 17.868	147.799
77	20	20 30.640	146.265
44	21	20 31.158	146.204
25	22	20 31.578	146.154
98	23	20 32.424	146.054
41	24	20 36.180	145.610
87	25	20 48.109	144.218
7	26	21 02.064	142.624
16	27	21 39.840	138.479
20	28	21 44.741	137.958
11	29	33 54.458	88.476
29	30	37 36.349	79.775
55	31	1 05 43.330	45.647

LAP NO. 30

CAR NO.	POSITION	ELAPSED TIME HR MN SECOND	AVERAGE SPEED
5	1	29 02.913	154.913
1	2	29 14.908	153.854
71	3	29 15.868	153.770
4	4	29 16.518	153.713
3	5	29 17.242	153.650
81	6	29 38.564	151.808
8	7	30 39.410	146.786
33	8	30 42.487	146.541
2	9	30 43.225	146.482
12	10	30 43.966	146.424
21	11	30 45.343	146.314
22	12	30 45.960	146.265
91	13	30 46.636	146.212
14	14	30 48.519	146.063
30	15	30 48.549	146.061
25	16	30 49.872	145.956
15	17	30 52.255	145.768
77	18	30 55.840	145.487
98	19	30 56.281	145.452
44	20	32 20.379	139.148
56	21	32 24.927	138.823
41	22	32 27.954	138.607
87	23	32 38.327	137.873
20	24	33 49.357	133.047
16	25	33 56.612	132.573
11	26	43 06.696	104.380
29	27	47 03.476	95.627
55	28	1 13 42.540	61.051

LAP NO. 40

CAR NO.	POSITION	ELAPSED TIME HR MN SECOND	AVERAGE SPEED
5	1	39 07.366	153.363
4	2	39 27.231	152.076
71	3	39 29.634	151.922
3	4	39 35.136	151.570
8	5	40 36.956	147.725
33	6	40 37.837	147.672
21	7	40 38.899	147.608
22	8	40 39.375	147.579
91	9	40 40.037	147.539
30	10	40 42.849	147.369
25	11	40 44.959	147.242
15	12	40 46.173	147.169
98	13	40 47.145	147.110
77	14	40 47.986	147.060
12	15	40 53.790	146.712
2	16	40 55.882	146.587
14	17	41 13.367	145.551
56	18	42 05.399	142.552
81	19	42 07.592	142.428
41	20	42 08.578	142.373
87	21	42 16.584	141.923
20	22	42 59.276	139.574
16	23	43 11.329	138.925
1	24	45 33.766	131.686
11	25	51 10.400	117.249
29	26	54 58.457	109.142
55	27	1 23 39.832	71.716

LAP NO. 50

CAR NO.	POSITION	ELAPSED TIME HR MN SECOND	AVERAGE SPEED
5	1	47 57.959	156.361
4	2	48 12.301	155.585
71	3	48 13.636	155.514
3	4	48 25.149	154.897
33	5	48 50.875	153.538
8	6	48 55.038	153.320
21	7	48 58.592	153.135
30	8	49 14.197	152.326
91	9	49 15.538	152.257
25	10	49 16.741	152.195
22	11	49 18.124	152.123
15	12	49 19.789	152.038
12	13	49 19.809	152.037
98	14	49 20.305	152.011
77	15	49 20.729	151.990
2	16	49 21.451	151.953
14	17	49 25.748	151.732
56	18	49 44.970	150.755
81	19	49 58.788	150.061
41	20	50 06.617	149.670
87	21	50 11.126	149.446
20	22	50 52.888	147.401
16	23	51 27.105	145.768
1	24	56 03.421	133.792
11	25	1 00 16.836	124.418
55	26	1 34 12.737	79.607

LAP NO. 60

CAR NO.	POSITION	ELAPSED TIME HR MN SECOND	AVERAGE SPEED
5	1	55 39.277	161.712
4	2	55 50.166	161.186
3	3	56 08.380	160.314
71	4	56 53.149	158.212
25	5	57 01.787	157.812
33	6	57 10.819	157.397
2	7	57 15.037	157.204
15	8	57 15.816	157.168
12	9	57 16.113	157.154
14	10	57 16.776	157.124
8	11	57 18.534	157.044
21	12	57 28.952	156.569
91	13	57 46.304	155.786
22	14	58 03.099	155.034
98	15	58 09.381	154.755
87	16	58 14.319	154.537
77	17	58 18.528	154.351
56	18	58 38.815	153.461
81	19	58 42.801	153.287
20	20	58 53.107	152.840
30	21	58 57.694	152.642
41	22	59 38.321	150.909
16	23	1 01 26.652	146.474
11	24	1 10 07.250	128.350
55	25	1 56 35.592	77.191

LAP NO. 70

CAR NO.	POSITION	ELAPSED TIME HR MN SECOND	AVERAGE SPEED
5	1	1 06 39.022	157.539
4	2	1 06 41.710	157.433
3	3	1 06 47.780	157.194
33	4	1 07 25.871	155.714
25	5	1 07 32.584	155.456
8	6	1 07 34.662	155.377
71	7	1 07 41.395	155.119
21	8	1 07 45.149	154.976
91	9	1 08 13.212	153.913
12	10	1 08 15.856	153.814
15	11	1 08 17.665	153.746
22	12	1 08 18.318	153.722
14	13	1 08 19.551	153.675
77	14	1 08 33.854	153.141
98	15	1 08 34.067	153.133
56	16	1 09 01.583	152.116
81	17	1 09 02.038	152.099
30	18	1 09 05.579	151.969
20	19	1 09 10.667	151.783
2	20	1 09 11.234	151.762
41	21	1 09 22.239	151.361
16	22	1 10 56.480	148.010
11	23	1 19 46.027	131.633
55	24	2 06 21.696	83.095

LAP NO. 80

CAR NO.	POSITION	ELAPSED TIME HR MN SECOND	AVERAGE SPEED
5	1	1 14 08.263	161.861
4	2	1 14 16.402	161.565
3	3	1 14 40.313	160.703
33	4	1 15 07.570	159.731
25	5	1 15 35.390	158.752
71	6	1 15 58.618	157.943
91	7	1 16 30.963	156.830
22	8	1 16 32.120	156.790
14	9	1 16 37.646	156.602
12	10	1 16 54.764	156.021
98	11	1 17 01.553	155.792
20	12	1 18 13.641	153.399
77	13	1 18 16.541	153.304
30	14	1 18 32.714	152.778
56	15	1 18 39.565	152.556
81	16	1 19 13.137	151.479
41	17	1 19 41.612	150.577
16	18	1 21 14.509	147.707
11	19	1 27 53.763	136.525
21	20	1 35 57.405	125.056
55	21	2 17 22.152	87.356

LAP NO. 90

CAR NO.	POSITION	ELAPSED TIME HR MN SECOND	AVERAGE SPEED
5	1	1 24 01.200	160.676
4	2	1 24 08.789	160.435
3	3	1 24 29.743	159.771
25	4	1 24 57.271	158.909
33	5	1 25 00.514	158.808
71	6	1 25 07.769	158.582
22	7	1 25 37.426	157.667
12	8	1 25 54.738	157.137
91	9	1 26 04.182	156.850
14	10	1 26 04.766	156.832
98	11	1 26 06.347	156.784
77	12	1 26 51.200	155.434
20	13	1 26 51.625	155.422
30	14	1 26 52.793	155.387
56	15	1 26 54.413	155.339
81	16	1 27 13.509	154.772
41	17	1 27 46.853	153.792
16	18	1 29 12.470	151.332
11	19	1 38 29.667	137.064
21	20	1 49 05.185	123.755
55	21	2 29 53.411	90.066

LAP NO. 100

CAR NO.	POSI-TION	ELAPSED TIME HR MN SECOND	AVERAGE SPEED
5	1	1 33 53.209	159.767
4	2	1 33 53.725	159.752
3	3	1 35 17.126	157.422
71	4	1 35 18.261	157.391
25	5	1 35 19.325	157.361
33	6	1 35 19.414	157.359
12	7	1 36 08.043	156.032
14	8	1 36 10.530	155.965
98	9	1 36 11.363	155.942
91	10	1 36 11.529	155.938
20	11	1 36 56.003	154.745
30	12	1 36 56.228	154.739
77	13	1 36 58.768	154.672
81	14	1 37 40.340	153.575
56	15	1 37 43.465	153.493
41	16	1 38 28.703	152.318
22	17	1 39 50.743	150.232
16	18	1 40 08.625	149.785
11	19	1 47 28.926	139.558
21	20	1 57 03.066	128.149
55	21	2 39 54.894	93.800

LAP NO. 110

CAR NO.	POSI-TION	ELAPSED TIME HR MN SECOND	AVERAGE SPEED
5	1	1 42 01.652	161.721
4	2	1 42 07.126	161.577
3	3	1 42 59.966	160.195
25	4	1 43 02.391	160.132
71	5	1 43 21.491	159.639
33	6	1 43 22.559	159.612
12	7	1 43 50.671	158.891
14	8	1 44 05.018	158.526
91	9	1 44 10.653	158.383
30	10	1 44 56.456	157.231
20	11	1 44 56.819	157.222
77	12	1 44 59.966	157.144
56	13	1 45 27.956	156.449
22	14	1 47 24.490	153.620
41	15	1 47 34.447	153.383
16	16	1 48 10.338	152.534
11	17	1 55 52.536	142.394
21	18	2 07 13.125	129.698
55	19	2 48 30.979	97.913

LAP NO. 120

CAR NO.	POSI-TION	ELAPSED TIME HR MN SECOND	AVERAGE SPEED
5	1	1 49 36.259	164.227
4	2	1 49 46.775	163.965
3	3	1 50 45.435	162.518
25	4	1 50 46.008	162.504
71	5	1 51 25.803	161.536
33	6	1 51 27.233	161.502
12	7	1 51 28.956	161.460
91	8	1 52 13.738	160.386
30	9	1 52 56.321	159.379
77	10	1 53 02.639	159.230
56	11	1 53 43.234	158.283
20	12	1 53 46.706	158.202
22	13	1 55 23.729	155.985
41	14	1 55 43.742	155.536
16	15	1 56 12.542	154.893
11	16	2 05 38.930	143.256
21	17	2 15 12.405	133.129
55	18	2 56 24.720	102.034

LAP NO. 130

CAR NO.	POSI-TION	ELAPSED TIME HR MN SECOND	AVERAGE SPEED
5	1	1 57 47.844	165.538
4	2	1 58 11.397	164.989
3	3	1 58 46.324	164.180
25	4	1 59 23.762	163.322
12	5	2 01 37.646	160.326
91	6	2 01 48.155	160.095
30	7	2 03 08.399	158.356
20	8	2 03 51.713	157.433
77	9	2 03 54.897	157.366
56	10	2 04 24.657	156.739
33	11	2 04 53.373	156.138
22	12	2 05 34.156	155.293
41	13	2 06 20.864	154.336
16	14	2 07 12.664	153.289
11	15	2 13 55.982	145.595
21	16	2 28 22.771	131.420

LAP NO. 140

CAR NO.	POSI-TION	ELAPSED TIME HR MN SECOND	AVERAGE SPEED
5	1	2 07 32.276	164.657
4	2	2 08 30.638	163.411
25	3	2 08 31.671	163.389
3	4	2 08 46.213	163.081
12	5	2 10 02.641	161.484
91	6	2 10 25.858	161.005
30	7	2 11 10.274	160.096
56	8	2 12 16.079	158.769
33	9	2 12 51.389	158.065
22	10	2 13 35.029	157.205
41	11	2 14 23.057	156.268
16	12	2 15 14.313	155.281
11	13	2 27 29.760	142.377
21	14	2 38 11.505	132.750

LAP NO. 150

CAR NO.	POSI-TION	ELAPSED TIME HR MN SECOND	AVERAGE SPEED
5	1	2 15 09.736	166.467
4	2	2 16 08.901	165.261
25	3	2 16 27.596	164.884
3	4	2 16 59.087	164.252
12	5	2 19 11.039	161.657
91	6	2 20 38.594	159.979
30	7	2 22 11.034	158.246
56	8	2 23 52.578	156.384
22	9	2 26 47.975	153.270
41	10	2 27 33.134	152.488
16	11	2 28 27.639	151.555
11	12	2 37 39.717	142.710
21	13	2 45 46.691	135.724

LAP NO. 160

CAR NO.	POSI-TION	ELAPSED TIME HR MN SECOND	AVERAGE SPEED
5	1	2 28 16.677	161.858
25	2	2 29 04.609	160.991
4	3	2 29 06.237	160.962
12	4	2 31 39.237	158.255
91	5	2 32 09.457	157.731
30	6	2 33 52.031	155.979
56	7	2 35 11.855	154.642
22	8	2 36 45.879	153.096
41	9	2 37 40.902	152.205
16	10	2 38 22.050	151.546
3	11	2 41 47.250	148.343
11	12	2 45 45.167	144.794
21	13	2 54 16.896	137.708

LAP NO. 170

CAR NO.	POSI-TION	ELAPSED TIME HR MN SECOND	AVERAGE SPEED
5	1	2 38 07.718	161.261
4	2	2 38 52.862	160.497
25	3	2 38 54.918	160.463
12	4	2 40 45.221	158.628
30	5	2 42 18.902	157.102
56	6	2 42 55.292	156.517
22	7	2 44 30.771	155.003
41	8	2 45 42.639	153.883
16	9	2 46 53.529	152.793
11	10	2 53 58.027	146.579
21	11	3 04 14.893	138.400

LAP NO. 180

CAR NO.	POSI-TION	ELAPSED TIME HR MN SECOND	AVERAGE SPEED
4	1	2 46 20.194	162.321
25	2	2 47 08.106	161.546
12	3	2 48 42.442	160.040
30	4	2 50 19.418	158.522
56	5	2 51 49.952	157.130
22	6	2 53 02.050	156.039
41	7	2 53 43.371	155.420
5	8	3 02 41.512	147.790
11	9	3 03 39.999	147.005

LAP NO. 190

CAR NO.	POSI-TION	ELAPSED TIME HR MN SECOND	AVERAGE SPEED
25	1	2 55 00.277	162.853
4	2	2 55 47.903	162.118
12	3	2 57 24.383	160.648
30	4	2 58 54.221	159.304
56	5	3 00 34.358	157.831
22	6	3 02 46.551	155.929
41	7	3 03 38.748	155.190

LAP NO. 200

CAR NO.	POSI-TION	ELAPSED TIME HR MN SECOND	AVERAGE SPEED
25	1	3 04 59.147	162.175
4	2	3 05 03.643	162.109

CARS BELOW DID NOT COMPLETE 200 LAPS

CAR NO.	LAST LAP COMPLETED	POSITION LAST LAP	REASON
12	198	3	END OF RACE
30	196	4	END OF RACE
56	195	5	END OF RACE
22	193	6	END OF RACE
41	192	7	END OF RACE
11	182	8	END OF RACE
5	180	8	MECHANICAL
16	171	9	MECHANICAL
21	171	11	END OF RACE
91	167	5	MECHANICAL
3	160	11	MECHANICAL
33	143	9	ACCIDENT
77	133	13	MECHANICAL
20	131	8	MECHANICAL
55	129	17	END OF RACE
71	125	8	MECHANICAL
14	117	9	MECHANICAL
81	109	17	MECHANICAL
98	109	20	MECHANICAL
2	76	18	MECHANICAL
8	75	21	MECHANICAL
15	71	22	MECHANICAL
87	68	23	MECHANICAL
1	57	25	MECHANICAL
29	45	26	MECHANICAL
44	34	22	MECHANICAL
18	28	23	MECHANICAL
23	25	13	MECHANICAL
7	21	28	MECHANICAL
24	8	31	MECHANICAL
84	0	33	MECHANICAL

Saturday, May 2

#18 Michael Andretti 210.772; 29 Pancho Carter 208.429; 71 Arie Luyendyk 208.188; 22 Dick Simon 208.188; 55 Josele Garza 207.708; 71T (43) Arie Luyendyk 206.280; 18T (38) Michael Andretti 206.138; 1 Bobby Rahal 203.860; 12T (52) Fabrizio Barbazza 200.490; 11 Jeff MacPherson 197.750; 59 Sammy Swindell 195.993; 23 Ludwig Heimrath Jr. 194.387; 42 Randy Lewis 194.1; 30"T" (50) Al Unser Jr. 193.215; 91T (37) Scott Brayton 192.760; 97 Rick Miaskiewicz 188.916; 81T (51) Rich Vogler 188.639; 15 Geoff Brabham (w/u); 81 Rich Vogler (no full hot laps) 19 cars/16 drivers; 7 yellows for 49 minutes; track open at 1:28/speed limit lifted at 1:39.

Sunday, May 3

#5 Mario Andretti 213.371; 1 BR 212.464; 18 MA 211.764; 30T AU 211.515; 29 PC 210.035; 71 AL 210.035; 22 DS 209.156; 4T (60) Roberto Guerrero 209.107; 55 JG 209.107; 5T (6) Mario Andretti 208.623; 8 Rick Mears 208.526; 21 Johnny Rutherford 207.510; 3 Danny Sullivan 205.291; 77 Derek Daly 205.058; 25 Danny Ongais 204.638; 20 Emerson Fittipaldi 204.605; 10 Dennis Firestone 203.850; 91T SB 203.389; 7 Kevin Cogan 203.022; 15 GB 201.793; 76 Rocky Moran 201.252; 12T FB 201.117; 56 Gary Bettenhausen 200.579; 97 RM 199.208; 11 JM 198.938; 87 Steve Chassey 198.587; 44 Davy Jones 184.162; 59 SS 180; 8T (28) Danny Sullivan (w/u); 23 LH (w/u) 30 cars/28 drivers; 17 yellows for 100 minutes; 35 cars out for month.

Monday, May 4

#10 DF 211.565; 4T RG 211.565; 30 Al Unser Jr. 211.317; 5 MA 211.069; 77 DD 209.205; 30T AU 207.852; 71 AL 207.277; 81T RV 207.182; 1 BR 206.991; 1T (31) Bobby Rahal 205.902; 21T (9) Johnny Rutherford 205.479; 18T MA 204.406; 7 KC 204.266; 91T SB 204.220; 22 DS 204.035; 56T (65) Gary Bettenhausen 203.481; 15 GB 202.657; 8 RM 202.611; 23 LH 202.383; 33 Tom Sneva 201.974; 11 JM 201.207; 44 DJ 200.044; 55 JG 199.512; 16 Tony Bettenhausen 197.657; 25 DO 197.281; 24 Randy Lewis 196.506; 41 Stan Fox 195.950; 3 DS 194.847; 20T (40) Emerson Fittipaldi 194.091; 56 GB 193.881; 81 RV 192.926; 2T (62) Jim Crawford 186.181; 14 A.J. Foyt (w/u); 15T (45) Geoff Brabham (w/u); 59 SS (w/u) 35 cars/30 drivers; 14 yellows for 73 minutes; 47 cars out for month.

Tuesday, May 5

#5 MA 218.204; 1T BR 213.017; 10 DF 212.929; 71 AL 212.665; 22 DS 212.164; 18T MA 211.069; 14 AJ 210.575; 2 Jim Crawford 210.378; 77 DD 210.329; 7 KC 210.102; 21 JR 209.790; 8 RM 209.497; 55 JG 208.188; 81 RV 207.809; 33 TS 207.660; 20 EF 207.230; 15T GB 206.849; 91T SB 206.403; 25 DO 205.902; 56T GB 205.479; 41 SF 203.665; 11 JM 203.570; 4 Roberto Guerrero 203.570; 44 DJ 203.343; 16 TB 202.702; 12T FB 202.657; 3 DS 202.429; 15 GB 201.658; 30 AU 200.660; 59 SS 200.044; 87 SC 199.885; 24 RL 196.5; 97 RM 194.2 33 cars/32 drivers; 18 yellows for 124 minutes; 49 cars out for month.

Wednesday, May 6

#5 MA 216.502; 2 JC 215.982; 1T BR 215.879; 4 RG 212.816; 18 MA 212.816; 22 DS 212.715; 71 AL 211.914; 8 RM 211.466; 2T JC 210.873; 18T MA 210.231; 14 AJ 210.133; 20 EF 209.448; 7 KC 209.253; 81 RV 208.574; 21 JR 208.478; 41 SF 208.092; 30 AU 207.421; 55 JG 207.134; 25 DO 206.422; 77 DD 206.327; 15 GB 206.280; 23 LH 206.091; 84 George Snider 205.245; 15T GB 205.138; 33T (73) Tom Sneva 205.058; 44 DJ 204.918; 3 DS 204.406; 91T SB 204.127; 16 TB 203.896; 11 JM 202.565; 12 Fabrizio Barbazza 200.982; 56T GB 200.803; 19 Dick Ferguson 200.578; 87 SC 198.763; 33 TS 198.6; 97 RM 197.591; 59 SS 195.270; 10T (90) Phil Krueger 195.180; 29T (95) Pancho Carter 194.3; 98 Ed Pimm 188.560; 20T Cogan 186.373 42 cars/37 drivers; 15 yellows for 120 minutes; 56 cars out for month.

Thursday, May 7

#5 MA 218.234; 1T BR 216.502; 71T AL 214.899; 4 RG 214.489; 22 DS 214.336; 18 MA 213.725; 71 AL 212.765; 1 BR 211.764; 2 JC 210.970; 20 EF 209.448; 21 JR 209.399; 23 LH 209.205; 33 TS 208.768; 77 DD 208.761; 30 AU 208.140; 44 DJ 208.044; 21T JR 207.564; 11 JM 207.564; 14 AJ 207.516; 41 SF 206.991; 15T GB 206.753; 8 RM 206.185; 84 GS 205.526; 3 DS 205.365; 8T Mears 204.638; 56T GB 204.452; 25 DO 204.359; 29T PC 204.081; 15 GB 203.850; 98 EP 203.804; 18T MA 203.665; 12 FB 203.619; 7 KC 203.2; 76 RM 203.114; 81 RV 202.931; 16 TB 201.929; 55 JG 201.929; 24 RL 201.297; 87 SC 200.892; 97 RM 200.356; 10T PK 198.281 41 cars/35 drivers; 15 yellows for 132 minutes.

Friday, May 8

#5 MA 216.242; 1T BR 215.568; 71 AL 214.951; 2 JC 214.438; 22 DS 213.9; 18 MA 212.264; 71T AL 211.964; 20 EF 210.329; 30 AU 210.084; 8TT (83) Rick Mears 209.594; 2T JC 208.913; 21 JR 208.574; 77 DD 208.092; 98 EP 207.852; 4 RG 206.991; 15T GB 206.891; 21T JR 206.753; 91T SB 206.185; 56T GB 206.091; 7 KC 205.573; 55 JG 205.291; 11 JM 205.058; 8 RM 204.919; 81 RV 204.731; 23 LH 204.638; 14 AJ 204.498; 44 DJ 204.313; 33T TS 204.1; 29T PC 202.850; 24 RL 203.619; 3 DS 203.481; 19 DF 203.297; 10T PK 201.432; 97 RM 200.892; 87 SC 200.000; 81T RV 198.037; 12 FB 197.889; 59 SS 196.936; 41 SF 194.8; 16 TB 192.802; 84 GS (w/u); 33 TS (no full hot laps) 42 cars/36 drivers; 20 yellows for 213 minutes; 57 cars out for month.

Qualifying Draw (May 8)

#18; 23; 81; 84; 33T; 8TT; 5T; 1T; 20T; 10T; 77; 71T; 2T; 29T; 22; 18T; 56T; 91T; 12T; 24; 71; 44; 16; 56; 11; 3; 1; 8T; 87; 81T; 59; 21; 30; 20; 30T; 97; 2; 98; 5; 7; 41; 42; 4T; 15T; 4; 21T; 55; 12; 15; 14; 8 (51 cars)

Saturday, May 9 (Morning Sessions)

#1T BR 216.606; 71 AL 215.879; 5 MA 215.879; 8TT RM 213.371; 18 MA 212.014; 22 DS 212.014; 29T PC 210.477; 2T JC 209.692; 84 GS 209.448; 14 AJ 209.055; 91T SB 208.381; 21T JR 208.044; 81 RV 208.044; 4 RG 207.852; 2 JC 207.852; 20 EF 207.612; 44 DJ 207.373; 98 EP 206.708; 15T GB 206.327; 23 LH 205.861; 33T TS 205.855; 55 JG 205.479; 56T GB 205.104; 12 FB 204.452; 7 KC 203.022; 3 DS 202.748; 81T RV 201.982; 30 AU 201.748; 21 JR 201.387; 77 DD 200.044; 11 JM 194; 16 TB 191; 30 AU 201.748; 21 JR 201.387; 77 DD 200.044; 11 JM 194; 16 TB 191.1; 41 SF 188; 24 RL 186.1; 97 RM (w/u) 35 cars.

May 9 (Afternoon Session—2:49 to 3:40)

#4 RG 211.1; 2T JC 210.5; 29T PC 205.339; 71T AL 204.3; 20 EF 204.3; 18 MA 204.3; 71 AL 204.1; 56T GB 202.6; 33T TS 202.5; 98 EP 202.3; 7 KC 201.0; 15T GB 200.7; 55 JG 200.6; 91T SB 200.5; 30 AU 200.0; 81 RV 198.8; 81T (Johnny Parsons) 196.9; 59 SS 183; 16 TB 178; 12 FB, 23 LH, 11 JM, 77 DD (no full hot laps) 23 cars. Saturday totals 37 cars/34 drivers; 14 yellows for 183 minutes; 4T did not practice but made a qualifying attempt.

Sunday, May 10 (All Sessions)

#91T SB 206.944; 56 GB 206.422; 81 RV 205.338*; 77 DD 205.198*; 84 GS 204.968*; 29T PC 204.824; 15T GB 204.824; 44 DJ 204.638*; 56T GB 204.452*; 30 AU 204.42; 11 JM 201.117; 7 KC 200.579*; 24 AL 200.33; 23 LH 199.600*; 12T FB 199.3; 97 RM 198.325; 55 JG 197.2; 87 SC 191.245; 17 Phil Krueger 190.961; 12 FB 190.667; 16 TB 185.375; 33T TS (no full hot laps) 22 cars/20 drivers; 10 yellows for 144 minutes; 58 cars out for month; 12T, 17, 56, 87 practiced in afternoon only; (*) speed turned in morning session.

Monday, May 11

#5T MA 211.714; 8TT RM 207.325; 18 MA 206.232; 77 DD 206.091; 91T SB 205.194; 4 RG 203.022; 20T EF 202; 71T AL 200.758; 24 RL 195.354; 2 (Gordon Johncock) 190.355; 17 (Dominic Dobson) 189.234; 7 KC 185 12 cars & drivers; 11 yellows for 122 minutes; Qualified cars out were: 4, 8TT, 18, 91T.

Tuesday, May 12

#5T MA 212.916; 1T BR 211.964; 4 RG 211.814; 8TT RM 211.665; 14 AJ 209.594; 18T MA 209.010; 91T SB 207.373; 23 LH 206.849; 20T EF 206.422; 12T FB 206.091; 77 DD 205.996; 81 RV 205.855; 30 AU 205.761; 98 EP 205.714; 7 KC 205.151; 44 DJ 204.778; 71T AL 203.573; 24 RL 202.520; 71 AL 201.746; 2 GJ 199.423; 16 TB 198.063; 59 SS 196.936; 42 RL 196.893; 17 DD 193.840 24 cars/22 drivers; 10 yellows for 81 minutes; Qualified cars out were: 1T, 4, 8TT, 14, 23, 71, 81, 91T; track opened at 11:03 under caution yellow, green at 11:10.

Wednesday, May 13

#18T MA 211.317; 8TT RM 211.019; 1T BR 209.302; 22 DS 208.140; 91T SB 207.852; 71 AL 207.708; 10T (49) Dennis Firestone 206.944; 14 AJ 205.808; 7 KC 205.667; 98 EP 205.658; 5T MA 204.964; 12T FB 204.731; 21 JR 202.702; 15 GB 200.668; 3 DS 198.326; 81T JP 197.671; 97 RM 197.411; 87 SC 197.281; 17 DD 194.510; 29TT (46) Pancho Carter 193.590; 10TT PK 176.678 25 cars/24 drivers; 14 yellows for 137 minutes; 62 cars out for month; Qualified cars out were: 3, 4, 14, 15"T", 22; 15T (45) was now practicing without the "T".

Thursday, May 14

#18T MA 209.399; 30 AU 208.913; 3T DS 207.900; 5T MA 207.277; 22 DS 207.182; 4 RG 206.469; 20T EF 204.498; 10T DF 203.665; 55 JG 203.665; 41 SF 202.931; 14 AJ 202.657; 7 KC 202.657; 24 RL 202.201; 25T AU 201.833; 59 SS 201.793; 44 DJ 201.117; 2 GJ 201.072; 15"T" GB 200.668; 3 DS 198.326; 81T JP 197.671; 97 RM 197.411; 87 SC 197.281; 17 DD 194.510; 29TT (46) Pancho Carter 193.590; 10TT PK 176.678 25 cars/24 drivers; 14 yellows for 137 minutes; 62 cars out for month; Qualified cars out were: 3, 4, 14, 15"T", 22; 15T (45) was now practicing without the "T".

Friday, May 15

#30 AU 210.231; 4 RG 209.937; 14 AJ 208.285; 77 DD 208.236; 55 JG 207.996; 12 FB 207.900; 3T DS 207.804; 25T AU 206.516; 29TT PC 205.996; 7 KC 205.667; 44 DJ 205.104; 12T FB 204.731; 22 DS 204.452; 24 RL 204.452; 15 GB 203.850; 11 JM 203.573; 16 TB 203.252; 2 GJ 202.201; 41 SF 201.117; 20T EF 201.0; 87 SC 200.982; 84 GS 199.971; 17 DD 199.115; 15"T" GB 198.719; 3 DS 198.719; 76T (57) Rocky Moran 195.524; 10TT PK 195.397; 10T EF 195.016; 59 SS 194.049; 56 GB 192.472; 56T GB 190.677; 98 EP 190.1; 22T (27) Dick Simon 189.6; 33TT (89) Tom Sneva (w/u) 34 cars/29 drivers; 13 yellows for 154 minutes; 65 cars out for month; Qualified cars out were: 3, 4, 11, 14, 15"T", 22, 56.

Saturday, May 16 (All Sessions)

#5T MA 215.930; 30 AU 210.182*; 12 FB 209.888*; 77 DD 209.205*; 25T AU 208.429*; 20T EF 208.333*; 44 DJ 207.948*; 33TT TS 207.5; 7 KC 207.182*; 3T DS 207.039*; 2 GJ 206.185*; 41 SWF 206.091*; 24 RL 206.091*; 29TT PC 205.761*; 16 TB 205.151*; 84 GS 204.266*; 98 EP 204.127*; 10TT PK 202.4; 55T (29) Garza 202.065*; 15 GB 202.0; 59 SS 201.658*; 87 SC 201.4; 76T RM 200.579*; 15"T" GB 198.7; 17 DD 195.100; 11 JM 193.3; 22T DS 192.9; 55 JG (no full hot laps) 28 cars/26 drivers; 18 yellows for 161 minutes; 5T, 10TT, 11, 15, 15"T", 22T, 87 practiced in afternoon only; Qualified cars out were: 11, 15"T"; The beige 55T ran on May 2 & 3 as the orange and white Hardee's 29; (*) speed turned in morning session.

Sunday, May 17 (All Sessions)

#29TT PC 208.962*; 21T JR 208.962*; 87 SC 207.660*; 20T EF 206.849*; 8TT RM 206.516*; 12 FB 204.824; 10TT PK 204.824*; 44 DJ 203.481* AND sNIDER 198; 76T RM 202.292*; 98 EP 202.065; 30 AU 201.929*; 11 JM 201.567*; 7 KC 201.387; 56T GB 201.387; 33TT TS 201.342; 15"T" GB 201.2; 84 GS 200.937*; 22T DS 200.713; 71 AL 200.668; 37 DS 200.356; 91T SB 199.733; 97 RM 198.3; 56 GB 195.6; 19T (69) Dick Ferguson (no full hot laps); 55 JG (no full hot laps) 27 cars/26 drivers; 12 yellows for 134 minutes; 66 cars out for month (total); 15"T", 19T, 22T, 33TT, 55, 56, 71, 81, 91T, 97 practiced in afternoon only; Qualified cars out were: 3T, 7, 8TT, 11, 12, 15"T", 21T, 30, 33TT, 5, 56, 71, 81, 91T; (*) speed turned in morning session.

Thursday, May 21 (Carburation Day)

#5 MA 211.515; 8 RM 207.134; 18 MA 205.885; 14 AJ 205.714; 12 FB 203.758; 21 JR 203.389; 1 BR 203.297; 71 AL 202.839; 3 DS 202.794; 55 JG 202.383; 91 SB 200.524; 2 GJ 199.379; 15 SB 199.071; 44 DJ 199.026; 33 TS 199.0; 29 PC 198.982; 25 AU 297.758; 81 RV 197.758; 11 JM 197.022; 7 KC 196.721; 23 LH 196.635; 22 DS 196.377; 16 TB 195.970; 24 RL 195.907; 30 AU 195.8; 56 GB 195.482; 77 DD 194.889; 98 EP 194.889; 20 EF 194.594; 87 SC 192.760; 41 SF 185.605; 4 RG (no full hot laps); 84 GS (tow-in) 33 cars & drivers; 8 yellows for 57 minutes; 2 changed from white to blue and red; track open from 11:00 to 1:00.

Evolution Of The
WINNER

The winning Penske 25 entry started May as the black PC-16 Ilmor-Chevrolet driven by Danny Ongais (top). Following the Ongais accident and withdrawal, late on Wednesday, May 13, 25 became an '86 March/Cosworth driven by Al Unser and sponsored by Hertz (second from top).

By Thursday morning, Cummins had replaced Hertz on the sidepods, while red trim had appeared on the rear wing and front flippers (second from bottom). Friday saw the black numbers and red trim transformed into blue (bottom), which was approximately the car's livery on race day (center). Center photo by Ron McQueeney-IMS; all others by David Scoggan.

IMS President Joe Cloutier and Five Hundred Festival Queen Pam Jones flank Karen and Al Unser in victory circle. (IMS-McQueeney)

THE WINNER'S INTERVIEW

Unser and Penske talk it over with the press.

Editor's note: The following is transcribed from a tape record-ing made in the Press Interview Room as Al Unser and Roger Penske held court with the media shortly after the conclusion of the 1987 "500." We wish to thank Bill Donaldson and Kurt Hunt of the Indianapolis Motor Speedway Publicity Department for making it available.

Q. If the resources are available, Ro-ger, would it at least be feasible for Al to run the other 500 mile races?

Penske: This is a tremendous load for the team and for Al. We are going to sit down, Derrick and the rest of the team, and if we can provide Al a ride with the team for the two 500's we're certainly going to look at that. I want to, and if Al wants to I can tell you he has been hired.

Q: Al, with all the problems people were having on the track during practice and qualifications, did you find any of those during the race?

Unser: No, with all the problems peo-ple were having all month with crashes and everything, I had no problems all day. I really didn't. I have no complaints

with the tires or the race car. I would like to have run down the straightaway about ten times as fast as I was so I could pass everybody but it just doesn't happen.

Q: There were several accidents today. Did you happen to come up behind any?

Unser: Yes, Josele on the first lap. He passed me down low going into the first turn, and luckily, I decided not to dive right down in there. He was on the paint and he spun and I had to make a very quick decision whether to try and outrun him to the straightaway, and I elected just to try and outrun him. And I barely made it by him, I'll tell you. In fact, I tensed up because I thought he was going to hit my left rear. It sure scared me.

Q: Al, can you tell us your feeling when you got the checkered flag?

Unser: I'll tell you, it is hard to put into words. It is just a great, great feel-ing. I was sitting in the car and thinking, I can't believe this has really happened today.

Q: How far were you behind Andretti when he dropped out?

Unser: I was a lap and about 10 seconds.

Q: Was that about as far as you were behind all day?

Unser: Well, I'm not sure, but most of the day Andretti had a lap on the field.

Q: Did you know that Guerrero was in trouble in the pit?

Unser: Well, Roger kept me informed

of that, yeah. He told me when Guerrero had his trouble in the pits we gained a lap on him and he kept saying, keep cool, stay calm and go fast!

Q: Do you have a ride for the rest of the year?

Unser: No, there isn't anything going right now. I think I can answer for Roger, and I don't think it would be fair to Roger to ask him to indicate it, because to run a three-car team for the rest of the year is impossible. To run a two-car team is hard, and I would never put the other two guys in jeopardy.

Q: What was your reaction, Al, when Guerrero unlapped himself?

Unser: Well, Roger kept me informed that he was a lap down, and as long as I kept him in sight, that was all I was trying to do. I was having trouble at the time, behind lapped cars, and I couldn't pass one car because I was pushing too bad at the time. I just couldn't get around him, and when Guerrero went around me it was just a matter of me trying to keep him in sight so I wouldn't lose him. I could look at the scoreboard, and of course Roger was telling me how many laps we had to go, so I knew that if I kept the pace he couldn't catch me. Then there was a yellow and I was worried.

Josele Garza's first lap spin came within inches of taking Al completely out just seconds after the start. (Part of a sequence by Bill Ferguson)

It was the first time since 1964 that Al Unser had come to the Speedway without a car assigned to him. The first week and a half proved to be tedious, but he handled the well- wishers graciously and took the needling in good stride. (IMS-Swope)

Q: Did you think you had a chance at this when Mario was running so good, and what were the thoughts in your mind when he went out and Guerrero went out?

Unser: No, Mario had us covered, let's not kid each other. He ran off and left us and there wasn't anything I could do with him. Guerrero was going to be a battle for me, I'll guarantee you. He could outrun me and I knew if he didn't have problems that I wouldn't be able to handle him. I could stay with him and that was about all I could do.

Q: When you didn't have a ride for Indianapolis, did you consider not coming here to look for a ride?

Unser: Oh, no. In no way did I not think about coming. As I said the other day after qualifying, if I didn't get a ride by a certain date I was going to go home and come back for the race. You get tired of standing around. It does get boring, I'll tell you. When Al, my boy, didn't get qualified the first weekend then I was going to stay. I wanted to make sure he got in the show.

Q: When the last green dropped, how did your car handle, and was that as hard as you drove it all day?

Unser: Well, from about the second fuel stop on I ran it pretty hard and then, of course, the last few laps I did squeeze a little bit more out of it. I was concerned, yes. We did run almost wide open around the place, and I'm not saying wide open 'cause if there had been a taillight on they probably would have seen me brake every once in a while. I ran it as hard as I could.

Q: Express a little bit of how you feel about A.J. coming back for his 30th race and trying to win his fifth race, and about you tying him on your fourth victory.

Unser: Well, I'll tell you, to be in a class with Foyt makes me very honored, it really does. As we both have said in regard to this, you wonder why you haven't won 10 of them or whatever the amount is, but it is a narrow group with the two of us now and being in that league makes me very happy, and yes, I am coming back. I still enjoy racing. I love racing and like I said several times, there is no way I could back off or retire. I love it and I do want to win. That is what this is all about. As you can see, what happened today with the team that Mr. Penske has is that it all comes together and it is hard for people sometimes to understand what a team is actually like. I'll tell you, once you have been here it is hard to look around and see what else is available. There isn't anything; because of the amount of new drivers and car owners there aren't any good teams forming right now.

Q: How confident did you feel coming in today?

Unser: Well, I felt very confident. I knew that we would be halfway competitive. In other words, you can never say that you are going to be totally competitive, when somebody like Mario is run-

Roger Penske's May, 1987 was filled with drama. (Whitlow)

ning as well as he is running, and I knew that Rick was going to be strong and Guerrero and the rest of them. I could get a whole list and say the ones that are going to be strong, but we knew if we behaved all day and if I could stay out of trouble and hoped to stay on the same lap, which I didn't, we could be very strong at the end. Of course, if Mario hadn't had his problems we wouldn't have won; but that's the way it goes.

Q: Could you recap why you were without a ride and why it took so long to get one?

A.J. Foyt and Al Unser run one-two in almost every all-time "500" category, and their combined record is phenomenal. (IMS-S. Scott)

Unser: It is kind of hard to put in words, because there are a lot of brand-new cars out there. Whether it is a Lola or a March or whatever, it takes a whole team to put one together, to make a car strong and to go fast. It takes people, and good people, and if you don't have that kind of effort . . . almost all of the teams out there think they do; but they don't. They are under budget and have problems and it makes it hard, and I'm not criticizing any team out there whatsoever, I'll guarantee you. Everybody that comes to this race tries to win this race. They have hopes of finishing and winning it, and so I'm not criticizing. There just wasn't anything that came together that I was happy with the people.

Q: You put a price tag on your ride, did you not?

Unser: No, like I said the other day, none of you work for nothing, do you? And I don't. It's not that I am over-priced, and I do not get into a price war whatsoever, and I mean that.

Q: Can you give us a rough idea of how many teams came to you to give offers?

Unser: No, I don't want to get into that. It doesn't make any difference. In other words, it is not a bidding contest, and I'm not trying to put out numbers. At one time I was requested to run the Buick and I turned that down. That was after Crawford [crashed] and nothing against Crawford, it was just circumstances that I was not happy with.

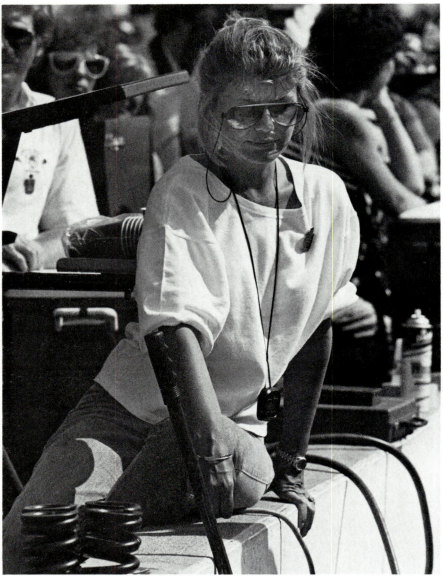

Karen (Mrs. Al) Unser. (Whitlow)

made on Thursday night to bring these cars in was a decision that you have to take with Derrick Walker, and we knew we had these cars back there and we had to have three; and unfortunately for the other fellows, their cars dropped out.

Q: Roger, can you reflect on laps as they unfolded at the end of the race and give your reactions on them?

Penske: Well, the big thing was we knew that Guerrero had his problems in the pits, and we had a lap on the field. I tried to tell Al to run the car just as strong as you can, but don't take a chance. It was very tough to pass for everyone and, of course, knowing that there could be a yellow, still with only 10 or 11 laps to go we weren't going to be concerned if Guerrero got by, knowing that he would be at the end of the pack, and I just told Al, run every lap the best you can and don't take any chances. And we ended up winning the race. Guerrero did a super job.

Q: Al, how did the cockpit feel when you first got in, and did they have to do much to get it ready for you?

Unser: The car was good right away. I made 6 or 7 laps Wednesday night and then Thursday we started working with the car, and then Friday morning I got it going better. Then Saturday morning it was better yet, so it was running good enough to get in the race, and that was all that we were concerned about. Sure, I would have liked to run 215 or whatever the speeds you want to put on it, but I couldn't; and the point was that we made the race, and that was all I wanted to do.

Q: Al, you had it in your mind that you were going to leave by a certain date, and what was that date, if you had one? Did you have a plane ticket to come back if you had to?

Unser: It was Wednesday, and after

Q: Roger, you had trouble with the cars you first came here with and you went back to your other cars . . .

Penske: Well, I think that if you go back and look, when we started here we came here with three drivers. We don't have a one, two or three driver; we give everybody exactly the best that we possibly can within our team and, of course, we came here with our own cars with high expectations and the Chevy engines certainly set the pace here today with putting a lap on the field. When Danny couldn't run—and you know Al and I have been pretty close for a number of years— and this guy has produced for us. I am sure that at the beginning of the season he was looking for a ride, and as it turned out he was in our garage a lot. Basically we knew when Danny couldn't run that Al was the guy. The decision we

Thundering on to the win, Al laps Dick Simon. (deBrier)

the first weekend of qualifying I said if I didn't have anything by Wednesday I was going to go home, because that would only give you two days to get ready. It is not that easy to get ready, but with a team like Penske's—because they are familiar with me and I am with them—that made it a lot easier. But I still would not have gone home because of Al, Jr. not being qualified. I did have reservations, yes.

Q: Al, later on did you have to make some adjustments? How well was your car running, and did you have to make some adjustment?

Unser: We made very few adjustments to the cars today. I think that I did most of the adjusting myself, because after the first pit stop I killed the engine and I was mad at myself. I had already gotten lapped and I was pretty unhappy with myself. I think I just finally got myself in gear, but we didn't change the car; it stayed the same all day.

Q: Can you tell us about the turbulence in the race and if you had a tough time with it?

Unser: I think that is probably the most trouble we had at the first of the race, getting used to the turbulence and knowing the car, because I hadn't run it on the track very much, so I was probably very easy on myself and the car so I wouldn't make a mistake. I think that is why I lost so much ground, I was just too conscious. I should have been a lot more aggressive, and I wasn't; but the turbulence was bad back there, the car was bouncing around quite a bit.

Q: Roger, how many times have you won with a car that is at least a year old?

Penske: Rick won in 1979, and of course Al today, so we have done it twice.

Q: Is it kind of helpless waiting for a ride and waiting for your son to get qualified? Did you feel useless?

Unser: This is the first time in my racing career that I came to Indianapolis without a ride. Helpless or whatever words you want to put on it, yes. It was a very empty feeling.

Q: Given the circumstances, how does this compare with the other three victories?

Unser: As I said earlier on the speaker outside, this one is a lot nicer. It is not just because it is number four; it's because I am older and I know how to cope with it, and I know now how hard it is to win these things. I think this one is a lot more gratifying because of the circumstances that occurred during the month, and yet it is just a great feeling to win.

Q: Do you have any sympathy for Mario Andretti for the long list of miseries he has had here at the Speedway since he won in 1969?

Unser: Yes, I do. It is an empty feeling to be as competitive and strong as he was today. He knew he had it won, but as we all know, you don't win until you get the checkered flag. He has got to feel very upset and mad, and I feel sorry for him because he has worked very hard, the team really has. It's a very strong team, and all I can say is I am sorry for him, and yet I am glad I was there.

Q: Roger, would you write a letter of recommendation for Al?

Penske: Let me say this: as far as if Al is going to have a ride with us the rest of the season, I think that question is open right now, and I will say this to him: he has a ride with us next year for sure.

Q: Given the fact that you don't have any hard feelings for Roger, do you feel some kind of harshness about the fact that a good driver had to come here

Al waits out the minutes before the start with his little-known crew chief, Clive Howell. (IMS-L. Young)

without a ride?

Unser: No, you have to understand that Roger can only come here with so many cars. He had Danny Ongais with a very good sponsor, and just like he told me on the telephone, ''I can't turn down the budget that is offered for sponsorship of the car,'' and I said, ''I know that and I respect that,'' so there were never any bad feelings whatsoever. When I came back here the first of May I walked in his garage, and I was in his garage the whole month. If there had been hard feelings, I guarantee you that I would not have been in his garage, so it is just a great feeling to have it come out the way it has.

Q: Al was the test driver for the Ilmor Chevrolet last year and they decided to switch back to the other power plant, so can you tell us who made the decision and how it came about?

Penske: Let me say this. Al and Rick did a tremendous job developing the Chevy engine. We only had three Chevy engines in those three cars and we just didn't have enough pieces to convert over. We had one car—an '86 which Rick broke the record with—and Al ran that car at Pocono. When it came down to changing the second car for Danny, we did that, and there just wasn't enough time to get ready for the second weekend. So we had to go with the Cosworth at this particular time, or otherwise it would have been a Chevrolet.

Al is greeted by his fourth-place finishing son at the finish. (IMS-J. Haines)

1

AL UNSER

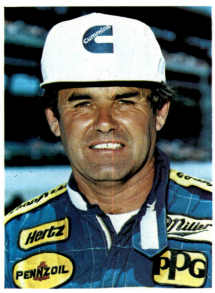

In a most unlikely scenario, Al Unser arrived at the Indianapolis Motor Speedway without a car to drive, finally secured the third seat on the Penske team after the withdrawal of Danny Ongais, and then proceeded to win the "500" for a record-tying fourth time.

It seemed preposterous to the general public that Al should be without a "ride". What they didn't realize was that several cars had been offered to him but he had politely turned them all down. He was past the stage in his career of merely wishing to "be" in the race. He is accustomed to having at least a fair shot at winning and understandably feels no motivation these days at going through all of the motions without that. He held out for one of the best.

Had Danny Ongais, a good friend of Unser's, not been forced to pass up the race, it is unlikely that Al would have driven at all this year. It is also unlikely that the Penske team would have bothered to field a third car for anyone else, since their obligation had been only to Ongais and his backer, Ted Field.

But out rolled the '86 March with a Cosworth engine, as the rumors of Al's inclusion on the team were confirmed with the official announcement just three days prior to the final qualifying weekend.

Race day didn't start out that well, as Al was almost taken out by Josele Garza on the opening lap and then was lapped by Mario Andretti after only 17! But he came back strong and led the final 18 laps for the amazing victory. His final circuit was his 613th career lap in the lead, thus pushing him to a tie with the late Ralph DePalma, who also paced for 613 laps between 1911 and 1921.

With four firsts, three seconds, two thirds and a fourth to his credit, Al Unser is the only driver in history to have made the top four on ten occasions.

CAR
March 86C-22/Cosworth

CHIEF MECHANIC
Clive Howell

SPONSOR
Cummins Holset Turbos

The 28-year-old Colombian now has one of the most extraordinary beginnings to an Indianapolis career of any driver in history, as he has never finished below 4th in any of his four starts.

His 1984 debut was most eventful as he stalled on two pit stops, ran over the rear wheel of Danny Sullivan during a yellow caution, spun a full "360" while trying to lap Bobby Rahal, and still ended up 2nd!

Roberto then finished 3rd in 1985 and 4th in '86 before embarking on his 1987 season.

At Phoenix in March of '87, he came all the way from the back row in devastating form to win an overdue first Indy car race, and the Indianapolis "500" came awfully close for him as well.

Apparently with the mysteries of matching the 1987 March to the radial tires solved, Guerrero qualified 5th and became the one person who could stay near Mario Andretti for most of the way.

Fate stepped in again, but it was to play both for and against Roberto before the day was out. He smashed headlong into Tony Bettenhausen's errant wheel on the 129th lap and lost the nose cone of his car.

He returned to the race with a replacement nose cone and continued to chase Andretti. Then Andretti dropped out and Roberto led!

Just 18 laps from the end and he was into his pit . . . AND HE STALLED. Fluid had been leaking from the master cylinder as the result of the jolt it had received from hitting Bettenhausen's wheel. He got back in, but was a lap behind Al Unser. Then he unlapped Al, and no sooner had he done so than the luckless Andretti stopped on the track to bring out the final yellow. Guerrero, therefore, came around to pack up behind the field and ended up losing the race to Al by less than five seconds.

He was upset for a few moments at the finish but then he weighed up the whole day and decided that perhaps 2nd wasn't so bad after all!

CAR
March 87C-30/Cosworth

CHIEF MECHANIC
Terry Gibbons/Tom Bloom

SPONSOR
True Value/STP

FABRIZIO BARBAZZA

Fabrizio Barbazza had never even heard of the Indianapolis "500" until his father told him about it not too many years ago, but Fabrizio certainly knew about motorsports.

His hometown in Italy is Monza, the venue for the Italian Grand Prix each year.

Son of a plastics manufacturer, Fabrizio took up racing himself in 1982 at the age of 19 and began competing in the Italian Formula Three series the following year. In 1985 he finished 2nd in the European Formula Three race, which precedes the Monaco Grand Prix through the streets of Monaco, and he finished third in the season's point standings.

He visited the United States through the encouragement of March Engineering's Robin Herd and met Frank Arciero, with whom he struck up a close relationship. Fabrizio spoke very little English when he arrived, but the Sicilian-born Arciero soon coached him. Fabrizio competed in nine of the 1986 American Racing Series events and won five of them plus the series title, for which one of the previously announced rewards was a "ride" in the Patrick Racing Team's ARS Buick March for the 1987 "500". It turned out that Fabrizio didn't need the car, as Frank had decided to field Fabrizio on the Indy Car circuit himself.

Fabrizio responded with one of the most impressive first-year performances ever, surviving a spin in which he touched nothing, and recovering to finish an outstanding 3rd.

During the summer of 1986, some of his new-found friends discovered that he enjoys fishing, so they took him up to Eagle Creek, a few miles northwest of the Speedway, for a day. He succeeded in landing a turtle, which explains why he is now nicknamed that and why several of the creatures are painted on his helmet.

CAR
March 87C-29/Cosworth

CHIEF MECHANIC
Paul Diatlovich

SPONSOR
Arciero Winery

It was a long, long month for Al Unser, Jr., and while it might not have FELT like his best "500", he did end up with his finest finish thus far.

After being in the minority for several seasons and relying on Lolas, the Doug Shierson team made the decision for 1987 to switch to Marches. Perhaps some other year would have been better!

The mystified team must have felt as if they had entered the Twilight Zone. They started out strongly enough, but the more they tried and the harder they tried, the slower they went. A 211 at the beginning of the month slipped further and further away, until by the first qualifying weekend they found themselves struggling just to get 201!

Diligent work during the second week resulted in a late breakthrough and they made the lineup safely.

A possible windup in 3rd was negated because of a stall during a stop plus a minor pit fire, but they came through for 4th anyway.

The full potential for Al Unser, Jr. has not nearly been realized yet, and "railbirds" generally agree that he is to be THE great driver of the future and should win the "500" several times.

He was racing go-karts at 9 and full sprints by 16. He was the SCCA National Super-Vee champion at 19 and the Can-Am champion at 20, making his Indianapolis debut right after his 21st birthday.

Al almost won the CART Championship in 1985, finishing 3rd in the final race, one position ahead of his challenging father, being nosed from the title by Big Al by a single point.

He came close again in 1986, completing more miles than any other driver, making the top ten on 13 occasions and winding up 4th in the final points. In other activity, he became the youngest driver ever to win the IROC (International Race of Champions) series.

CAR
March 87C-(No chassis #)/Cosworth

CHIEF MECHANIC
Neil Micklewright

SPONSOR
Domino's Pizza

It was the 16th time out of the gate for Gary Bettenhausen, who has now driven in the "500" more times than his father, and he ended up with one of his best finishes ever.

The former Tinley Park, Illinois resident who now lives in Monrovia, Indiana almost won the "500" in 1972, his Pens-

ke McLaren failing eighteen laps from the end after having led for 138 of them. One of the great sprint car drivers of any era, Gary had battled back and forth for the USAC title over four consecutive seasons with his close friend Larry Dickson, alternately being nosed out by Dickson, then beating him each year between 1968 and 1971. Once he was on board with Penske as Mark Donohue's teammate, pressure was put on Gary to give up sprints and dirt track racing, but he would have none of it.

Gary suffered two sidelining injuries (one in 1972, the other in '74) and that was it for Penske. Coming back in 1975 with one arm that was rendered almost useless, Gary had to practically start all over again. He made his comeback in a USAC midget race on the indoor track at Fort Wayne, Indiana and won the feature!

In 1980, Sherman Armstrong took Gary on at Indianapolis as a FIFTH driver, already being committed to Tom Bigelow, Howdy Holmes, Jerry Sneva and Greg Leffler. Gary was given a four-year-old Patrick Wildcat, which he and a group of friends independently set up for the race. He finished third!

Things looked bleak for Gary's future after he failed to qualify for the 1983 and

'84 races, and even bleaker when he didn't even have an assignment for '85. He came back in '86 with the Leader Card team and made the lineup for the first time in four years, placing 11th. This year he was retained by his old friends Dick Hammond and Galen Fox and the happy, close-knit little operation came home fifth.

CAR
March 86C-35/Cosworth

CHIEF MECHANIC
Galen Fox

SPONSOR
Genesee Beer

DICK SIMON

Driving in the "500" for his 16th time and now officially the oldest driver ever to have started at Indianapolis (at 53 years and eight months), the amazing Dick Simon enjoyed his best month of May ever.

Placing his faith yet again in the Lola chassis rather than the rival March, Dick was rewarded with a starting position on the outside of the second row after several years of braving cars into the lineup on the final qualifying day. He then hung in there all day for a 6th-place finish and scored his first-ever appearance within the top twelve. Had he not run out of fuel at the halfway point and required a tow-in, the effervescent veteran could easily have finished 3rd.

Born in Seattle, Washington and for many years a resident of Salt Lake City, the athletic Simon attended the University of Utah on a skiing scholarship and later won several championships both in skiing and parachuting!

He began racing super-modifieds in 1962 and divided his time between supers and SCCA road racing events prior to entering the USAC Championship division in 1969. His Indianapolis debut came the following year.

Dick finished 10th in the USAC Championship standings in 1970, bolstered by a 3rd-place finish in the inaugural Ontario "500" behind Jimmy McElreath and Art Pollard. For the most part, however, he has seemed forever hampered by mechanical failures, but nothing has ever dampened his spirits. Many a time he has slaved away in the pit area during a "500", supervising major stops that sometimes have taken 45 minutes, his policy always having been, "We owe it to our sponsors to make as many laps as possible. If we can fix it, we'll fix it."

He gave up a lucrative position as an insurance executive years ago in order to pursue racing on a full-time basis and his phenomenal salesmanship obviously persists, as he is never without sponsorship for what is usually a two-car and occasionally a three-car team.

CAR
Lola T8700-10/Cosworth

CHIEF MECHANIC
Gilbert Lage

SPONSOR
Soundesign Stereo

It seemed as if Stan Fox was fourth in the pecking order on the A.J. Foyt team behind Foyt, George Snider and Davy Jones, but it ended up with Stan being the only one of the quartet around at the finish. He avoided the first-lap tangle with Josele Garza and Pancho Carter, and while he laments that he never passed a car all day, the bottom line is that he was 7th at the payoff.

It was actually Stan's second shot at Indianapolis, an incomplete qualifying attempt coming when he tried to qualify for Leader Cards prior to making five Indy car starts for that team in 1984.

His forte has been short track oval racing, primarily with midgets and dating back to 1971. He was a mainstay with the USAC Midgets series for several years and was the 9th ranking driver of 1979, 8th in 1980 and 5th in 1982. He has won seven USAC Midget features and still makes an occasional appearance. He started in 101 USAC Midget "mains" through the end of 1986 and had placed within the first five in exactly one third of them.

He competed with the SCCA Super-Vee series in 1981, '82, and '83, placing 9th in points in the latter year as he built on his experience with rear-engined cars.

Stan's long-time midget car owner has been Steve Lewis, who promotes the Indy Motorsports Expo in Indianapolis each May, and Stan works with Steve on the promotion of that event.

On the personal side, the Janesville, Wisconsin driver is in a very select group of "500" drivers who have attended a military academy. Stan attended St. John's.

CAR
March 86C-8/Cosworth

CHIEF MECHANIC
Jack Starne/John Fisher

SPONSOR
Kerker Exhaust/Skoal

Jeff MacPherson, from the romantic-sounding venue of Rancho Santa Margarita in California, ran into difficulties almost as soon as the 1987 "500" began and had already lost about eight minutes from four stops before he'd reached 30 laps. He complained of excessive vibra-tion and handling problems and seemed to have his hands full keeping the car straight even on the straights. He was forced to settle for laps in the 180 mph range for much of the journey, but he stayed out of trouble and kept his Brabham-Honda engine- powered car running all day, being flagged in with 182 laps completed for an 8th-place finish.

Like Rick Mears, Jeff got his start in the rough and tumble world of off-road racing, driving a mini pickup. He was very successful in off-road racing events, and stayed with it for ten years until 1983, when he tried Formula Atlantics and liked them.

He moved into the Super-Vee class in 1984, won in a thrilling, extremely close finish at Michigan, finished 3rd in the season's points and was declared Rookie of the Year.

He travelled to Australia and New Zealand for the Tasman series in the winters of 1984 and '85, winning the series in the second year. He then pursued the 1986 European Formula 3000 series, but returned home after eight races and subbed for the injured Randy Lanier in Frank Arciero's Indy car at Mid-Ohio at the end of August. He also competed at Laguna Seca and Elkhart Lake and then made the arrangement to join the Rick Galles team as a teammate to Geoff Brabham for the 1987 season.

CAR
March 87C-17/Brabham-Honda

CHIEF MECHANIC
Mike Arnold

SPONSOR
Team MacPherson

Mario Andretti was far and away the class of the 1987 field, starting from the pole and leading at will for almost 90% of the race. He had led all but seven of the first 177 laps and had forfeited those only when making pit stops. He frequently lapped in the 203/204 mph range when no one else was above 200,

and had it not been for yellow caution periods, Mario would have lapped the field several times. Then it all came apart.

The fuel-metering device malfunctioned and Mario was forced to quit after struggling in and out of the pits for three more laps.

"It is not my deepest disappointment here," lamented one of racing's greatest-ever champions, "only my most recent."

It was the fifteenth time in his 22 starts that Mario had not been around to take the checker in a race in which it had seemed he would finally repeat the win he scored back in 1969.

The Italian-born Andretti is perhaps the most versatile driver who ever lived, having been victorious in virtually every form of motorsports. Between 1966 and 1971, for instance, he had won the Indianapolis "500", Championship races on superspeedways, flat paved ovals and dirt tracks, sprint car and midget races, major sports car enduros, including the Sebring 12-hours, plus the Daytona "500", the South African Grand Prix in Formula One and even the Pikes Peak Hill Climb!

In 1974 and 1975 he was routinely competing in USAC dirt car races and

SCCA Formula 5000 races on the same weekend in different sections of the country, commuting back and forth and still winning at both.

In 1978 he realized a boyhood dream by winning the World Championship, taking the Argentinian, Belgian, Spanish, French, German and Dutch Grand Prix for Lotus.

USAC Champion in 1965, '66 and '69 as well as CART Champion in 1984, Mario has won the prestigious Driver of the Year Award three times, each in a different decade.

CAR
Lola T8700-09/Ilmor Chevrolet

CHIEF MECHANIC
Colin Duff

SPONSOR
Hanna Auto Wash

The decision to stick with a year-old March and hope for the best worked out pretty nicely for the conscientious, business-minded Tony Bettenhausen in 1987. He wasn't running at the end, but he had enough laps in for 10th place. But that was overshadowed heavily by the fact that a wheel which had come from his right front during the leader's 129th lap ended up taking the life of a spectator.

The third son of the late Melvin Eugene "Tony" Bettenhausen, young Tony B. used to stooge for his older brothers, Gary and Merle, and then started out on his own with go-karts. Relocated from Tinley Park, Illinois to Houston with his remarried mother, he got going in NASCAR and was 2nd behind Jack Ingram in the Late Model Sportsman series of 1972. He turned 21 at just about the time the season was ending. He went on to the Grand National cars, drove in the 1974 Daytona "500" and was 20th in points that year.

His first "500" start (after being bumped in 1980) came in 1981, and he finished 7th driving for a team he put together himself. As later expenses increased, the sponsoring Aat Groenvelt of Provimi Veal took over himself as car owner, and as the team grew and changed direction, Tony ended up at the end of 1984 on the outside looking in.

He raised enough money during May of 1985 to take over a Lola from Mike Curb and Dan Gurney, and then sold it back after the race for the same sum! Not many people have been able to recoup the outlay for an Indianapolis car!

With a growing list of "car owners" which ended up numbering something around 45, Tony obtained a brand-new March for 1986 and then leased it for the part of the season to Provimi. Many of his 1986 and '85 owners came back for another shot in '87, but were still advised by Tony, "I want you to be involved, but we are not going to get rich. Only do this if you could stand the loss and can afford to do it just for fun."

CAR
March 86C-33/Cosworth

CHIEF MECHANIC
Rick Duman/Rob Stark

SPONSOR
**Nationwise Auto Parts/
Payless Markets**

Al Unser joined A.J. Foyt as a four-time winner of the Indianapolis "500" but, for a twist of fate, it might have been Johnny Rutherford instead. The Texan ran strongly throughout the race and was one of the fastest people on the track in the closing stages. Unfortunate-ly, he had lost 30 laps just before the midway point to change a distributor rotor and a heat shield, and so was merely trying to get in as many laps as possible. He salvaged 11th.

A "rookie" in the 1963 "500", Rutherford, along with Johncock and Foyt, are the only three active drivers to have driven front-engined "roadsters" in a "500" (Mario Andretti drove "roadsters" at some tracks in 1964 and '65 but never here) and Rutherford's total of 23 starts ranks him second only to Foyt's 30 on the all-time roster.

The 1965 USAC Sprint Car champion was forced to miss the 1966 and 1983 races because of injuries and was known as one of the "hard luck" drivers for his first decade at Indianapolis. A front-row qualifier in 1970, his fortunes changed when he hooked up with McLaren in 1973, winning the pole the first year and the race itself in '74. He was runnerup in 1975 and then won (in the rain) in 1976 from his second pole spot. After McLaren withdrew at the end of 1979, J.R. replaced the departing Al Unser on Jim Hall's Chaparral team and triumphed with his third pole and a third "500" win.

A talented artist who is proficient both in oils and pencil sketches, Rutherford is also a WWII aircraft buff who once own-ed not one, but two P-51 Mustangs, the upkeep of which proved to be VERY expensive.

Articulate and extremely personable, Rutherford represents motorsports with great dignity, while indicative of his so-cial standing these days is the fact that he has been entertained at the White House on no less than four different occasions by Presidents Nixon, Ford, Carter and Reagan!

CAR
March 87C-10/Cosworth

CHIEF MECHANIC
John Capels

SPONSOR
Vermont American Tools

This was neither Scott Brayton's best start nor his highest finish, yet it had to rank as his finest performance on an overall basis thus far. He had climbed all the way to 5th at 170 laps just before mechanical failure sidelined him.

The son of former driver Lee Brayton,

Scotty was only 22 when he had his first Indianapolis start in 1981. Two years later he made the top ten with a 9th-place finish.

The Brayton team went with Buick power in 1984 and a year later they almost grabbed the pole. Scott turned a single-lap track record of 214.199 during his early qualification attempt in '85, but a failing transmission on the final lap dragged the four-lap average down to 212.354 mph. That was still a record for the time being, but it didn't hold up as the single lap did. Pancho Carter, also utilizing Buick power, went out and posted a 212.583 mph average which snatched away both the pole and the record as, for the first time since 1958, the one-lap record and the four-lap record were held by different drivers.

Scotty ran strong in the early stages of the '85 race, even leading for one circuit, but he was sidelined by 19 laps with a turbocharger failure.

The Coldwater, Michigan driver is in a sand, gravel and concrete related business with his father. He started racing go-karts in 1975 at the age of 16 and four years later won the Skip Barber-pro series prior to moving into SCCA Formula Fords.

He had started 50 Indy car races and earned almost three-quarters of a million dollars by the end of 1986 and had finished within the first ten on ten occasions, the highest being a 6th in the Pocono "500" in 1984 and another 6th on the Portland road course in 1985.

CAR
March 87C-33/Cosworth

CHIEF MECHANIC
Darrell Soppe

SPONSOR
Amway/Autostyle Cars/LivingWell

It was an up-and-down month for Danny Sullivan, who would dearly love to have another good run at Indianapolis to back up his strong win of 1985.

He struggled with the PC-16 Ilmor Chevrolet combination and settled for a qualifying run at 205. After noting the superior handling characteristics of teammate Rick Mears's '86 March and the subsequent switch to it the night before the first qualifying day, a second '86 March was sent for. Sullivan soon worked this car up to better speeds with greater comfort, and so the qualified PC-16 was "pulled". Danny put the March in at 210 and, after sorting it out in the race, came up to a strong 3rd and even led some laps under caution. Perhaps to be forever haunted for spinning in front of Mario Andretti on his way to winning the 1985 race, Danny had another spin while running 3rd this year. He maintained 3rd for a while after that and was still 4th, just a lap down, when entering the final 100-mile sprint to the finish. He was out immediately after that, however, ending a possible run for the win, since Andretti was only minutes away from being sidelined himself.

Continuing to do much for the image of motorsports, Sullivan routinely makes appearances on the nation's leading network television talk shows, as well as having performed acting roles in "Miami Vice" and the daytime soap opera, "All My Children".

He gets needled unmercifully by his colleagues, but takes it all in good stride, and has never wavered from being most gracious with the fans in spite of his considerable notoriety.

CAR
March 86C-37/Ilmor Chevrolet

CHIEF MECHANIC
Chuck Sprague

SPONSOR
Miller Beer

The "up and down" description for the fates of several "500" drivers this May could certainly be applied to Tom Sneva. He crashed several cars in practice and then looked as if he'd be "just another driver" in the race. But he did what he has done so many times before: from out of the ashes, he worked pit stops to his advantage, put his superb racing savvy to work and ran 4th for many laps until it started to go away.

The V-6 Buick engine began to sound sour and he stopped to have a loose turbocharger hose tightened. He later lost control of the car when the handling went away and he was into the concrete again to rudely halt a valiant attempt.

The former school teacher has an envious record in the "500" but one for which he has worked extremely hard. He won the race (1983) and has also finished as runner-up three times. He was the first person to break an official 200 mph lap and did it on his way to winning the first of his three pole positions. Inasmuch as he was also the fastest qualifier for the 1981 race (but started far back by virtue of not qualifying until the second weekend), Tom and A.J. Foyt are the only two drivers to have been the fastest qualifier in four different years.

It is more than just going out and driving hard for Sneva. He has made a study of handling and setups, constantly seeking information from others, probing in a very Bobby Unser-like manner, relentlessly searching for an improvement that will help him towards a win. Late at night, long after the other drivers have left Gasoline Alley, Sneva is still there, working, probing, learning.

CAR
March 86C-2/Buick

CHIEF MECHANIC
John Anderson

SPONSOR
Skoal

Derek Daly had just moved into 8th place when he had to drop out of the 1987 "500", ending his bid in his fourth start.

He came within just a minute or two of qualifying for the 1986 "500", only to have a torrential rain storm move in while he was on the track as a substitute for the injured Herm Johnson while moving just fast enough to force his way into the lineup.

Derek began his career in Dublin, Ireland, racing what are loosely referred to over there as "stock cars" but are the equivalent of jalopies in the United States. He was only 16 at the time, and the surface on which he was racing was grass!

He travelled to Australia with another Irish driver, David Kennedy, in the winter of 1974/75 and began working in iron ore mines, earning some of the fantastic salaries he had read were possible down there.

He returned to England one day in late April and read that the International Trophy Formula One race was being held at Silverstone that same day. He went up and watched James Hunt lead the race for the flamboyant and colorful Lord Hesketh, never dreaming that three years later he would lead the same race for the same Lord Hesketh!

Now a full-fledged British star himself, Derek moved to the Tyrrell team at the end of 1979 and finished 4th in the Grand Prix of Argentina and Great Britain in 1980. Two years later, he was taken on to the Williams team as Keke Rosberg's teammate following the re-

tirement of Carlos Reutemann, but was definitely cast in the role of "number two" driver there. Rosberg won the World Championship, while Derek could only muster a trio of 5th-place finishes and a brace of mechanical DNF's.

He drove in his first "500" in 1983 and had to recover from a terrible leg-shattering accident at Michigan in late 1984, but later married an Indianapolis girl and settled just north of the city.

CAR
March 87C-27/Buick

CHIEF MECHANIC
Ken Winning

SPONSOR
Scheid Tire/Superior Training/ Metro Link

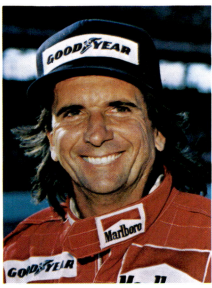

It was not a happy May for unretired two-time World Champion Emerson Fittipaldi. The Brazilian, who ran near the front in both his second and third starts here in 1985 and '86, did not qualify that well in his fourth go-around. Then he wiped out his car during an accident in the final practice session just three days before the race, forcing the withdrawal of his damaged car and pushing him back to the 33rd starting position with a substituted backup car.

He ran steadily during the race and the continual attrition permitted him to advance to 8th place before a mechanical failure put him on the sidelines as well.

Fittipaldi was only 23 when he went on to the Lotus team in 1970, following the death of Lotus's posthumous World Champion, Jochen Rindt. The team was still reeling from the shock of Rindt's loss when young Fittipaldi scored an outstanding win in the U.S. Grand Prix at Watkins Glen. Two years later he became the youngest-ever World Champion.

He started out 1973 in strong fashion by winning three out of the first four races. But a change in fortunes at Lotus caused him to lose the title to Jackie Stewart. Amidst much criticism, he left for McLaren at the end of the year, but had been able to duplicate the uncanny ability of his mentor and idol Juan Manuel Fangio to "jump ship" at precisely the right time. McLaren was on the upswing and Fittipaldi won back the World Championship!

He left after being runner-up again in 1975 and formed his own team, Copersucar, a team which had very little good fortune. Discouraged after several seasons, he retired and returned to Brazil.

He unexpectedly showed up for the 1984 Miami Grand Prix sports car race after several years' layoff and won the pole. Then he made his Indy Car debut at Long Beach and placed 5th. He's been Indy car racing ever since, with wins coming in the Michigan "500" of 1985 and the Elkhart Lake 200 of 1986.

CAR
March 87C-19/Ilmor Chevrolet

CHIEF MECHANIC
Gary Rovazzini

SPONSOR
Marlboro

The 1981 "Rookie-of-the-Year" and his crew deserve all the credit in the world for stick-to-itiveness. They could easily have given up after sustaining damage during Josele's first lap, first turn spin and subsequent tangle with teammate Pancho Carter. Instead, they persistently made a go of it.

They made a total of ten stops, the first of which lasted 27 minutes. Two others were in the region of 15 minutes and the total time lost was over one hour. In spite of that, they were around for the checker with 129 laps registered and a 17th place finish instead of the 32nd they would have received had they given up at the beginning.

A similar situation prevailed in 1986, when Josele was forced to stop at 132 laps to have a right front wheel bearing replaced. He'd been running 6th for over 20 laps when it happened. He lost 25 minutes, but they got him back in there and he was 18th at the finish.

It was generally believed that Josele, the first Mexican ever to drive in the "500" (Pedro Rodriguez tried but never made it), was 22 years old when he made his Indianapolis debut. In fact, he was three years younger than that and was actually 19 years, two months and nine days old when he led the 1981 race!

Josele was having his best season in Indy car racing in 1986 when he crashed on the Mid-Ohio road course and broke his leg in a horrible-looking accident. He missed five races but was back before the end of the year. Just before his accident he had scored a career high by placing 2nd to Johnny Rutherford in the Michigan "500".

This eligible bachelor continues to commute back and forth to Mexico City, where he has interests in an ice cream company, real estate and a sun-tanning product line.

CAR
March 87C-5/Cosworth

CHIEF MECHANIC
Mark Bridges

SPONSOR
Bryant Heating & Cooling/ Schaefer Beer

Arie Luyendyk of Holland had an extensive background in European road racing before he made his first visit to the United States. Motor racing was something he grew up with because of his father's involvement. The elder Luyendyk drove himself and was a mechanic for several Dutch drivers, including Carel De Beaufort, whom road racing

enthusiasts will recall as a spirited privateer who drove an orange 1500cc Porsche in 1961-64 Grand Prix races.

Arie started in 1973, competing in dozens of Formula Ford, Formula Vee, and Formula 1600 events during the next four years. In 1977 he won the European Super-Vee title and for the next two seasons contested for the European Formula 3 championship. In the French and Dutch rounds of 1979, he was runner-up both times, beaten only by Alain Prost, who in 1985 and '86 became the World Champion in Formula One.

Arie was 2nd in the 1980 European Super-Vee championship and then ventured over to the United States for the 1981 Robert Bosch Super Vee series, in which he finished 4th.

He was back and forth across the Atlantic for the next couple of seasons, but had formed a strong friendship with the American-based Dutchman, Aat Groenvelt, of Provimi Veal. Under Aat's sponsorship, Arie won the 1984 Super-Vee title and placed 8th in his Indy Car debut at Elkhart Lake. Groenvelt's Indy car team was completely revamped for the 1985 season and Arie became the driver. He finished 7th in his first Indianapolis "500", won the Rookie of the Year title and later secured the CART rookie

award.

The handsome and personable Luyendyk, who speaks several languages, qualified on the inside of the third row for his third "500" and ran 3rd for many laps. He even outsprinted Bobby Rahal after a yellow caution just past the 30-lap mark and held 2nd for four laps, later fading and finally being knocked out after hitting a wheel in the pits and damaging his left front suspension.

CAR
March 87C-01/Cosworth

CHIEF MECHANIC
Larry Curry

SPONSOR
LivingWell/Provimi Veal/WTTV

It looked better than it had in several years for the amazing A.J. Foyt, who was going into the "500" for an unprecedented and unbelievable 30th consecutive time. A.J. had won his third and fourth 500's exactly ten years apart, in 1967 and 1977, from the fourth starting position. Another ten years had passed and now he was starting from there again.

He didn't win and he didn't finish, but he was running 9th when he dropped out and he extended his amazing record of career laps completed to 4,248, which works out to 10,620 miles in competition.

A.J. had to move over and have Al Unser join him as a four-time winner of the "500", but as A.J. pointed out to Al at the Victory Banquet, he did get there first!

It was Foyt who took Al Unser under his wing on the final qualifying weekend of 1965 and ended a frustrating "rookie" month for Al by supervising the then 26-year-old into the lineup for his initial start. Unser had been needling Foyt about that ever since!

Several of the drivers against whom Foyt drove in his "rookie" year of 1958 are no longer living, while several of the 1987 starting field were not even born at the time Foyt made that debut. It is hard to believe that he has now competed in almost half of the 500's ever run!

Idolized by millions of fans (and by most of the other drivers, as a matter of fact), Foyt continues to return to the Speedway as an almost ageless, larger-than-life legend whose competitive spirit and will to win seems never-ending.

CAR
Lola T8700-4/Cosworth

CHIEF MECHANIC
Jack Starne

SPONSOR
Copenhagen/Gilmore

None of the current "500" drivers attempt a schedule anywhere close to that of Rich Vogler in terms of number of races competed in during a season. Vogler, who lives close to a small airport and flies his own plane, routinely makes in the region of 75 dates per year and sometimes more.

In 1986 alone he won the USAC Midget Championship for the fourth time with six wins from 19 starts; was 4th in the Sprint standings with three wins in ten starts; was 8th in the Silver Crown (dirt car) series, and finished runnerup in the Indianapolis Speedrome "regional" midget series with five wins in 14 starts, losing the seasonal title on the final turn!

The Glen Ellyn, Illinois native, who now resides just outside of Indianapolis, had won 70 USAC National Midget features, 25 Sprints, three Silver Crown and 23 Speedrome "regionals" through the end of 1986, not to mention perhaps 100 more main events with various other associations. He has finished within the top four of the USAC Midget standings for nine consecutive years, and in 1980 became the only driver ever to win the USAC Sprint and Midget titles in the SAME season!

He passed his Indianapolis "rookie" test in 1980 but did not make it into the lineup until 1985, when his friend and sponsor, Jonathan Byrd, purchased a Patrick team backup car near the end of qualifying.

Rich was on a roll in the '86 "500" and had climbed to 8th out of 25 cars still on the track when a wheel came off and sent him hurtling into the wall. Back with a Buick- powered car in 1987, Rich emerged from the first round of pit stops in 6th place but almost immediately fell to the back with a mechanical problem and struggled on from there until just past the halfway mark.

CAR
March 87C-26/Buick

CHIEF MECHANIC
Larry Curry

SPONSOR
Byrd's Kentucky Fried Chicken/ LivingWell/VALPAK

A Cornell University graduate who excelled as a high school athlete, Ed Pimm seems equally as adept at equestrian sports as at motor racing.

After several seasons of racing SCCA production classes and then Formula Fords, he won the Robert Bosch Cup for Super-Vees in 1983. He tried unsuccessfully to qualify for the 1984 "500" with a stock block-powered car, but later hired on with Dan Gurney to drive an All-American Eagle. He seemed to be hampered by accidents and injuries but came through to finish 9th in the 1985 "500" and later finished 5th in the Michigan "500", with a career high 3rd coming in the fall 200-miler also held at the Michigan International Speedway. He finished 13th in CART points that year.

Released by Dan Gurney for 1986, it began to look as if he would be without a car to drive at Indianapolis. He managed to put a team together with a variety of sponsors, however, and after running remarkably quickly throughout practice, he went into the race pretty much as a dark horse, with some people even looking to him for a possible top-three finish. He was 8th at 10 laps, but electrical trouble stepped in almost immediately and he ran at the back of the pack until dropping out near the end.

It was more of a cliff-hanger in 1987, when Ed failed to find speed until just about the last minute and squeezed into the field with only about a quarter of an hour left on the clocks. He had to come from the back on race day and had reached 9th place by halfway, just before the dreaded electrics came in to spoil another day for him.

CAR
March 86C-11/Cosworth

CHIEF MECHANIC
Bob Morris

SPONSOR
Skoal

Gordon Johncock dramatically announced his retirement from racing on the day before the first qualifying day at the Speedway in 1985.

He served as the color announcer on the race day radio broadcast and then returned to the ranch he had purchased in Arizona, where he had wanted to spend more time.

He'd still watch races on television, and as the summer wore on he began to regret his decision more and more. He attended the Phoenix 200 near the end of the year and announced that he was making a comeback.

He thought he had sponsorship lined up and came close to obtaining a back-up car from Roger Penske for the 1986 "500". There wasn't enough financial backing there to swing the deal, however, and a couple of other possibilities had to be passed up as well. A team was put together for 1987, but apparently without much substance. The car had not arrived when the track opened, nor was it about to.

Then Jim Crawford was injured in the ARS Buick, but the team decided to regroup with its backup car. Al Unser was approached, but no deal could be struck.

Johncock was on the ranch in Arizona with his family when the call came.

In the most emotional qualifying run of 1987, Gordy Johncock returned to the racing wars and the white March was transformed into the blue and red STP trim of old by race day.

The 50-year-old two-time winner had the Buick rolling and ran as high as 7th before he became one of a whole legion of people to fall victim to electrical maladies. But he'd had fun.

CAR

March 86C-18/Buick

CHIEF MECHANIC

Tom Anderson

SPONSOR

STP Oil Treatment

A two-time winner of the "500" and a top-three finisher in half of his ten starts, Rick Mears continues to add accomplishments to what has already become one of the most significant careers in the track's history.

A member of the Penske team for each of his starts (he missed the '77 race driving for another team), Rick has started on the front row no less than seven times and has never ranked out of the ten fastest qualifiers. He has also led the race in seven different years and is the only driver in history to have led in six consecutive years (1979-84). Not only did he win the "500" in 1979 and 1984, he was on the losing end of the closest finish ever (sixteen one hundredths of a second to Gordon Johncock in 1982), as well as the closest one-two-three finish ever (less than two seconds behind Bobby Rahal and Kevin Cogan for 3rd in 1986). He has won the pole position three times, while his one and four-lap track records for qualifying went unbroken in 1987.

Rick, who won all of the greatest honors the sport of off-road racing had to offer, made his Indianapolis car debut in the Ontario "500" of 1976, driving a Bill Simpson-owned car to 8th. In 1979, he won the inaugural CART championship and added a second and third title in 1981 and '82.

Severe foot and ankle injuries sustained during an accident in Sanair, Canada in 1984 kept Rick out for much of the 1985 season. Al Unser had to sub for him in the road racing events, and then Rick voluntarily passed up the later oval track races as Al became a contender for and ultimately won the CART championship. Even so, Rick won the Pocono "500", thus having recorded at least one Indianapolis car victory for eight consecutive years.

CAR
March 86C-41/Ilmor Chevrolet

CHIEF MECHANIC
Peter Parrott

SPONSOR
Pennzoil

The son of three-time Australian World Champion Sir Jack Brabham, Geoff is carving out quite a career of his own and is part of a quartet of "rookies" from the 1981 "500" starting field who have yet to miss a race between them. The other three are Josele Garza, Kevin Cogan and Tony Bettenhausn.

Geoff ran as a teammate to Garza in his first run and ended up 5th. His best finish in his seven starts thus far, however, came in a race he almost didn't start. He came to the track in 1983 without an assignment and the chances of obtaining one were becoming slim.

John Paul, Jr. sustained a broken leg while driving for the VDS team, for whom Geoff had driven in the Can-Am series, and Geoff was taken on as a replacement.

He went from 26th to 4th in the 1983 "500", and had it not been for a stall during a pit stop, he might have been able to outrun Al Unser and Rick Mears for 2nd.

He was runnerup to A.J. Foyt in the 1981 Pocono "500" and was also 2nd at Long Beach and Portland in 1984, and 2nd at Cleveland in 1985.

He did not finish the 1987 "500", although it is quite possible that he could have. He had just moved into 11th place when he came in to retire, reporting that the oil light was on. He did not wish to blow one of the expensive Honda engines developed by a firm in which his father had an investment. The teardown revealed a glitch in the electrics, causing the light to be on for no reason. The oil supply had been fine—and so had the engine.

CAR
March 87C-7/Brabham-Honda

CHIEF MECHANIC
Owen Snyder

SPONSOR
Valvoline

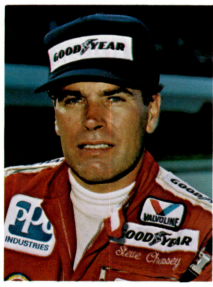

Few drivers have appreciated qualifying for a "500" more than did Steve Chassey when he made the starting field for the first time in 1983. It was an ambition he had harbored from the time he was around five years old. His father used to take him to races while the family was still living in Massachusetts and a little later on, after a move to California.

Steve started racing in 1964 and served a stint in Vietnam with the U.S. Army before returning and moving into West Coast sprint car racing. He relocated to the Midwest in 1973, gathered momentum and in 1980 was runner-up to Rich Vogler for the USAC Sprint crown.

He qualified for the 1981 "500" but his speed failed to hold up and it was '83 before his starting debut came. He ran all day in Dick Hammond's normally-aspirated Chevrolet- powered car (the only car in the race without a turbocharger) and seemed just as happy taking the checker in 11th place as if he had won.

He crashed two cars trying to make the '84 race and was "bumped" after posting a seemingly adequate run in '85. It took until 1987 for him to make it for a second time, thanks to the team put together with lady car owner Lydia Laughrey.

Steve appeared in several television commercials and television shows as a child and, as a teenager, also sang as a backup singer on some pop records in the early 1960's. He still shows up occasionally in ads, modeling sporting clothes, etc.

He feels his biggest accomplishments in racing to this point have been qualifying for the "500" and leading all 100 laps of the 1984 Hoosier Hundred from the pole.

CAR

March 87C-25/Cosworth

CHIEF MECHANIC

Hywel Absalom

SPONSOR

United Oil/Life of Indiana

Studious Bobby Rahal was strongly favored to repeat his 1986 Indianapolis "500" win and he got off to a fine start. Choosing Lola over March certainly played in his team's favor and he qualified second fastest only to Mario Andretti. He then ran either third or fourth for the first 75 miles, but then electrical troubles cropped up and they finally threw in the towel after struggling until the 57th lap.

The son of an SCCA "regional" racer, Bobby grew up knowing many of the better-known sports car drivers of the 1960's. He began his own career in 1973 while attending Dennison College (where he was a history major) and by 1975 had won SCCA's Formula Atlantic title, along with the prestigious President's Cup.

With backing from his father's friend, Jim Trueman, he went to Europe in 1977-8 and raced in the European Formula III series for Walter Wolf, whose Formula One Grand Prix driver was Jody Scheckter. A second car was provided for Rahal for participation in the 1978 Grand Prix of Canada and the United States.

He then became one of the front runners in the Can-Am series and in 1981 co-drove the winning car in the Daytona 24 hours.

He made his first Indianapolis start in 1982, and after winning Indy Car races at Cleveland and Michigan, was runner-up to Rick Mears for that season's CART championship.

Rahal led the "500" in both 1983 and '85 before storming home to win the '86 running. He has never finished lower than 5th in the CART standings in any year, and the six wins he scored on his way to the 1986 championship brought his five-year total in that series to 14.

A history buff who enjoys reading and studying the choreography of famous battles, Bobby inadvertently stumbled upon golf around 1984 and now takes that game VERY seriously.

CAR
Lola T8700-06/Cosworth

CHIEF MECHANIC
Jim Prescott

SPONSOR
Budweiser

Nineteen eighty-seven's month of May is probably one that Pancho Carter would just as soon forget entirely. He escaped injury after his first Hardee's March spun, became airborne and completely inverted. He then qualified a second car but found himself more comfortable in yet a third, and qualified that after the second had been withdrawn. Then he raced for less than a quarter of one lap before he found his own teammate sideways in front of him. He clipped the sliding car, damaged his own suspension and struggled around to the pits. He returned to the race, was in and out with electrical problems and finally fell out after 45 laps with an engine failure. Not a happy month.

Pancho's "500" career was off to a flying start when he finished 7th, 4th and 5th in his first three years, but several lean years followed. His high points so far have been finishing 3rd in 1982 and winning the pole in '85.

Pancho won the USAC Midget title in 1972, when he was still only 22 years old and attending college. Two years later he won the USAC Sprint crown as well and in 1978 was also the Dirt Car (forerunner of Silver Crown) champion.

Pancho won the inaugural Michigan "500" in 1981 and was also 3rd in the 1986 race, the same year he placed 3rd in the Pocono "500". In 1978 he finished 2nd in the Ontario "500", thus having finished within the top three at least once in all four of the recent 500 mile races for Indianapolis cars.

His father is former driver Duane Carter, his step- brother Johnny Parsons, and his father-in-law Carl Forberg, against whom his father drove in the 1951 "500".

CAR
March 87C-35/Cosworth

CHIEF MECHANIC
John Barnes

SPONSOR
Hardee's

DAVY JONES

The fastest "rookie" to qualify for the 1987 Indianapolis race was also the youngest driver in the lineup, newcomer Davy Jones being just over a week away from his 23rd birthday when he sped under Duane Sweeney's green flag. He's had quite a career for one so young.

Davy grew up in McGraw, NY, about thirty miles south of Syracuse and had already participated in motocross and snowmobile events when he took up driving quarter-midgets at the age of 11!

He went through the Bertil Roos racing school at Pocono International Raceway at age 15 and after a few races in Formula Fords, had to start racing in Canada because it had been discovered that he was underage.

Running legally in 1982 at the age of 18, he ran for the SCCA Super-Vee championship but had to miss the first two races because of his age. He was then runner-up at Elkhart Lake, Mosport and Riverside, won at Laguna Seca and finished 3rd in the points behind Michael Andretti and Ed Pimm. The next year he travelled to Europe and was 3rd in the Formula III standings behind Ayrton Senna and Martin Brundle!

He won three more Super-Vee races at home in 1985, placing 2nd in the standings, and in 1986 partnered Mario Andretti's nephew, John Andretti, on the short-lived BMW GTP program. They contested for the IMSA Camel GTP series and, in one of racing's great upsets, won the Watkins Glen 500 - kilometers round with the Porsche of perennial champions Al Holbert and Derek

Bell finishing 2nd and in the same lap.

Davy drove a Dick Simon car in the 1987 ROP prior to moving into the A.J. Foyt camp for May and he seemed to have no difficulty in adapting to the big oval. He qualified at 208 and was running 20th in the race when he had to quit with what was mysteriously described as "a hole in the engine".

CAR
March 86C-23/Cosworth

CHIEF MECHANIC
Jack Starne

SPONSOR
Skoal/Gilmore/UNO

The 1987 "500" was the fourth one for Michael Andretti and the first in which he failed to land a finishing position within the first eight. He hadn't completed any less than 196 laps in any of his three previous races, but he was knocked from competition after only 28 laps this time around.

Michael was off to a rousing start in his "rookie" year of 1984, when he qualified for the inside of the second row and overtook Tom Sneva for 2nd early in the going. He finished 5th and split the Rookie of the Year balloting with Roberto Guerrero. He finished 7th in CART points after placing 3rd in five races.

He had a disappointing year in 1985 but highlighted it with a 2nd-place finish at Elkhart Lake. The Kraco team, for whom he drove, elected to concentrate on a single car entry for 1986, and Michael leaped into the forefront. He broke down leading the Phoenix opener but won the following week on the streets of Long Beach. He qualified for the front row of the "500" and led the first 42 laps, winding up 6th. He then won at Milwaukee and battled for the season with father Mario and Bobby Rahal for the CART point lead, several times dropping out of the race while leading. He wound down the season with a string of top-three finishes and his third win of the year (at Phoenix), but a DNF in the finale at Miami gave the title to Rahal. He had led at least a portion of 12 of the 17 races.

Mario got him started racing go-karts at ten years of age, and in 1980 Michael drove his first Formula Ford. He was the SCCA Northeast division FF champion in 1981, the Super-Vee champ in '82 and Formula Mondial champ in '83.

CAR
March 87C-24/Cosworth

CHIEF MECHANIC
Barry Green

SPONSOR
Kraco/STP

Son of German-born Canadian Ludwig Heimrath, Ludwig, Jr. took up racing go-karts in 1972 while his father was still racing. Ludwig, Sr. drove in several USAC Championship events between 1969 and '71 but never entered for Indianapolis.

Ludwig, Jr. aspired to run Indianapolis

himself, however, and remembers going to a Toronto theater to watch the live closed-circuit telecast of the 1967 "500". The race had originally only gone for 18 laps before being stopped by a downpour, and his father was unable to return to the theater when it was rescheduled for the following day. The inquisitive ten-year-old therefore scooped up his father's "raincheck" from the kitchen table and headed downtown with it!

He won several national honors in kart racing while attending college, and after graduating with a bachelor's degree in mechanical engineering, began racing Porsches in IMSA events and some of SCCA's Trans-Am series. He also did some single-seater time with the Super-Vee series and won the 1983 rookie award in that class. He had a single Indy car start (at Elkhart Lake) in 1984 and one more (at Mid Ohio) in '85.

He hooked up with Dick Simon for Indianapolis in 1987 and was very impressive for the short time he was in the race. He held down 10th for the first 50 miles but had a wheel come off right after making his first pit stop. He was out for the day.

Ludwig has no difficulty in justifying racing to his spouse, as she is the outstanding female driver, Kathy Rude,

who once tested an Indianapolis car at Ontario for Rolla Vollstedt.

CAR
Lola T8700-05/Cosworth

CHIEF MECHANIC
Peter Roband

SPONSOR
MacKenzie Financial/
Tim Horton Donuts

Kevin Cogan has taken some hard knocks at the Indianapolis Motor Speedway.

He made an early pit stop in his "rookie" year of 1981, dropped to 33rd, came up through the pack, lost a wheel under yellow and still finished 4th.

In 1982, drafted onto the Penske team alongside Rick Mears, Kevin turned the fastest practice lap of the month and qualified second only to Mears. Coming down for the start, his car inexplicably veered to the right, bounced off the car of A.J. Foyt, spun and then was hit by Mario Andretti, bringing out the red flag.

In 1983 he managed to place 5th as teammate to Tom Sneva, but in a car some crew members felt was geared incorrectly and should have finished 2nd to Sneva.

In 1984, he signed on with the French Ligier team, which brought their own car to the track and then quickly withdrew when it proved to be woefully uncompetitive. He then subbed for the injured Michael Chandler in Dan Gurney's Pontiac- powered Eagle and was forced out, not with mechanic trouble, but because the right rear wheel could not be removed. He had run until he was virtually out of rubber.

In nineteen eighty-five he struggled home to 11th in a poorly handling back-up car that he had qualified late after his original mount had been bumped.

In nineteen eighty-six he almost had one in the bag. He grabbed the lead late from Rick Mears and then was snookered by Bobby Rahal after a late-race caution left the front runners with only two laps of green.

From 2nd in 1986 to 31st in '87 was quite a tumble. But should Kevin ever win the "500" (and many feel that that is in the cards), it'll be something he REALLY appreciates.

CAR

March 87C-018/Ilmor Chevrolet

CHIEF MECHANIC

Cole Selva

SPONSOR

Marlboro

RANDY LEWIS

Randy Lewis strikes one as certainly being one of the most JOVIAL drivers the Indianapolis Motor Speedway has ever seen, his bubbling enthusiasm emphasizing the realization of finally having made it to the track as a partici-

pant. The 41-year-old Lewis had been racing for 16 years and had been eyeing the Speedway for at least a dozen, back to the time when he was one of the mainstays of the SCCA Formula 5000 series and the Can-Am series.

Randy had attended the "500" before as a guest of the late Lindsey Hopkins and had actually been entered for the '84 "500". That "ride" failed to materialize, however, when the Rattlesnake Racing team, for whom he was to have driven, had their final race car wiped out in total by Don Whittington in an accident at the Speedway in the spring.

Randy had his first Indy car start at Monterey, California in 1983 and had three more the following year, but failed to finish in any of them. He had no starts in 1985 but put together a program for eight road races in '86 and finished 10th twice. He opened the '87 season with an 8th at Long Beach.

The 1987 "500" was his first race ever on an oval track, but he adapted nicely and was the 18th fastest qualifier in the field. Race day was over in a hurry, however. After running the first five laps under caution because of the Garza/Carter accident, he found himself victim

to a transmission problem as soon as the green unfurled. He was out after turning only eight laps.

CAR
March 87C-31/Cosworth

CHIEF MECHANIC
A.J. Watson

SPONSOR
Toshiba/Altos

Although George Snider did not start in the 1981 "500" (he turned his car over for race day to Tim Richmond), he had certainly qualified for it and in 1987 extended his string of consecutive successful qualification runs to 23! Only A.J. Foyt has more. In terms of starts, George shares third ranking with Mario Andretti and Al Unser, each of them having 22 starts while Johnny Rutherford has 23 and Foyt, 30.

The amazing thing about Snider is that he usually has very little practice prior to qualifying and due to a series of circumstances in 1981, not the least of which was deteriorating weather conditions, George ended up qualifying with NO practice whatsoever, his maiden lap of the month being his first qualifying warmup.

Unfortunately, George has only a pair of 8th place finishes to show for all of those starts and recent years have usually found him among the first to be eliminated. A turbo fire this year knocked him out during the pace lap and for the third time in five years he was forced to accept a finishing position of either 32nd or 33rd. His strongest runs have been when he started from the outside of the front row in 1966 and ran third for a while, and in 1977 when he ran in the first six and led during the first round of pit stops.

George was on his way to winning the 1975 USAC Sprint title when he cleared the outer retaining wall at Winchester, IN and broke both of his arms. He had finished 3rd in Sprints the year before.

George, who is often to be found in the Garage Area far into the night as a crew member on all of the Foyt cars, including his own, won the 1971 USAC Dirt car title and has finished 10th or higher in six other years, including 1986, in that same series, now known as the Silver Crown series. He won the 1981/82 USAC Gold Crown title and has six sprint wins and four midget wins to his credit.

CAR
March 86C-34/Chevrolet V-6

CHIEF MECHANIC
Jack Starne

SPONSOR
Calumet Farm/Copenhagen

MISSED THE SHOW

Swindell squeezed 202 out of John Buttera's non-turbo Pontiac. He was the last to be "bumped".

Dobson went for broke and was second alternate at 201.

Moran's ex-Truesports March was bumped.

Ex-Machinists Union March, intended for Bigelow, waved off a 198 and finished out a 196 with Miaskiewicz.

It was a great month for Jim Crawford—until qualifications.

Sullivan went ahead and posted 205 with the PC-16. It was later "pulled".

Mears started out with the PC-16.

145

Mears even tried a PC-15!

Poor Dennis Firestone met the wall twice in Raynor Lolas.

Phil Krueger was Raynor's crew chief AND second driver. He hit the wall qualifying at 204.

Dick Ferguson only had an '85 March but reached 203 before crashing.

Bad month for Tom Sneva. This March/Buick was destroyed.

Tom Sneva also tried a March/Cosworth.

Bloodlines of the winner. Ongais wiped out his PC-16, suffered a concussion, was "parked" by the medics, and opened the door for Al Unser.

Lewis tried the second Leader Card March. Bigelow and Swindell were rumored to get it. Neither did.

Moran's original '86 March for the Walthers came from Morales. It was destined for the wall.

Johnny Parsons started as a Luyendyk/Brayton/Vogler teammate but crashed hard, sidelining himself.

Luyendyk didn't need his backup.

Barbazza had twin Marches from which to choose.

Another Lady Entrepeneur Materializes

When her professional race driving husband, IMSA's Mike Downs, started looking around for a special bag in which to carry his helmet, Kathy Fox Downs turned on her imagination and her sewing machine and whipped one up.

It wasn't long before other drivers were asking where they could get one just like it, so she started filling orders. Kathy subsequently formed Fox Fabrique.

Kathy had graduated from UCLA as an English major but couldn't find any jobs, so she went into personnel to start with and eventually purchased a decorating firm. It was here that she sharpened her business acumen and first learned about color and fabric. Her lifelong talent for sewing, her business sense, a practical flair for design and a love of motor sports each seemed destined to sell into something, so when the subject of a new gear bag for Mike came up, the light went on!

Kathy's mainstay is still the gear bag, but she has now added timing totes, fire extinguisher holsters and a range of jackets, aprons and team shirts at her recently expanded facility, located at Sears Point

Kathy checks in with a customer, five-time LeMans 24-hours victor Derek Bell. (Fox collection)

International Raceway. That's the track utilized by the famed Bob Bondurant racing school and in fact, Bob uses several of her items.

Most of Kathy's customers so far have been IMSA drivers, but George Snider uses one of her gear bags and so does Dominic Dobson. NASCAR standout Darrell Waltrip is another customer, as are such outstanding road racers as Hurley Haywood, Al Holbert, Derek Bell, Brian Redman, Chip Robinson, John Morton, Bob Tullius, Gene Felton, Craig Carter and Doc Bundy.

More and more women are becoming part of the Indianapolis car scene these days, and Kathy Fox Downs is on her way to being right in there with them.

SPIN AND WRECK REPORT

1. **DATE:** 5/3 **CAR NO.:** 29
TIME: 2:50 P.M.
DRIVER: Pancho Carter
CAR NAME: Hardee's March
CAR CONDITION: Damage to tub area when roll bar was torn off. Suspension damage on all four corners.
DESCRIPTION: Car broke loose in turn 3, spun one time (660'), became airborne (100'), upside down, slid 600', hit the fourth-turn wall, slid another 260', stopping upside down on the track. No driver injury.

2. **DATE:** 5/5 **CAR NO.:** 10
TIME: 5:58
DRIVER: Dennis Firestone
CAR NAME: Raynor Motorsports Lola
CAR CONDITION: Heavy damage to tub and front half of car.
DESCRIPTION: Car went low in turn 4, slid 600' with a 3/4 spin, hit the outside wall with the left side, slid 80' along the wall, then slid an additional 500' with a half spin. Firestone broke two small bones in his left foot.

3. **DATE:** 5/6 **CAR NO.:** 7
TIME: 1:22
DRIVER: Kevin Cogan
CAR NAME: Marlboro Patrick Racing March
CAR CONDITION: Damage to right front corner.
DESCRIPTION: Coming out of turn 1 (little high), out of groove, 100' to wall (light contact). Slid for 60' along wall. Continued on 1040' across south chute, nudged wall a 4th time entering turn 2. Driver released.

4. **DATE:** 5/6 **CAR NO.:** 91T
TIME: 4:39
DRIVER: Scott Brayton
CAR NAME: Amway/Autostyle Cars/LivingWell March
CAR CONDITION: Right front suspension broken.
DESCRIPTION: Made contact with the wall of turn 4.

5. **DATE:** 5/6 **CAR NO.:** 77
TIME: 5:15
DRIVER: Derek Daly
CAR NAME: Scheid Tire/Superior/Metro March
CAR CONDITION: Continued into the pits
DESCRIPTION: Brushed the wall in the south short chute.

6. **DATE:** 5/6 **CAR NO.:** 19
TIME: 5:15
DRIVER: Dick Ferguson
CAR NAME: Los Angeles Dry Wall Special March
CAR CONDITION: Continued into the pits
DESCRIPTION: Brushed the wall in the north short chute.

7. **DATE:** 5/7 **CAR NO.:** 25
TIME: 11:44
DRIVER: Danny Ongais
CAR NAME: Panavision Penske Chevrolet
CAR CONDITION: Extensively damaged.
DESCRIPTION: Came high out of turn 4 (360' to wall), hit the wall with the right side, slid on top of the wall 80', (broke light bracket) slid away from the wall, across the track through the pit entrance 480', then 200' hit the inside pit wall and slid 135' along the wall. Ongais escaped with a concussion.

IMS-B. Scott

8. **DATE:** 5/7 **CAR NO.:** 76
TIME: 5:49
DRIVER: Rocky Moran
CAR NAME: George N. Walther March
CAR CONDITION: Heavy damage in the rear.
DESCRIPTION: Came high off turn 2, hit the outside wall, slid 540' to the inside wall with one spin, hit the inside wall and slid 260' along the wall. Moran received minor abrasions on his left knee.

IMS-M. Young

9. **DATE:** 5/8 **CAR NO.:** 33
TIME: 11:22
DRIVER: Tom Sneva
CAR NAME: Skoal Bandit March
CAR CONDITION: Extensive damage to right side and rear.
DESCRIPTION: Got high out of turn 1, 320' to the wall, hit with right side, slid across south short chute 1160' and contacted the turn 2 wall, sliding 280' with a 1/4 spin away from the wall.

10. **DATE:** 5/8 **CAR NO.:** 56
TIME: 2:06
DRIVER: Gary Bettenhausen
CAR NAME: Genesee Beer Wagon March
DESCRIPTION: Made one complete spin out of turn 4 and continued to the pits.

11. **DATE:** 5/8 **CAR NO.:** 19
TIME: 3:01
DRIVER: Dick Ferguson
CAR NAME: Los Angeles Dry Wall March

CAR CONDITION: Extensively damaged.

DESCRIPTION: Came out of turn 4, did one spin, hit the inside wall 800 feet down with the left side, slid through the pit entrance 200 feet and hit the back side of the inner track wall.

12. **DATE:** 5/8 **CAR NO.:** 10T
    TIME: 5:21
    DRIVER: Phil Krueger
    CAR NAME: Raynor Motorsports Lola
    CAR CONDITION: Right rear suspension damage.
    DESCRIPTION: Hit the wall in the south short chute with the right rear and slid into the infield grass with one spin. He continued to pits.

13. **DATE:** 5/9 **CAR NO.:** 41
    TIME: 9:25
    DRIVER: Stan Fox
    CAR NAME: Kerker Exhaust-A.J. Foyt Enterprises March
    CAR CONDITION: Light damage
    DESCRIPTION: Came high out of turn 3, spun, slid 900 feet across the north short chute into the inside wall, 195 feet, slid back on to the track.

14. **DATE:** 5/9 **CAR NO.:** 81T
    TIME: 3:05
    DRIVER: Johnny Parsons
    CAR NAME: Kentucky Fried Chicken/LivingWell/Valpak March
    CAR CONDITION: Minor damage.
    DESCRIPTION: Coming out of turn 2, brushed the wall and continued to the pits.

15. **DATE:** 5/9 **CAR NO.:** 2T

TIME: 3:56
DRIVER: Jim Crawford
CAR NAME: American Racing Series March
CAR CONDITION: Extensive damage to right side and front.
DESCRIPTION: Came through the middle of turn 1, spun once 360 feet and hit the wall with the right side, then slid through the south short chute 860 feet. Crawford sustained dislocation and fractures of both ankles and a fracture of the lower right shin bone.

16. **DATE:** 5/10 **CAR NO.:** 33T
    TIME: 10:30
    DRIVER: Tom Sneva
    CAR NAME: Skoal Bandit March
    CAR CONDITION: Sustained right-side damage
    DESCRIPTION: Hit the wall coming out of turn 1, did one spin into the infield grass and stopped at the edge of the track in turn 2 (980 feet).

17. **DATE:** 5/10 **CAR NO.:** 56T
    TIME: 11:11
    DRIVER: Gary Bettenhausen
    CAR NAME: Genesee Beer Wagon March
    DESCRIPTION: Spun 1 1/2 times coming out of turn 1, 840 feet through the south short chute grass, stopping at the edge of the track in turn 2. No contact.

18. **DATE:** 5/10 **CAR NO.:** 84
    TIME: 5:29
    DRIVER: George Snider
    CAR NAME: Calumet Farm March
    CAR CONDITION: Damage to right rear.
    DESCRIPTION: Got high out of turn 2, 760 feet (1 1/2 spins) hit inside wall with right rear, slid additional 100 feet along inside wall and stopped.

19. **DATE:** 5/13 **CAR NO.:** 15T
    TIME: 5:28
    DRIVER: Geoff Brabham
    CAR NAME: Team Valvoline Special March
    CAR CONDITION: Both right side wheels broken, no other apparent damage.
    DESCRIPTION: Got high coming out of turn 3. Drove into wall 580 feet with right side. Slid along wall 340'. Slid away from wall to middle of track an additional 240'. Right rear wheel came loose; backed off to safety lock, broke wheel.

20. **DATE:** 5/14 **CAR NO.:** 81T
    TIME: 11:59
    DRIVER: Johnny Parsons
    CAR NAME: Kentucky Fried Chicken/LivingWell/ValPak March
    CAR CONDITION: Extensive damage to right side.
    DESCRIPTION: Low in turn 1, spun one time 420', hit wall with right front, 60' along wall, then away from wall across track to infield grass (680', 2 spins). Parsons sustained fractured left heel and right ankle.

21. **DATE:** 5/14 **CAR NO.:** 97
    TIME: 5:23
    DRIVER: Rick Miaskiewicz
    CAR NAME: Pizza Hut/WENS/R.C.V. March
    CAR CONDITION: Light damage
    DESCRIPTION: Came low off the second turn, did one spin 540 feet to inside wall, hit with left side, continued along wall 180 feet with half-spin, tore right sidepod loose.

IMS-Swope

22. **DATE:** 5/15 **CAR NO.:** 10
    TIME: 2:00
    DRIVER: Dennis Firestone
    CAR NAME: Raynor Motorsports Lola
    CAR CONDITION: Extensive damage
    DESCRIPTION: Low in turn 4, slid 340' into wall (1/2 spin), along wall 100', (spun 1 1/2) hit again with right side. Slid an additional 500', stopped against outside wall. Dazed but awake, Firestone complained of neck and shoulder pains. Taken to Methodist Hospital. Emergency/Trauma Center revealed a concussion and several neck fractures, with some minor weakness of his arms and hands.

IMS-Sellers

23. **DATE:** 5/17 **CAR NO.:** 10T
    TIME: 12:22
    DRIVER: Phil Krueger
    CAR NAME: Raynor Motorsports Lola
    CAR CONDITION: Extensive nose and right-side damage
    DESCRIPTION: Got low in turn 1, hit the outside wall, slid across the track to the infield grass and hit the wall with a half-spin (800 feet), then spun 3 1/2 times and came to a stop. Krueger was released after examination of abrasions on both knees.

IMS-Newman

24. **DATE:** 5/21 **CAR NO.:** 14
    TIME: 11:34
    DRIVER: A.J. Foyt, Jr.
    CAR NAME: Copenhagen-Gilmore Lola
    CAR CONDITION: Extensive left front damage and moderate damage to rear.
    DESCRIPTION: Did a half spin in turn 1, 320 feet to the wall, hit the wall with the left side, did a half-spin across the south short chute to the infield grass 600 feet.

25. **DATE:** 5/21 **CAR NO.:** 20
    TIME: 12:19
    DRIVER: Emerson Fittipaldi
    CAR NAME: Marlboro Patrick Racing March
    CAR CONDITION: Extensive damage to the right side of the car.
    DESCRIPTION: Spun one time in turn 3 400 feet to the wall, hit the wall with the right side and continued along the wall 420 feet.

The 1987 winning car is readied for display along with a pair of Cummins Diesel cars Dave Evans drove in the 1930s.

CUMMINS/AL UNSER DAY

The winning sponsor entertains its own.

Photos courtesy of Management Resources

So what do you do when the car you've sponsored wins the Indianapolis 500 Mile Race?

Well, you celebrate, of course; and if you happen to be the Cummins Engine Company, you joyfully share the celebration with your employees—every single one of them.

With arrangements made almost as suddenly as the surprise, last-minute sponsorship itself, Saturday, June 20 became designated as "The Day." The proceedings were scheduled to start early, so Al and Karen Unser drove down the night before in order to spend the night in Columbus. They met with Cummins

executives for breakfast at the corporate headquarters the following morning and then were taken to where Al's wining car had been on display outside since about 8:30 a.m. The mayor arrived, and with approximately 1,000 onlookers in attendance, he proclaimed it "Cummins/Al Unser Day."

Next, it was out to CERAland, the Cummins-owned private 345-acre park which derives the first half of its name from the Cummins Employees Recreational Association.

Accompanying miniature golf, swimming pool and go-kart track facilities at CERAland are a pair of adjoining gymna-

siums. Both of these were converted for other uses on "The Day." One side was utilized as a 300-seat viewing theater in order for guests to see films of past Indianapolis races, while the other one was transformed into a display area.

Freddie Agabashian's 1952 pole-winning Cummins Diesel Special was there, as was the Dave Evans "non-stop" car of 1931 and also another Cummins entry driven by Evans in 1934. Around lunchtime, the 1987 winning car was brought from downtown and it was placed in the center of the floor on a raised rostrum which revolved. A half dozen of the 1987 Five Hundred Festival

Thousands of yellow Cummins balloons ready for distribution.

Cummins President Jim Henderson (left) and Chairman of the Board Henry Schacht (right) discuss the huge turnout.

The Five Hundred Festival was represented by five princesses and 1987 Queen Pam Jones (front seat center).

Cummins employees, families and friends begin to gather!

princesses were on hand to greet the guests and there was a Holset turbochargers trade show exhibit nearby.

Al Unser? While the public address system continuously replayed a five-minute excerpt from the closing moments of the race day radio network broadcast, Al was set up in a booth with stacks upon stacks of four-color victory lane shots, which he tirelessly autographed with just a couple of breaks during the next few hours.

Outside there were still more displays with approximately a dozen or so Cummins or Holset-related items, including the Miss Madison Unlimited Class propeller-driven Hydroplane. Long lines of children formed as they anxiously waited for their turns to climb up into the cabin of a massive truck, wrestle with the steering wheel and honk the horn!

Food was served buffet-style in marquees with Cummins executives manning no less than 24 food lines, even the top brass donning aprons and chef's hats.

After several hours of autographing (estimates are that he did 15,000), Al and Karen were taken "down the hill" to where music ranging from Dixieland jazz to country and western had been performed throughout the day in an amphitheater area. The country band playing at the time stopped as Al came into view and led into "The Ballad of Big Al," a number which had been commissioned especially for the occasion.

Al becomes an honorary Cummins employee. Jim Henderson is about to present the first of a 25,000 run of commemorative caps.

There were 24 food lines.

Al got a standing ovation as he came in.

Next came a brief presentation in which Cummins president Jim Henderson gave Al a service pin and proclaimed him an honorary Cummins employee, a gesture which brought a warm response from the crowd. Mr. Henderson next announced that a special run of 25,000 commemorative caps had been prepared and would be distributed among the employees, with Al getting the first one.

More cheers.

Al hadn't planned on such an extensive day, and he started becoming concerned about driving back to Indianapolis in order to catch a flight he had booked out for later that evening. Cummins came up with a solution to have him stay longer. They flew the Unsers to Indianapolis on the corporate jet at about 5:00 p.m. and had somebody else drive the car back for them later!

It was quite an occasion.

As far as the turnout of employees, families and friends was concerned, it was more than double the size of any crowd previously handled by the park.

The final count was 26,059!

Consumed during the day were 15,000 hot dogs, 20,000 hamburgers, 4,000 pounds of baked beans, 22,000 ice cream bars and no less than a full ton of cole slaw!

It was a day the Cummins employees will never forget.— DCD

Part of the throng crowding to see and hear Al Unser. (Telematrix)

Live music was continuous throughout the afternoon.

Hey, Mister!

Emerson Fittipaldi. (Wendt)

Al Unser, Jr. (Wendt)

Ludwig Heimrath, Jr. (Wendt)

Can I Have Your Autograph?

Tom Carnegie. (Wendt)

Fabrizio Barbazza. (Wendt)

Tony Bettenhausen. (Wendt)

154

Josele Garza. (Wendt)

Arie Luyendyk. (Wendt)

Ed Pimm. (Whitlow)

Mario Andretti. (Strauser)

Davy Jones and Stan Fox both made it in on A.J. Foyt's team. (Bonwell)

ROOKIES: THE CLASS OF '87

by Al Stilley

There were several "rookie days" at the Indianapolis Motor Speedway in 1987.

The first significant days for rookies took place on May 16-17, the final weekend of qualifications for the 71st Indianapolis 500, and continued on race day itself as three first-year drivers posted finishes among the top 10.

Almost to the driver, this year's rookie crop remained in the background during practice. Once again, they came mostly from various road racing venues. However, two open- wheel oval specialists on pavement and dirt added a traditional flavor to the rookie class of 1987.

On race day, the six rookies included five with road racing experience and only one (Stan Fox) with open wheel short-track oval experience.

The 33-car starting field for the 1987 500-mile classic included rookies Ludwig Heimrath, Jr., Jeff MacPherson, Fabrizio Barbazza, Randy Lewis, Fox, and Davy Jones. Each rookie brought a touch of class to the starting lineup. Heimrath, a second-generation race car driver, was entered as a Speedway teammate of veteran Dick Simon in the MacKenzie Financial Services-Tim

Horton Donuts/Lola-Cosworth. The 30-year-old driver made his championship car debut in 1984 at Elkhart Lake. In recent years, the Canadian native competed in IMSA road races. His father, Ludwig Sr., raced in ten Indy Car races in 1969 and 1970 but never drove at Indianapolis.

MacPherson, also 30 years old, was a teammate of Geoff Brabham on the Honda-powered Galles Racing team. The Californian driver's roots go back to off-road racing in his native state. He was rookie of the year in SuperVees in 1984. MacPherson competed in three Indy Car races in 1986 and raced in the European Formula 3000 series.

Barbazza was among the more familiar rookies to American open wheel followers, mostly because the young Italian driver captured the 1986 American Racing Series championship. Barbazza began racing at the age of 19 in Formula Monza cars. The 24-year-old driver later competed in the Italian Formula III championship series for two years. Barbazza captured five of nine A.R.S. races in 1986 to earn his first ride at Indianapolis, where he joined Arciero Racing and drove the Arciero Winery March-

Cosworth on race day.

Lewis had the distinction of being the oldest rookie in the starting lineup at the age of 41. Lewis began his racing career in the early 1970s, winning five Formula III races in the U.S. The Californian driver was the best rookie in the 1975 Formula 5000 series. Lewis made his Indy Car racing debut in 1983 and opened the 1987 CART season by finishing eighth at Long Beach. Lewis drove the Toshiba-Altos/March- Cosworth entered by the famed Leader Cards stable on race day.

Fox was the only rookie among the six first-year Indianapolis drivers with a wealth of open wheel short track experience. The 34-year-old Wisconsin driver began his racing career in midgets in 1971, eventually winning 50 feature races in eight years. Fox raced SuperVees from 1981 through 1983 and was waved off a qualifying run by his crew while making his debut at Indy in 1984. In 1986, Fox raced in four A.R.S. events. Fox was one of two rookies on A.J. Foyt's four-car team.

Jones, a teammate of Fox on the Foyt team, was the youngest of the six rookies at the age of 22. Jones made his Indy Car debut

Fabrizio Barbazza. (IMS-Goode)

Dominic Dobson. (IMS-Francis)

Ludwig Heimrath, Jr. (IMS-Goode)

at the Speedway after winning the 1986 IMSA GTP race with co-driver John Andretti at Watkins Glen. Jones's racing background includes Formula Ford, British Formula II, SuperVees, and Formula Atlantic competition.

And so it was that those five drivers with vast road racing experience and a lone open wheel short track veteran carried the first-year banner on race day—but only after they discovered the actual thrill of qualifying for their first Indianapolis 500.

Heimrath became the first rookie to qualify for the 71st Indianapolis 500 on may 10 with a run of 207.591 miles per hour for fast qualifying time for the day.

His run had been delayed one day because the rear wing was too high on both Dick Simon-owned team cars when they went through inspection one day earlier. Although with high winds and a very slippery track, the first day of qualifying was not one that was attraftive to first-year drivers at the Speedway.

Nonetheless, Heimrath recorded a top lap of 208.011 mph and earned a spot on the inside of the fourth row. His first qualifying run was not without a scare. When Heimrath started his qualifying attempt, the oil pressure light flashed and remained on during his complete four-lap run. Heimrath wisely ignored it.

"As soon as I got the green, the oil light came on," Heimrath recalled. "I chose to ignore it as long as the car ran good. I have learned something here with every lap . . . This is a dream come true."

Heimrath was one of the earliest rookies to be announced for the Indianapolis 500 on an established team.

Car owner Simon attested that Heimrath "is a real sleeper and we're honestly looking for a possible win from him late in the year."

Heimrath was joined only by MacPherson as a rookie qualifier on opening weekend as the "weekend for rookies" was still one week away.

Randy Lewis. (IMS-Goode)

Jeff MacPherson. (IMS-Goode)

Rick Miaskiewicz. (IMS-D. Young)

Sammy Swindell. (IMS-Goode)

Rocky Moran. (IMS-Francis)

Ludwig Heimrath, Jr. is married to lady race driver Kathy Rude. (IMS-L. Young)

MacPherson turned in a creditable four-lap run of 205.688 mph and qualified only four-hundredths of a second quicker than teammate Brabham. The road racing veteran was proud that he had conquered the Speedway.

"This track is a real experience for me," MacPherson said. "Getting up to speed at any track is tough, but Indy, because of its tradition and the fact that it is the dream of every driver to compete here, provides some psychological barriers that all rookies must overcome."

MacPherson's first qualifying run in the Team MacPherson March-Honda put him in the middle of the fifth row.

Barbazza added a lot of color to the rookie class and to qualifications. Barbazza picked up the nickname "Turtle" after the always smiling driver-fisherman caught a turtle while fishing at nearby Eagle Creek. The nickname stuck and Barbazza had several turtles drawn on his racing helmet.

Like the rookies who qualified before him, Barbazza made steady improvement during practice. None of the rookies were spectacular during practice runs dominated by veterans. To a driver, they were at the Speedway to learn, and that's what they concentrated on early in the month. Barbazza was no exception.

Barbazza averaged 208.038 mph on his qualifying run, to start in the middle of the sixth row between former winners Danny Sullivan and Gordon Johncock.

Describing his first qualifying run at Indianapolis, Barbazza said, "The track changed from the practice session. I ran 210 then and the car felt real good, but in qualifying it developed a bad push and it wasn't possible to run fast. I have to run a different line each lap because of the push."

Barbazza admitted to being awed by the Speedway and said, "I never see 400,000 people in one place. This place . . . it's the best in the world."

The rookie from Italy discussed the 2.5-mile oval with fellow Italian native drivers Teo Fabi and Mario Andretti.

"They tell me to take it easy and take my time," Barbazza said. "I must learn the track."

Barbazza learned with apparent ease. Within one week of practice, the veteran road racing driver improved his lap speeds from 197 mph to 210 mph.

It was, as usual at the Speedway, part driver and part car improvement. Chief mechanic Paul Diatlovich admitted that it took a week "to figure things out" with the new March chassis and Goodyear radial tires.

Diatlovich was impressed with his rookie and praised, "He's as good as the best driver I've ever had here. He's fantastic. What makes him so good is his driving ability, to communicate what the car is doing."

Lewis turned in a creditable four-lap run of 206.209 mph and became the third rookie qualifier on the third day of time trials. The North Carolina resident made his qualifying try despite "teething" problems with the gears.

After his run, Lewis admitted, "The crew had the car set up perfectly. We were shooting for consistent 205s. To be honest, we would have taken 204s."

By making the 33-car starting field, Lewis and his crew overcame earlier problems that included two blown engines and the popoff valve. Those problems prevented him from turning practice laps in excess of 205 mph until it came down for the real thing on qualifying day. Lewis had earned

his starting spot in the middle of the eighth row.

And Lewis had all the excitement of a kid after qualifying when he remarked, "Being 41, it's a kick being a rookie. It's like being a kid again. Today, I took a big breath before I took the green."

With extensive oval track experience, Fox put together a qualifying run of 204.518 mph in the Kerker Exhaust March-Cosworth from the Foyt stable.

Fox qualified at 204.518 mph, a personally disappointing run after practicing above 208 mph.

"I wasn't happy with our run," Fox admitted bluntly after qualifying for his first Indianapolis 500. "We dropped some speed on the last lap, and I felt in jeopardy of bumping the wall."

Fox revealed his advice from Foyt by saying, "His advice about qualifying was to go out and run four smooth laps and run the car hard, because you can't do anything unless you run the car hard."

Then the former Badger midget champion added, "The other day A.J. was adjusting the wing and I mentioned that it felt like he was taking too much out. A.J. said, 'I'm working on the car and you're driving it.'"

Being a rookie, Fox admitted to feeling the impact of qualifying at the Speedway for the first time by commenting, "I feel more pressure from worrying about other guys than getting in the race."

At the end of the third day of qualifying, a total of six rookies, including Sammy Swindell, had completed qualifying runs. Only the fourth day loomed and it would be turned into a day for rookies—one that some would like to forget.

Only one more rookie successfully qual-

Fabrizio Barbazza's hard work paid off with an outstanding 3rd-place finish. (Wendt)

Jeff MacPherson (with chief mechanic Tracy Potter) was 8th at the finish. (IMS-L. Young)

ified for the 500 on the final day of time trials.

Jones stole the show, to say the least, on the fourth day of time trials.

On his second attempt, Jones qualified at 208.117 mph, a speed that would hold up as the fastest of the day to make Jones the second recipient of the daily fast-qualifier award. Heimrath was the first on the second day of qualifications.

Jones astounded the crowd with his qualifying run, which became faster and faster with each lap. His initial lap was 207.135 and his final lap was a blistering 209.176. Jones would start on the inside of the 10th row as the youngest driver in the field. It was a great recovery from his first try one day earlier, when he tapped the outside wall in the fourth turn and saved the car from spinning.

And the word spread quickly that Foyt, perhaps at long last, had discovered a protege. After qualifying the No. 44 Copenhagen March-Cosworth, Jones finally revealed that he listened attentively to Foyt, who "coached" two rookies into the lineup.

"The coaching that A.J. gave me controlled me and showed me that I could do it," Jones said.

Jones had an up-and-down month as he went from below 200 up to 209 and down again in practice.

Finally, Foyt told him that, "You've got 10 million people telling you what to do and you just can't listen to them." "Coach" Foyt even took Jones around the track in the pace car before qualifications began.

"He was trying to make eight corners out of four," Foyt said. "I showed him the groove and told him to just let the car have

its head. The next practice session he turned in a 203 lap . . . I don't know if he saw me or not, but before he went out (to qualify), I pointed out at him and told him to use his head."

"On race day, three of the six rookies performed as veterans on a track that was a little cooler than earlier in the month, but still produced its skittish moments lap after lap on race day.

Surprisingly, with their abundance of road racing experience, two veteran road racers wound up in the top 10 with the short track veteran Fox.

Barbazza drove to a third-place finish and left no doubt that the Italian-born driver with the flashy smile and exciting wave was indeed the 1987 Bank One Rookie of the Year.

Barbazza presented car owner Frank Arciero with his second straight top rookie title at the Speedway on race day. Despite spinning on the frontstretch late in the race, Barbazza managed to finish only two laps behind winner Al Unser.

Sipping champagne with his crew after the race, Barbazza fully realized a dream come true and admitted, "This is an incredible race. I start in the middle of the field and I finish third. Everything is possible in this race."

The 24-year-old rookie even discovered "all the possibilities" when the heat of the exhaust burnt and cracked the carbon fiber on the wing and forced him into a wild spin down the frontstretch.

Barbazza relived the spin by saying, "When I spin, I close my eyes; then I said, 'No, no, open the eyes,' because if I see the straightaway I push the gas . . . This race, you don't know what's going to happen to

you."

In one short year, Barbazza went from falling asleep in the first turn while watching the 1986 race as a spectator to being the 1987 Indianapolis 500 Rookie of the Year.

Fox became the second rookie member of the top 10 by finishing seventh, also the best finishing driver of the four-member Foyt team.

Afterward, Fox admitted, "It was pretty uneventful for me. We weren't contenders, but we were consistent . . . I sure wish A.J. had won No. 5; then he, and everyone, would have been happier."

MacPherson completed 182 laps and finished eighth in the Honda-powered Galles Racing March despite being bothered by the methanol fumes on starts and restarts during the race.

"We used mechanical band-aids all day. Either something broke, bent, or got loose, but it wasn't that bad out there," MacPherson said afterward.

Jones mustered only 34 laps from the Foyt car to place 28th. His race began by avoiding the spinning Josele Garza car in the first turn.

"Josele spun but I was high on the track when it started to come around on him, so I missed him," Jones recalled. "I could run anywhere, but we lost an engine going hard down the backstretch into (turn) three . . . I can't wait to come back."

Heimrath completed 25 laps before losing a wheel and spinning out in the fourth turn following his first pit stop.

Lewis completed only eight laps before the gearbox went out.

The six rookies who finished the race were among ten first-year drivers who qualified at the Speedway in 1987.

Rick Miaskiewicz came awfully close for the second year in a row. (Whitlow)

Rocky Moran and Sammy Swindell both posted qualifying times but were "bumped" from the starting field in the closing moments. (Wendt)

Swindell attracted much attention and sentiment in his gallant try to get a naturally aspirated "true" stock-block Pontiac V-8 into the starting lineup. Swindell was the first rookie qualifier on the third day of time trials with a run of 201.840 mph.

Surprisingly, Swindell, of World of Outlaws sprint car fame, was not disappointed in the run and continued his Don Quixote approach to the Speedway.

"Being a pioneer, you have to do what you can," Swindell said philosophically.

Swindell remained in the field in the Buttera-Center Line-Machinists Union/March-Pontiac until 34 minutes of qualifying on the final day, when he was "bumped" by Ed Pimm.

Swindell stood by his under-horsepowered car and said, "I'm disappointed because I wanted very much to make this race. I'm convinced I got the most that was in the car and that John (Buttera) and the crew had the car as close to perfect as it could be . . . We're all proud that we came as close as we did with as little as we had to work with."

Ironically, Swindell was one of three rookies who did not make the race on the final day of qualifying as the spotlight once again struck first-year hopefuls.

Californian Rocky Moran was the fifth rookie to complete his rookie test on May 3 for the 1987 race. Moran was entered in a year-old March Cosworth owned by George N. Walther.

Moran officially became the 33rd qualifier for the 500 with a four-lap average of 199.157 mph on May 17; however, he did not fill the field because two previous qualifiers had withdrawn their cars to re-qualify different cars.

With only two Indy Car races in his background, Moran was "bumped" from the field by Foyt teammate George Snider.

Rick Miaskiewicz made a bold try at qualifying, but his speed fell considerably short of making the field in the Pizza Hut March-Cosworth on the final day.

With only 39 minutes left to qualify and needing a run in excess of 201.2 mph, Miaskiewicz could only muster two laps at 198 on his first try and finally completed a four-lap run with only 10 minutes to go at 196.192 mph.

The 10th rookie to be entered and the second rookie to be "bumped" from the field was Dominic Dobson, a German-born driver who earned the 1986 Vandervell PPG Indy Car Series Rookie of the Year title.

Dobson qualified the Intersport March-Cosworth with about one hour to go in time trials at a speed of 201.240 mph. The 28-year-old driver lasted through two incomplete attempts before being "bumped" by Steve Chassey's run of 202.488.

The rookie class of 1987 went into the 500 history book as one that placed three first-year drivers among the top 10 finishers on a race day that was fit only for those who could finish.

Tom Sneva, Derek Daly, Rich Vogler and Gordon Johncock each ran the compact V-6 turbocharged Buick. (Strauser)

The 2.65 liter four-cam, 32-valve Ilmor engine carries the Chevrolet logo on its heads. (Allen)

POWERPLANTS

Some welcome variety in the 1987 engine department.
by Al Stilley

In 1975, the Cosworth was a challenger to the mighty engine "establishment" at the Speedway. Today, the Cosworth of designers Mike Costin and Keith Duckworth is being challenged long after the powerplant changed the face of racing in the USA.

The 2.65-liter (161.27 cubic inch) double overhead cam, turbocharged, four-valves-per-cylinder Cosworth V8 faced many formidable challengers in the 1987 Indianapolis 500. The list included the well-publicized Ilmor-Chevrolet V8, the well-tested turbocharged stock block Buick V6, the Galles Racing Honda V8, a pure stock block normally aspirated Pontiac V8, and an ill-fated Foyt turbocharged stock block Chevrolet V8.

The Ilmor-Chevrolet became the odds-on race day favorite to dethrone the Cosworth. The British-built Ilmor-Chevrolet occupied two spots on the front row in Mario Andretti's pole- winning Newman-Haas Lola and Rick Mears's year-old Roger Penske-owned Pennzoil Z-7 March on the outside of row one.

Andretti kept the Ilmor-Chevrolet in the headlines all month. On five of six practice days that the car was on the track, Andretti set high-speed marks for each day. His top run was 218.234 mph on May 7, the fastest unofficial lap in Speedway history. Andretti earned the pole with a four-lap average of 215.390

mph on a hot Hoosier day and on a slippery track.

The engine that powered Andretti's qualifying run was the same one that powered his 218-plus laps on May 7 and May 8, according to Chevrolet publicist Brian Wilson. The motor was the 10th and final engine the team received from Ilmor Engineering of Brixworth, England.

Franz Weiss of VDS Engines, which prepared and rebuilt the Ilmor-Chevrolets, admitted that Andretti's engine "ran really hard." Chevrolet liaison engineer Alan Hayman pointed out that it was not a special qualifying engine because "our emphasis is on reliability and durability and we are not interested in taking the time to build qualifiers."

A second Ilmor-Chevrolet joined Andretti on the front row when Mears qualified a race car that was on display at a Pennsylvania Sheraton Hotel just three days before his remarkable qualifying run. The March 86C was the same car that Mears drove 233.934 mph to break the USA closed-course speed record in November 1986 at Michigan International Speedway. Mears had only eight laps at speed to break the car in after its belated arrival at the Speedway. Penske ordered the car after scrubbing the new PC16 chassis for Indianapolis.

Mears qualified for his seventh front-

row starting spot at 211.467 mph and afterward said he could have gone over 214 with more preparation time and practice.

The efforts by Mears and Andretti were the lone bright spots for the Ilmor-Chevrolet on qualifying weekend. The marriage of the new engine with Penske's PC16 and Patrick Racing's March 87C had been a struggle all month, especially after some very promising performances during private practices in the spring.

Handling woes forced Penske to call up year-old March chassis for Mears, Danny Sullivan and Unser, who replaced the injured Danny Ongais. Penske, a principal backer of the Ilmor-Chevrolet project, was forced to place a Cosworth in Unser's year-old car because of a lack of replacement components for the new engine.

The new powerplant had won at Long Beach with Andretti and there was plenty of confidence in the engine before its first Indianapolis 500.

Weiss said, "I really feel like it is on the right track, especially with the caliber of the three teams involved."

However, Weiss cautiously added, "You can't expect a brand-new engine not to have problems."

Reviewing the engine's characteristics, Hayman said, "It's the very flat torque curve that gives the Chevy the advantage

Mario Illien (right) and Chevrolet Special Products Liason Engineer Alan Hayman were on hand for the Long Beach Grand Prix on April 5 when Mario Andretti led flag to flag to post the inaugural win for Ilmor power. Hayman provides a link between Chevrolet and the company Illien formed with Paul Morgan. (Chevrolet)

duct of Formula One and packed 740 horsepower at nearly 11,000 rpm.

The Honda engine powered the Galles Racing cars driven by Geoff Brabham and rookie Jeff MacPherson.

Before making his first qualifying run, MacPherson attested, "The engine has been performing very well. It is proving to be quite reliable and we have high hopes. One of our biggest advantages is Honda's electronic fuel management system that increases our fuel economy."

Brabham practiced at 206-plus and MacPherson got into the 207 bracket. Each driver qualified successfully on the second day of time trials as MacPherson edged teammate Brabham 205.688 mph to 205.503 mph.

A lot of attention was focused on the Ilmor-Chevrolet, but the development of the all-American turbocharged Buick V6 continued with renewed enthusiasm during the 1986 summer testing season and private tests at the Speedway leading into the month of May.

The engines were prepared by Fischer Engineering and VDS with Buick "heavy-duty" parts under the direction of Buick Special Products Engineering. In its racing form, the 209- cubic inch six-cylinder turbocharged engine produced 750 horsepower at 9,000 rpm. The engine featured a Buick cast- iron Stage II block, an even-firing forged Buick crankshaft, Buick Stage II aluminum cylinder heads, forged aluminum pistons, roller-type valve lifters and dry sump pumps fitted to the block.

The Buick V6 was impressive in 1985 when it was qualified 1-2 in the starting lineup by Pancho Carter and Scott Brayton. But disappointing performances in 1986 resulted in a renewed effort to

over the Cosworth. The Cosworth is more peaky. You need to apply the throttle before you need it and the power comes suddenly. With the Chevy, transitions are smoother and quicker."

Andretti added, "The one thing I noticed the most is that if they wouldn't have a rev-limiter, I could keep right on revving. It doesn't peak out at 11,500 or even 12,000 (rpms) . . . All they got from me is me begging them to put the rev-limiter up more and more and more."

The engine is a joint venture of Penske, designers Mario Illien and Paul Morgan and Chevrolet, which provides engineering assistance.

On race day 1987, five cars powered by the Ilmor- Chevrolet lined up for the start of the 71st annual classic.

Hampered by a lack of testing in early 1986, Rick Galles's Honda V8 project was in evidence at the Speedway. The engine was built by John Judd with assistance from Honda. The 161-cubic inch double overhead cam V8 is the pro-

Cosworth was still on top in 1987 and powered the first seven finishers. (Strauser)

162

produce longevity. Buick made a major switch in its program by moving from McLaren engines to Fischer Engineering and VDS for its 1987 Indianapolis 500 assault.

Private tests at the Speedway put 3,350 miles on the Buick V6 and prompted Buick SPE manager Joe Negri to comment, "Our people have worked long and hard to analyze and improve the mechanical integrity of this engine. It's an engine that has impressed in the past, but our goal is to have its best performance come on race day."

Negri explained, "The biggest thing we did was make a slight change in the bore and stroke. We knew we were pretty close last year [1986], but we had a lot of problems in May."

Looking at the Ilmor-Chevrolet, Negri offered, "The Chevy engine is a purpose-built racing engine . . . The Buick is a modification of a stock block engine, so they're really not comparable. One is an engine built for racing to go heads up against the Cosworth, but our engine falls into the stock block rules where we're allowed to make certain modifications to a production engine. But we still have to keep most of the basic dimensions the same. In my estimation, it takes more technology to make a stock block engine work well at Indy than it does to make a racing engine work well. A lot of people question whether there should be stock block engines because they feel it's old technology. Well, it's a lot harder to make a stock block run for 500 miles and win the race than to make an overhead cam engine designed specifically for the purpose, to win the race . . . Buick is in motorsports and we're here to stay."

Driver-team combinations using tur-

George Snider qualified the A.J. Foyt-entered Chevrolet V-6, but a turbocharger fire knocked it out on the pace lap. (Strauser)

bocharged Buick V6 power on race day included two-time Indianapolis 500 champion Gordon Johncock in the American Racing Series March 86C as a replacement driver for injured Jim Crawford, who had tested the engine extensively through early May; 1983 winner Tom Sneva in the Skoal/Curb Products March 87C; USAC midget car champion Rich Vogler in a March 87C sponsored by Jonathan Byrd's Kentucky Fried Chicken Restaurants and LivingWell Fitness Centers and owned by Ron Hemel-

garn; and Derek Daly in the Scheid Tire/ Superior Training/Metrolink 1411 March 87C.

Crawford's testing efforts netted a hot lap of 215.982 mph on May 6, the second-fastest practice lap to date in the ARS Buick V6 housed in a "Second-Hand Rose" March.

After his high-speed run, Crawford beamed, "The handling was almost perfect. We made a change in the settings right on pit road. There's more left in this Buick engine. Everything is really coming about quite nicely."

Unfortunately, it fell apart on the first day of qualifying. Crawford suffered two fractured ankles and a broken shin bone in a horrendous first-turn crash on a May 9 qualifying attempt. The car (2T) was extensively damaged and Johncock was summoned from his ranch in Arizona to replace the injured Crawford.

Two crashes drastically slowed any progress of the Buick V6 driven by Sneva, who eventually qualified at 207.254 on the last weekend.

Vogler took advantage of private testing time for the first time in his three 500s. The midget and sprint car veteran was the first driver to qualify a Buick V6 with a run of 205.887 mph on the second day of qualifying. On the final weekend Johncock qualified, tearfully and joyfully, at 207.990 mph. Daly qualified at 207.522 mph.

Again there was confidence among the Buick V6 teams. Hemelgarn, who provided free LivingWell physical rehabilitation equipment for Crawford's recovery, boldly stated that a Buick V6 would fin-

There were two Brabham Hondas in the race, with Jeff MacPherson finishing 8th. (Whitlow)

John Buttera's normally aspirated V-8 Pontiac missed the starting lineup cut-off by one position. (Strauser)

ish the 500 for the first time. After making two bold charges near the front with Cosworth power, Vogler predicted he "would be able to stay close to the leaders and pass them at the end." Sneva contended that the off-season changes in the Buick V6 "would make last year's woes ancient history." And Daly admitted that the Buick V6 "is by far the strongest engine I've ever had in any form of racing."

A fourth different engine challenger joined the fray on the last day of qualifications as veteran George Snider qualified A.J. Foyt's Calumet Farm/Copenhagen March 86C turbocharged stock block Chevrolet V6 at 203.192 mph to bump rookie Rocky Moran.

One of the most interesting driver-car-engine combinations at the Speedway in 1987 was the normally aspirated stock block 350-cubic inch Pontiac V8 fielded by car owner John Buttera and veteran dirt-sprint car driver Sammy Swindell. Pitted against the exotic Cosworth, the Buick V6 and the Honda, the Pontiac V8 team dreamed the impossible dream under existing rules at the Speedway.

Center Line and Machinists Union provided the March chassis for Buttera's adventure. The engine was built by Buttera, Randy Scovill and Ronnie Saver. Eventually, Swindell drove the March-Pontiac about as fast as it could go in a gallant effort to re-establish the future of normally aspirated stock block engines at Indianapolis. It was an uphill battle.

"We didn't know it was going to be this difficult," Buttera said. "We didn't think we would be as handicapped as we were."

Technically, Buttera thought the torque

would overcome a lack of horsepower. The Pontiac was about 50 horsepower under the Cosworth, 100 less than the Ilmor-Chevrolet and 125 less than the Buick V6. Buttera bravely turned up the rpms to 8,300 on the stock block rocker arm Pontiac, compared to a range of 11,500 to 11,800 rpm for the exotic double overhead cam racing engines.

Misfortune, too, hit the team one day before the final weekend of time trials when the Pontiac V8 dropped a valve. Swindell had practiced in the 201 mph range before qualifying at 201.840 mph. They had attained the "impossible dream" for one day until they were bumped by Ed Pimm on the last day. A non-turbocharged stock block engine would not make the field.

"Being a pioneer, you have to do with it what you can," Swindell attested. "I wanted very much to make this race. I'm convinced I got the most that was in the car . . . This just proves that a naturally aspirated engine is playing into a stacked deck against the turbocharged cars."

If there was a "stacked deck," it appeared ominously on race day as Andretti and the smooth-flowing Ilmor-Chevrolet dominated almost all phases of the race by leading 170 of the first 177 laps. But the secret to winning at Indianapolis or anywhere else is to be around at the finish. The Cosworths were and most of its challengers were not.

With Unser's March Cosworth leading the way home after engine failure ousted Andretti, the final scorecard showed Cosworth among eight of the top 10 finishers. The Honda and unheralded rookie MacPherson finished eighth and Andretti officially placed ninth.

The top seven Cosworths were driven by Unser, Roberto Guerrero, Bank One Rookie of the Year Fabrizio Barbazza, Al Unser, Jr., Gary Bettenhausen, Dick Simon and rookie Stan Fox.

Andretti at first thought his car went out because of a fuel-feed problem. Shortly after the race, Andretti explained that "all of a sudden, it backfired . . . It was spewing raw fuel into the engine." The post-race tear-down by Weiss revealed that a broken intake valve spring was the culprit.

The Ilmor-Chevrolet race day "report card" showed an oil pump leak that sidelined Kevin Cogan, a cracked oil pump casing which ended Fittipaldi's race day run, a "lower end" engine failure on Sullivan's car, and a broken ignition coil on Mears's car.

Sneva had the longest lasting Buick V6 on race day, completing 142 laps before hitting the second turn wall. The fate of the Buick-powered cars included an engine failure for Daly, a broken rocker arm for Vogler and a valve problem for Johncock.

Disappointed after failing to finish his third 500, Vogler explained, "It felt like it was running out of fuel . . . Something happened to the pick-up in the tank. There was a lot left in my Buick and I was saving it for a hard charge at the end. The car was running good, but unfortunately, something began to rattle in the engine."

Snider, the 12th driver-engine combination to challenge the Cosworth, never completed a lap in the turbocharged stock block Chevrolet V8. A fuel leak developed on the parade lap, causing a fire to break out and burn through the rear suspension parts.

There was a "twist" to the 1987 engine war. It was brought about by the Penske team as Unser won his history-tying fourth Indianapolis 500 for a car owner heavily involved in the Ilmor-Chevrolet project. Unser's car was powered by a Cosworth.

It was not planned that way. As Penske explained, "Al would have been in a Chevrolet had it not been for switching all the cars from the PC16 to the March 86C. We didn't have enough pieces left to change a third car. So we had to leave the Cosworth in the third car."

Cosworth powered 21 cars on race day and had four engine failures, according to the official finish.

After looking at their 1987 race day experiences, General Motors executive vice president Lloyd Reuss admitted that "we're here to stay. We'll be back."

And so will the Cosworths, the Buicks, the Hondas and, for the first time in modern-day racing history, Porsche, with defending champion Unser. The Cosworth challengers, old and new, will try again in 1988.

GASOLINE ALLEY

An overgrown back road transforms into a racing headquarters.

by Jep Cadou

This used to be Roena and Vermont. (Mahoney)

"Gasoline Alley" was hardly an original name, but it is certainly an accurate one to apply to an area where race-car-related businesses have sprouted up like spring dandelions.

Formerly known as Roena Street, Gasoline Alley runs from Rockville Road up to Vermont Street and is dotted with racers and racing businesses on both sides of the street.

It is a living tribute to a hustling racer named Charlie Patterson who bought his first property on the street back in 1978.

Patterson remembers it well. "I bought a piece of property on that street, land everyone said was totally useless," Patterson recalls, "It was covered with brush and trees and was being used as a dump, a definite eyesore to the community. It took a lot of time and a lot of hard

Charlie Patterson. (Patterson collection)

work, but now I am quite proud of my accomplishments."

Patterson put up his first building in 1979. He now owns five buildings along the street. He had the space in the first building sold to racing teams and suppliers before it was finished.

Patterson, who runs a thriving driveshaft business on Dan Jones Road near Avon, had originally purchased ground on Roena Street with the thought of moving his driveshaft business there. But he realized that a lot of Speedway teams needed a place where they could work without any restrictions.

Original tenants included the Alex Foods racing team of Alex Morales and Johnny Capels, Jud Phillips's engine business and Rick Muther's racing team.

Now, there are a total of 27 race-related businesses that have set up shop in the new Gasoline Alley, so named by the Indianapolis City Council in 1985 after Patterson led a successful campaign for the change.

Vince Granatelli Racing, formerly Cotter Racing, has one of the largest and most completely equipped buildings to maintain the CART Indy Car World-Series car driven by Roberto Guerrero.

Some of the other businesses located along the street include Jackie Howerton's fabrication shop, Herb Porter's engine shop, Gambler Speed Shop, Elouisa Garza's fiberglass shop, Mike Fanning's engine shop, Frank Weiss's machine shop, Rick Hendrick's Mr. Goodwrench team, which runs the IMSA GTP circuit with Indianapolis-based driver Sarel Van Der Merwe, and Donnie Ray Everett's sprint engine building business.

Patterson had a rich and varied back-

ground in racing, which allows him to understand the problems and needs of his tenants as well as those who build their own buildings along Gasoline Alley.

Gasoline Alley, of course, was the name applied originally to the Garage Area at the Indianapolis Motor Speedway. It also was the title of an early comic strip and also had been applied to

Charlie shades Paul Newman from the sun during the making of "Winning" at the Speedway in the summer of 1968. It was here that Newman became "hooked" on racing. Note the camera attached to the side of the car for closeup action shots. Newman would get the car up to speed and then activate the camera himself. (Patterson collection)

Charlie helps push Bob Wente out for a practice run in 1964. Crew chief Bob Higman is at left. (Patterson collection)

Charlie checks on the progress of a building in August, 1984. (Patterson collection)

a concentration of midget race car shops at Paterson, N.J., which seems an unlikely coincidence.

Patterson (the one with two t's) began his racing career in 1958, working with Bob Sowle, who owned a midget driven by the popular and colorful Eddie Sachs, known as the "clown prince of racing".

Charlie hung around Sowle's garage, which was in Avon, and washed parts and did odd jobs, never receiving any pay but attending a lot of races and meeting a lot of people, learning all along the way.

After Sowle sold the midget, Patterson in late 1959 landed his first paying job with Rolla Vollstedt, the West Coast lumberman and race car builder and enthusiast.

Charlie began working for the Bob Higman garage in 1963. Higman was the chief mechanic for a car owned by Gil Morcroft.

Patterson went to work for Walt Flynn in 1966 and then for Dick Cecil, who was chief mechanic for the MVS Indy cars owned by three Indianapolis businessmen.

In the late 1960's, Patterson helped the filming crew prepare the race car for Paul Newman for the movie "Winning."

After traveling with the MVS cars in 1970, Patterson went to work at Joint and Clutch Service Inc., where he learned the art of driveshaft repairing.

With the uncertainties of racing, he de-

Every one of the industrial-looking buildings in this shot, with the exception of the mini-storage, contains a racing-related business, and most are owned by Charlie. Photographer Mike Grider took this shot as a passenger in former "500" driver Bob Harkey's Stearman bi-plane.(Grider)

cided to get into a more stable occupation which would insure making a living for his family.

He opened his own driveshaft shop — Patterson's Driveshaft Inc. — in 1972 on the farm where he grew up near Avon. He helped his family milk 40 head of cows daily and farmed nearly 300 acres.

In April 1980, he and his uncle opened another driveshaft shop near Sarasota, Fla., which is considered one of the better shops in the state.

In 1981, Patterson opened another business, the Stitching Post just across 16th Street from the Indianapolis Motor Speedway. The business featured racing jackets, shirts, drivers' uniforms, patches and many other racing items. The successful business was sold to Jim and Susan Luebbert in 1982 in order for Patterson to devote more time to racing and the driveshaft business.

Patterson's favorite form of racing is the Championship Dirt cars, but he also enjoys the midgets very much.

In 1973, Arnold Knepper drove the Patterson Driveshaft Special to a third-place finish in the USAC Dirt Championship Division. The team's best finish was a second at Syracuse, N.Y.

During the winter months of 1979, Charlie designed and built Super Pro ET Bracket drag racing cars. He first built, from the ground up, a Chevy with a 1972 Vega body, which he drove at Indianapolis Raceway Park.

Looking south at Charlie's mini-storage, with another Patterson-owned building behind it. (Mahoney)

Legendary Herb Porter uses his initials for a double entendre on his shingle along Gasoline Alley. (Mahoney)

(Above)Gambler Competition (Center) is on the right in the foreground, while looking north is Jackie Howerton's building with the Arciero truck in front of it. (Mahoney)

The fabrication shop of Canadian Frank Weiss (a former Indy car driver) is in the foreground, while the other half belongs to engine builder Mike Fanning. Mike built Tom Sneva's winning Cosworth in 1983 and later, in this facility, developed in secrecy the turbocharged V-6 Renault Doug Shierson commissioned but never raced. (Mahoney)

Further south and right next to Vince Granatelli Racing (formerly Bignotti-Cotter) is the attractive building used by Johnny Capels and the Alex Morales team. (Mahoney)

He also built a Super Pro Buick Roadster which won several trophies at car shows. From 1979 to 1981, Patterson actively sponsored Lonnie Caruthers, one of the front-runners in USAC midgets.

Charlie then bought his own midget and had Bob Meli and Andy Hurtubise as the driver. In 1985, he had a new midget built, powered by a new V-6 Renault engine. It was driven by Hurtubise and by Johnny Parsons on occasion.

Patterson has been associated with many driving greats through his 25-year racing career. In addition to Sachs, Meli, Hurtubise and Parsons, they include Len Sutton, Ernie Koch, Ed Kostenuk, Bob Wente, Al Miller, Bob Harkey, Ralph Liguori, Johnny Rutherford, Arnie Knepper, Rick Muther, Norm Brown, Ronnie Duman, Steve Chassey, Mark Alderson, Dana Carter, Jerry Sneva, Bill Whittington, Bob Williams, Bob Meli, Tracy Potter, Dennis Firestone and Tom Bigelow.

Patterson now has hopes that Gasoline Alley may be extended from Vermont Street all the way north to 16th Street. The city is committed to building a new roadway to connect Grande Avenue at 10th Street to Polco Street at 14th Street.

Jack as a 13-year-old in 1938. He and friend Harvey Guttry carved these model cars out of balsa wood. (Craig-Alvarez)

JACK FOX...

A Tribute

The world of motorsports lost one of its most eminent historians on Wednesday, June 3rd, 1987 with the passing of our good friend, Jack C. Fox.

Jack, who was 61, had plunged into a coma following a massive heart attack suffered some six days earlier, and he never came out of it.

Well-known to readers of Hungness publications, Jack was the author of three substantial books as well as being a contributor to the Indianapolis 500 Yearbook each year. In 1967, the original version of Jack's marvelous "The Illustrated History of the Indianapolis 500" was published by World Publishing Company and immediately greeted with critical acclaim. It was updated by World in 1968 and subsequently republished by Hungness in 1976 and 1986.

Another masterpiece was unveiled in 1977 when Hungness published Jack's highly cherished "The Mighty Midgets," while more recently his "The Illustrated History of Sprint Car Racing, Volume One, 1896-1942" has gone into the catalogue.

In addition to producing those delightfully "meaty" historical pieces for the "500" Yearbooks each year, Jack delayed his return to San Jose, CA in 1982 after his annual Speedway pilgrimage and stayed over to undertake the entire editing job for the '82 book. It was not a totally new type of assignment for him, since back in 1959 and 1960, he and the former Carol Anderson (now Carol Sims) had pooled their efforts to produce what were probably the two best ever of the Floyd Clymer "500" Yearbooks.

Jack also went it alone on occasion to produce yearbooks for the Bay Cities Racing Association and, in the mid-1950's, for the United Racing Association (both midget groups), featuring not only his own writing and intricate statistics but also largely his own photography.

His sometimes caustic and pointed comments appeared in a regular column over a period of more than 30 years in the now defunct Illustrated Speedway News and also in several other publications which are no longer in existence. His total output of columns probably numbered several thousand.

A man of many talents, Jack was a very accomplished painter who turned out oils of 1920's and 1930's Indianapolis cars, sprints and midgets, not only with great accuracy for color and detail but with very little time required.

While his great interest in the Indianapolis "500" was rivaled by a passion for Gilbert and Sullivan operas, both were outranked by more than a half century of pure love for the sport of midget racing.

Over a period of many years, numerous authors and would-be authors had set out to write a history of midget racing, but nobody had progressed very far with such a huge undertaking. Jack had mused about it for years and was certainly far more qualified than most to give it a shot. Carl Hungness had been keen to publish such a work and eventually talked Jack into doing it.

What Jack turned in as the first draft a few months later was a well-written, factual, straightforward textbook history of the sport.

"This isn't really what I had in mind," Carl told him. "The anecdotes you used are great, but it needs more of them. Put in some of the great stories you've told me in the past that I don't see here. You lived this history for all of these years and knew all of the people. The history is great, but do it as seen through your eyes. Put more of yourself into it. Think about all of your favorite stories, what you thought was right, what you thought was wrong, what made you laugh and, by golly, put it ALL in there. Keep this draft with you for a while and have fun with it."

What Jack submitted not too long after that was the absolute winner which was soon available to the public in its first of several printings.

With that in mind, and by way of a little more biographical background on Jack, here is a sampling from "The Mighty Midgets" in his own words.

I guess that every youngster has a close family friend whom he calls "Uncle" as a term of endearment. Dad's best friend, my "Uncle Earl" Gilmore, also happened to be the richest man to regularly visit our home. I could always tell when he had been there as he was the only cigar smoker we knew. The evidence of his visits lingered in the air long after his departure. He was a kind, slightly gruff, bashful man who sent me toys and presents addressed to "my darling little boy."

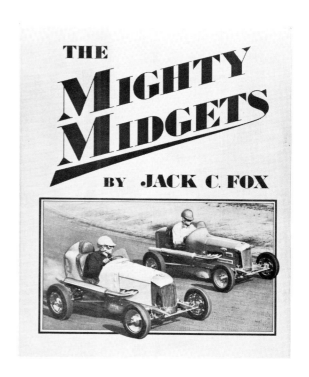

My father, Bill Fox, came to Los Angeles early in the 1900's. He was born in New Orleans and left home to live in New York where he learned physical culture work from Billy Muldoon, trainer of John L. Sullivan. A not-too-successful career as an outfielder with Happy Hogan's Vernon Tigers was sandwiched between service tours; in first the Navy, and later as an army sergeant in World War I. The early 1920's found him marrying, settling down and raising a family (me). He became director of athletics at the University Club, later moving to the equally prestigious Jonathan Club where he knew most of the local athletes as well as the city's businessmen. At the University Club Dad met Earl Gilmore and a mutual interest in sports and physical conditioning spawned their friendship.

Dad regularly attended the board track races at the Beverly Hills Speedway but lost interest in auto racing when his big Irish heart couldn't stand to see drivers killed or injured. As a result he didn't go to the Legion Ascot Speedway nor would he take me despite my persistent pleading.

My mother, Grace, had been a real race fan before World War I when she and her girl friends used to watch Ralph DePalma, Eddie Pullen, and Teddy Tetzlaff compete on the popular Ascot mile track. It is even possible that she saw Alex Pabst and his young friends in some of their exhibition races. She was also in the crowd at the 1916 Corona road race in which Wild Bob Burman lost his life.

Possibly, there was some pre-natal influence which made me a motor racing fan almost as far back as I can remember but for the first seven or eight years of my life my actual exposures to the sport were restricted to watching Saturday afternoon movie serials which had auto racing themes. "The Crowd Roars" (a Warner Bros. feature film still appearing regularly on TV) really lit my fires and I'm sure that it would have been only a matter of time before I persuaded my parents to take me to Ascot—had not a mutually agreeable alternative presented itself.

One night, late in 1933, my father came home from work with some exciting news. "Uncle Earl" was going to build a stadium on the northwest corner of his ranch just southwest of Hollywood. Of prime interest to me was that one of the uses to which the stadium would be put was that exciting new sport . . . Midget auto racing!

And he continues on a little later in the book:

Were you a spoiled child? I was and I'm damn glad I was. In fact, I wouldn't have had it any other way!

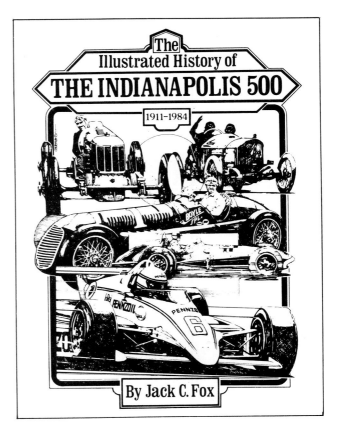

My parents were in their forties when I was born and by that time they had most of the running around out of their systems. They were in the perfect position to spoil their only child and being rather precocious I took full advantage of the situation. I don't think I particularly abused the privilege but we did do many things together and these were mostly the things I wanted to do . . . like going to as many races as possible. It took a little planning to work our vacations around the every Thursday night Gilmore races—and I didn't miss a race there from August, 1936 until the place was torn down in 1950. We usually vacationed in San Francisco where I had learned via the Bergen Herald that races were being held at Neptune Beach on Tuesday nights. This was convenient, since we could leave for the north on Friday morning and then return the next Wednesday, catching the Neptune races just before heading home.

Those who knew Jack and his gentle, laid-back manner were usually surprised to learn that he had flown 35 missions with the 99th Bomb Group of the 15th Air Force in Europe during WWII as a B-17 tailgunner! Jack Fox???!!!

It was also rather ironic that one of the world's most outstanding historians for American oval track motorsport would never get around to learning how to drive a passenger car!

It was all part of Jack's mystique.

Jack attended every Indianapolis "500" from 1951 until 1986, but the recent years had become a little tougher for him to take because he could never quite accept the changing trends at the Speedway and still felt as if all the drivers should have to have come up through the ranks of midgets and sprints! Consequently, he'd spend much of his time in the Oldtimer's trailer, talking over the old days but constantly on the alert for snippets of information he hadn't known of from the past to add to his vast knowledge.

Gracious and witty, Jack was very generous in sharing that knowledge, not only in person but also through the painstaking procedure of writing it down. It is our good fortune that Jack was so prolific, and while we certainly miss him a great deal, perhaps we can take some consolation in the fact that we can always reach for the shelves, take down something Jack has written, and muse over his entertaining words.—DCD

AL UNSER ...IMAGES from the past

Photos by John Mahoney

Sporting a brand-new crew-cut at Atlanta, GA, August, 1965. (Donald Davidson)

The crew cut is growing out by the time Sacramento rolls around in October, 1965.

Taking the Willie Davis sprinter out on its maiden voyage at Terre Haute, IN, August, 1965.

Bye-bye, crew-cut. Trenton, April, 1967.

Dominating the 1970 season and heading for the win on the road course at IRP, July, 1970.

Yet another victory in the 1971 Hoosier Hundred.

The late Sid Collins interviews Al after the '71 Hoosier Hundred.

Hiking the front left during the 1973 Hoosier 100, a race which Al won for the fourth consecutive year.

Al and George Bignotti made a tremendous combination. Check the sideburns.

The top drivers make concentrated efforts to learn the on-track as well as off-track idiosyncrasies of their rivals. These two already had that handled.

How many times has Al Unser wrecked a race car? Not very often. He luckily escaped with just a shaking from this one after a punctured tire sent his VPJ backup into the concrete during practice for the '77 "500." The car was totalled.

Al's 22nd "500" results in a record-tying fourth win. (IMS-McQueeney)

Al won many, many dirt races with Johnny Capels.

Father of a son who is now preparing to start a fifth "500", in 1987 Big Al contemplates his own 22nd. (John Strauser)

INDY MOTORSPORTS EXPO

The Hoosier Dome is the home of the NFL's Indianapolis Colts.

Linda gets a chuckle out of a Mario Andretti quip. Also seen are John Andretti, the son of Mario's twin brother, Aldo, plus Mario's two sons, Jeff and Michael.

Two-time "500" winner Rick Mears is Linda's guest.

Parnelli checks out an exhibit. Looks like the lady staffing the booth has realized who he is.

SPEEDWAY

PEOPLE PEOPLE PEOPLE

Yearbook publisher Carl Hungness learns the latest Wichita Falls news from Lloyd Ruby. (deBrier)

Famed artist Leroy Neiman spent a day at the track. (Wendt)

Indianapolis Star Assistant Sports Editor Robin Miller was a "500" devotee long before entering his teens. (Strauser)

National Speed Sport News editor and publisher Chris Economaki probably has more sources than any other motorsports person in the world. (deBrier)

While A.J. Foyt was celebrating his 30th "500" as a driver, Lou Palmer was doing the same thing as a member of the IMS Radio Network. (Strauser)

Lovely Cynthia Engelstadt created the magnificent montage friends of Clint Brawner commissioned (See: "Guess Who's Staying At Our House?" starting on page 184). (Strauser)

Richard Petty makes his annual visit. (IMS-Binkley)

Drag racer John Buttera almost saw his non-turbocharged Pontiac V-8 make the lineup. (Wendt)

Another Andretti? Don Henderson listens as Mario talks with his youngest son, Jeff. (Wendt)

Stock Car legend and mechanical wizard Henry "Smokey" Yunick used to enter cars at Indianapolis. (Wendt)

Chris (Mrs. Rick) Mears takes a break. (Wendt)

Sonny Meyer built the engines for Vince Granatelli Racing this year. (Wendt)

Duane Carter (Pancho's dad) drove in 11 Indianapolis races. (IMS-Hunter)

Ludwig Heimrath, Sr. drove in some USAC Championship races, but never at Indianapolis, as did his son in 1987. (Wendt)

Lola designer Nigel Bennett and Raynor driver/crew chief Phil Krueger ponder. (Wendt)

Michael Chandler, injured here in 1984, would like to return. (Wendt)

Pete Halsmer checked out the ''backup'' situation but didn't stay around long. (IMS-Binkley)

Ron runs an idea by his team manager, Lee Kunzman, a four- time starter in the "500" and the 1973 USAC Sprint Car series runner-up. (IMS-Binkley)

RON HEMELGARN

Fitness king's racing team gathers momentum.
by Philip LeVrier

"There are no tricks to being a success," says Ron Hemelgarn. "You just have to have a positive attitude. You can't look back. When you begin to doubt yourself or have any negative attitudes, that's when you fail."

So says the owner of LivingWell Fitness Centers and Hemelgarn Racing. Since his early childhood years, Ron Hemelgarn strenuously followed a positive mental attitude, a dedicated determination, and plain hard work and has become one of America's most successful entrepreneurs.

The Toledo, Ohio resident has put the same efforts into his Indy car racing and is well on his way to successfully obtaining his goal of forming a winning racing team that will someday capture a victory in the prestigious Indianapolis "500."

"I know that our day is coming," he says about that particular dream. "Our victories are coming and when it happens, we'll deserve it. I don't compare myself to a Penske or a Patrick— I'm gonna do my own thing. But we'll get there."

Hemelgarn's "own thing" consists of developing a racing stable the same way in which he successfully developed his multi-million dollar fitness center business. "You've got to start out by building a strong foundation before you build a strong building," Hemelgarn points out. "We have built a good foundation for a racing team and hired good, strong employees and mechanics and good drivers. Now all of a sudden our 'building' is looking pretty nice. At Indy this May, Arie (Luyendyk) was fourth quick all month. And the first day that the track opened for practice, we had all five of our cars running. We entered seven cars and actually had seven running cars. Not many teams can say that. It's a pretty nice accomplishment to get all of our cars qualified up front." (Arie Luyendyk

qualified the LivingWell Fitness Centers/Provimi Veal/WTTV Special on the inside of the third row; Rich Vogler put the Jonathan Byrd's Kentucky Fried Chicken/Val-Pak of Indianapolis Special on the inside of the fifth row; and Scott Brayton qualified on the outside of row five in the Amway/Autostyle Special).

Feisty Ron Hemelgarn has been an outstanding businessman since before he entered the first grade, when he gathered newspapers and magazines from his Dayton, Ohio neighborhood and, with the help of his father, delivered them to the local salvage yard.

By the time he was eight, little Ron decided he should have his own paper route. He had to fib about his age, saying he was eleven, and immediately built up his route to the maximum number of deliveries, 100. He accomplished this an amazing three times, selling the routes off to the other carriers as separate routes. The enterprising youngster had already mastered the art of delegation and money management.

At age 12, Hemelgarn moonlighted in the evenings, setting pins at a local bowling alley. At 16, he stocked groceries after school and all day on Saturdays. He learned that if he was going to get ahead in the world, it was entirely up to him to get the job done. "I've always said," Hemelgarn pointed out with a determined grimace, "If I want something to happen, I have to make it happen."

Obsessed with making money and being his own boss, Ron Hemelgarn did not get along with his teachers as a teenager. "I wasn't a good student," he admits. "All I've ever wanted to do since I was a small boy was make money. To me, money is a reward and I've worked very, very hard to get it."

Upon graduation from an all-boys Catholic high school in 1965, Hemelgarn was ready to challenge the world after his counselor had told him, ''You'll never be successful.''

Securing a low-paying job as a maintenance man and a part-time instructor at a fitness center, Ron worked as much as 90 hours a week in the club, hoping to stockpile enough money to be independent. He has never liked being under someone else's employment and in 1972, he decided that he knew enough about the fitness business to manage his own club. He soon took over three financially troubled clubs in Toledo, Ohio. Within 18 months Hemelgarn had all three operations making money and opened a fourth club.

In 1977, Ron bought four clubs in Indianapolis and began to expand. By 1983, he had several hundred clubs.

Still working hard and possessing a dream of forming a major national health and fitness operation, Hemelgarn met Texas fitness entrepreneur Tom J. Fatjo in 1984. They merged their club interests, forming the LivingWell Fitness Centers as they are known today.

A long-time auto racing fan, Hemelgarn has loved Indy car racing since the 1950s. ''I've always liked racing,'' he smiles. ''I listened to Sid Collins's radio broadcasts of the Indy 500 since 1956.''

In 1964, young Ron hitchhiked from his home in Dayton to Indianapolis to see the ''500.''

''I couldn't afford the price of a ticket,'' he remembers. ''I walked into the infield and stood on a garbage can in turn four to watch the race. I had dreams of someday being involved in the race.''

As he grew older, Ron Hemelgarn stuck with his auto racing interests and even became involved as a competitor when he raced ''semi Late Model Stock Cars between the age of 18 and 20 in the Ohio area.''

While perched atop that garbage can and witnessing the spectacular 1964 Indianapolis ''500'', a spellbound Ron Hemelgarn decided that he would someday be a part of the race, and fourteen years later, after obtaining his many fitness center businesses in Indianapolis, his dream came true when he sponsored Dick Simon's entry. He renewed that agreement in 1980, then sponsored Spike Gelhausen in 1981, and later Josele Garza.

''I sponsored cars in the '500' because I knew that would promote my Indianapolis clubs,'' says Hemelgarn. ''Everybody responds to the Indy 500. It was always exciting to see our club members on the sidelines saying, 'Hey, there goes our car!' They had the same feeling of pride and ownership as I did.''

In 1984, Hemelgarn's Spa*erobics was the sponsor of the Primus Team and driver Chris Kniefel. That was also the year that Hemelgarn decided to form his own racing team, and he bought the Primus operation.

''The reason I bought Primus was because I wanted to get control of the direction of the team,'' Hemelgarn says. ''I wanted to organize a team that could compete and eventually win. I knew it was going to be a lot of hard work, but I'm used to that. As a matter of fact, I thrive on it.''

Hemelgarn also thrives on proving that he can do the impossible. ''Racing is a brutal business,'' he says. ''There's a lot of back talk and back-stabbing that goes on. I've learned to ignore that. I just sort of keep to myself. I do my own thing and try to run a good team.''

There were a lot of negative comments about Hemelgarn's decision to form an Indy car team, yet he persevered. ''I hate negative talk,'' he said sternly. ''I always try to keep a positive attitude and I stress that in my fitness centers and racing team. I have a saying: 'If you speak from the heart, you'll never have to worry about what you said because it comes from the heart.'''

Hemelgarn has been assembling his operation one piece at a time, not cutting any corners. Rather, the stress has been on quality and not making the same mistakes twice.

''Everything is a learning process,'' he says. ''And you're always going to make mistakes in anything that you venture out into that's new, but the biggest thing is learning from your mistakes. The last couple of years we've had a few failures and we've learned from those failures. We've picked up the pieces and moved forward. We've built a very strong foundation, with all of our team members

A typical Hemelgarn spa. (Van Sickle)

Hemelgarn Racing headquarters on Country Club Road, Indianapolis. (Van Sickle)

Part of the spacious race car shop. In the foreground is the March driven in 1986 by Jacques Villeneuve. (Van Sickle)

179

The first time Silhouette appeared as a partial sponsor was on the Rolla Vollstedt/Dick Simon effort of 1979. (IMS)

Johnny Parsons drove the Silhouette-sponsored Wysard March in 1982. (IMS)

Ron put a deal together with Josele Garza and the Machinists Union in 1983. (IMS)

from 1986 back with us in 1987. They've worked together as a team and developed as a team. They know how each other thinks. They know what the car needs and how to service it properly. The rapport they have built with Arie Luyendyk in just a short period of time has been phenomenal.

"I believe in working on one project at a time," says Hemelgarn. "If you put someone on one project at a time you get 110%. If you put him on three projects at a time, you only get 33%. That's why all my drivers have separate cars, engines and crews. That is the reason we succeed."

After purchasing the Primus operation, Hemelgarn fielded cars for Michael Roe and Enrique Mansilla in 1985, with Spa*erobics as the primary sponsor. Roe and Mansilla, both rookies, were competing for the Vanderwall Rookie of the Year Award, along with Hemelgarn's present driver, Arie Luyendyk. That same year, Hemelgarn put veteran Spike Gehlhausen in the seat for superspeedway events, later adding Scott Brayton to his stable of racers.

A busy man who thrives on work and projects, Hemelgarn continued expanding his fitness center business as well as his racing operation. "I work better in multitudes," revealed Hemelgarn. "I like working with multiple operations like my fitness centers. The challenges are more and the results are better. It's the same in racing. You get a broad base of good ideas when working with a lot of people, and I like that.

"I've been able to take over bankrupt health clubs and turn them into a success. That's how I respond. I thrive on impossible situations. That makes me respond. When people say I can't do something, then that makes me want to do it. When I started my health club business many people said, 'No, you can't do that. You'll fail!'

"Everybody said the same thing when I started my own Indy car team. They said, 'There's no way you'll survive.' Then all of a sudden they were saying, 'Hey, maybe you can do it.' I don't look at myself as being a normal car owner. I look at myself as a businessman."

Highly motivated and a man who knows exactly what he wants, Ron Hemelgarn wants no excuses from his employees, only results. "I don't like the word 'maybe.' To me that's a negative word. I want 'yes' or 'no'. Those words are simple to understand. There's no confusion. Everything I do is real simple and works out well. That way I can have several thousand people I can run simply.

"This racing is not a part-time thing, for sure. It's a business and I run it that way. Each of my race cars has a separate crew. It's just like a health club. They all have separate facilities. When I start a new health club, I don't take equipment out of one club to start a new one; I buy brand new equipment. That's the same way I run my race car team. Each one gets their own separate equipment and crew."

In 1986 Hemelgarn continued expanding his racing team and hired Canadian Jacques Villeneuve as his primary driver, with Scott Brayton handling the driving chores on the ovals. Crashes, which totalled his race cars at Toronto, Pocono and Mid-Ohio, would have closed the doors of other operations; but Hemelgarn, upon witnessing Villeneuve's crash at Toronto, had purchased another March 86C before the day was over.

Near mid-season, Hemelgarn hired veteran crew chief Larry Curry to work with crew chief Graham Donaldson to prepare the race cars under the supervision of team manager Lee Kunzman. Curry had been chief mechanic for Kevin Cogan in 1986, when he came so close to winning the Indianapolis "500."

The same year Hemelgarn, a CART board member, became involved in the new Buick American Racing Series (ARS) and hired young Steve Millen to drive, moving Donaldson over to the ARS car as chief mechanic.

At the end of the 1986 racing season, Hemelgarn regrouped and hired Luyendyk to be his driver for the upcoming schedule. Another addition to building his foundation for a successful racing team was the hiring of engineer Tim Wardrop, who assisted in the design of the March 87C.

"I don't want anything but professionalism in my racing team," says Hemelgarn. ''That's the kind of team I want. My whole drive is to win races, and I don't sit there and point fingers. I want a positive team with positive results. We've been very fortunate so far. We've been able to build a team that works together well and will be a winner very soon.

''As long as all our efforts are positive and not negative, I'll probably be in racing for many, many years. I do things to win. I am successful and I will continue to be successful. As long as I have pride and my team stays that way, we will be winners.''

Has the Indy car racing involvement helped Hemelgarn's fitness business, or has the high cost of the sport hindered it? ''The racing has done nothing but help my business,'' he quickly points out. ''My LivingWell business doubled in the month of May from all the promotion the month before the race. We're very promotion minded . . . take our half- million dollar May promotion, for example. It's paid off well. Our sponsors have all gotten good exposure from it. We've got TV, radio and press coverage because of all the promotion. Our name is constantly in the limelight in May. It's just unbelievable the amount of exposure we get from the Indy 500.''

Hemelgarn has brought many co-sponsors into his racing efforts and he makes sure they get as much media exposure as possible for their money.

''I'm very conscious of my sponsors. To me, the guy who spends $10,000 on sponsorship is as important as the guy who spends a million dollars. They're all part of the team and this is their race car.

''I like to see my sponsors when they're pleased with the pride of ownership. That's what I want—that pride.

''All their support, whether it's large or small, is what makes our team a success and makes our guys go out and run competitively. Positive attitude and pride of ownership—to me, that's the key.''

Ron Hemelgarn and his wife Helen have five children; Brian, 18; Rhonda, 12; Amie, 11, Greg, 7 and Brent, 4. They have always supported his hardworking habits and his racing interests. ''They come to all the races as a sort of family outing,'' he says. ''They all like the atmosphere and challenges and they have my positive attitude. Their backing of me really helps. They're a major factor in my success.''

Hemelgarn Racing has been on the scene for three years now and is recognized as a viable racing team. ''We have definitely moved up over the years,'' says Hemelgarn. ''We are now challenging the top teams in Indy car racing and they know it. I think within five years I should have won or been able to win the Indianapolis 500. Nobody comes in and wins the race right away; it takes time and experience, and that's what we've been doing, building our organization and gaining the experience.''

It has taken a lot of hard work and extreme sacrifices and

The original Bignotti-Cotter building, now owned by Vince Granatelli Racing, is expected to be occupied by Hemelgarn Racing by the end of 1987. (Mahoney)

Six foot six inch Chris Kneifel couldn't fit into the average Indy car and so the Primus team built its own for 1984. Ron took over the Primus team shortly thereafter. (IMS)

challenges for Ron Hemelgarn to reach the plateau he has in Indy car racing, but he has loved every minute of it. ''My feelings toward hard work are: the harder I work, the luckier I get. No matter what business — health clubs or racing.''

With his penchant for hard work and organization and his exuberant positive attitude combined with that particular little bit of luck it takes, it will not be long before Ron Hemelgarn achieves his dream of fielding a race car that will capture an Indy 500 win.

Arie Luyendyk is Hemelgarn's number one driver for 1987. (VanZant)

Designer/Engineers
Designer/Engineers
Designer/Engineers
Designer/Engineers
Designer/Engineers
Designer/Engineers
Designer/Engineers
Designer/Engineers
Designer/Engineers
Designer/Engineers
Designer/Engineers
Designer/Engineers
Designer/Engineers
Designer/Engineers
Designer/Engineers
Designer/Engineers
Designer/Engineers
Designer/Engineers
Designer/Engineers
Designer/Engineers
Designer/Engineers
Designer/Engineers

All photos by Doug Wendt

Designer/Engineers
Designer/Engineers
Designer/Engineers
Designer/Engineers
Designer/Engineers
Designer/Engineers
Designer/Engineers
Designer/Engineers
Designer/Engineers

Famed Lee Dykstra was on with Patrick this year.

Ex-Lola designer Nigel Bennett served as engineer for Raynor.

EVERYBODY wanted Adrian Newey's services. Newman-Haas had him.

Ian Reed worked with Shierson and Al, Jr.

Much sought-after ex-Newman-Haas man Tony Cicale alligned himself with Skoal right before the final qualifying weekend.

Alan Mertons, co-designer/engineer with Peter Gibbons for Kraco.

Eric Broadley IS Lola.

Geoff Ferris, long time Penske designer/engineer.

Peter Gibbons.

Past credits for Hemelgarn's Roman Slobodynskyj include the '72 Gurney Eagle, the Romlin Lightnings and the Ongais "Batmobile."

Former Gurney Eagle designer John Ward was with the Machinists team.

Grant Newbury of Truesports.

The Indianapolis Motor Speedway is surrounded by residences in which the participants routinely used to stay during May and part of the summer. (Indiana State Police)

GUESS WHO'S STAYING AT <u>OUR</u> HOUSE!

It was a time when race cars were housed in garages down almost every alleyway around Speedway and the race drivers were literally "the guys next door."

by Donald Davidson

Back before the city of Indianapolis began bursting forth with multi-million dollar sporting complexes and convention centers and expensive modern luxurious hotels, and back before race teams were figuring budgets that ran well into seven figures and were taking cars to race tracks in $200,000 transporters, and back before race drivers could either command massive retainers and sign lucrative product endorsements or else were considered ''marketable entities'' and were able to produce their own six and seven figure sponsorships, there used to be a very different, simple, straight-forward existence around the Indianapolis Motor Speedway.

The race cars used to come in on open trailers towed by trucks or station wagons, usually driven by the chief mechanic, who was very often the only full-time employee of the team. The drivers were rarely from well-to-do backgrounds, were usually hired strictly on a race-to-race performance basis, paid a standard 40% of all prize money earned by the team, and they very often derived no income during the year other than what they could win at race tracks. They had never heard of personal managers and very a few drivers even had any inkling as to what a retainer was.

Of course, a few affluent ''gentlemen'' race drivers of the pre-WWI era, some of whom were from quite wealthy families, had ensconced themselves in great comfort during May downtown at the Claypool Hotel, the Athletic Club and so forth, and this was still the procedure into the 1920's for those few who could afford such luxury. It had already become desirable for the general rank and file, however, to seek shelter closer to the track. The problem was that there weren't any hotels anywhere out there, and with finances tight anyway, the solution was to make an arrangement with a nearby family willing to rent either a room or a corner of their basement for the month.

When the so-called Championship ''trail'' began to expand in the late 1940's, and the Midwestern sprint and midget racing became enticing enough to lure drivers in from other parts of the country, Indianapolis became a centrally-located ''home base'' for much of the activity. It meant that not all of the drivers and mechanics would leave after the ''500'' was over. They'd stay on in the area by the track for the summer, some drivers taking on menial jobs for the weekdays between races and some perhaps maintaining a sprint or a midget driven in races either by themselves or a colleague.

Visit a drug store soda fountain or lunch counter on any day within the shadows of the Indianapolis Speedway during the summers of the 1950's and 1960's and one would find a variety of drivers and crew members gathered around in groups, either in heavy discussion or throwing good-natured barbs back and forth. Check the parking lot of the White Front tavern on down 16th Street on any night and one would not only see all kinds of hopped-up vehicles (the exotic ones bearing California plates), but the commotion from within was often an indication that a spirited ''500'' driver or two were about to be asked to leave!

The locals thought nothing of it. These were merely the guys who came in during April and left in September, sometime after the Hoosier Hundred. The USAC office was located upstairs on the corner of 15th and Main for a couple of years in the late 1950's and in Kepler's garage, just down the alley from there, a variety of sprints and midgets were kept. Race cars were housed and worked on in garages next to houses all around the neighborhood, and it was just about heaven on earth for anyone who wanted to be a part of racing and for the wide-eyed school kids enthusiastically riding their bikes up and down the alleys. Race cars and race people were all part of the scenery.

The Indianapolis Motor Speedway is not in Indianapolis. It's actually in a suburb named Speedway.

Out-of-towners generally have no idea that such a town exists, and most of them usually believe the name to be some kind of joke upon first hearing it. The name probably evolved more or less as a working title shortly after the construction of the race track and the Prest-O-Lite factory across the street, and it was certainly in use before WWI. Speedway was officially named in 1926.

Speedway has its own town board, town hall, police force, fire

Fifteenth and Main as it appears in 1987. The upper floor of the corner building was home for USAC headquarters during the late 1950's and for Carl Hungness Publishing in the mid-1970's. When Duane Carter was USAC Director of Competition, his young son, Pancho used to tie pieces of string to unused entry blanks and fly them out of the rearward bathroom window as kites. Two houses further down is where Jim and Betty Packard lived. Parnelli Jones lived with them, while visitors at this house included A.J. Foyt, Rodger Ward, Jim Clark, Jackie Stewart, Jochen Rindt, Eddie Sachs and Bobby Marshman among many, many others! Betty's baby-sitter in the mid-60's was Joyce DeWitt. (John Mahoney)

department and water company. Fine color paintings of past ''500'' winners hang from many of the street signs immediately west of the track. The four grade schools are named Fisher, Allison, Newby and Wheeler, for the original quartet of partners who built the track in 1909. Allison and Fisher also have streets named for them, as do three-time ''500'' winners Wilbur Shaw and Louis Meyer, as well as such early automobile firms as Cole, Cord, Auburn, Cadillac, Winton, De Soto, Ford, Lincoln, Buick, and Nash. There's even a street named for Crosley!

The heritage is still there today, but sadly, it is rather different now. Speedway has grown. It is no longer the tight little community

The old homestead on the corner of Norfolk and 16th in 1942. The trees hadn't grown much yet. (Otte collection)

The other corner of 15th and Main. A drug store and lunch counter used to be downstairs. Eddie Sachs, Jimmy Reece, Don Freeland and Howard Kelley once shared one of the upstairs flats. The Charger racing paper was downstairs in the rear in the late 1960's, Kepler's garage was just down the alley and all kinds of race folk stayed in the houses on down the street from the 'teens through the sixties. (John Mahoney)

---

where everybody knew everybody else. Apartment buildings, shopping centers and fast-food restaurants have shot up to occupy the sprawling acres that were farmland not so long ago. The police force has expanded considerably from merely the chief, two patrolmen and the single squad car it began with in 1953!

And, along with the changing face of racing, sad to say, the drivers no longer stay around here anymore.

But cruise the streets between 16th and 10th, and all of those others with the car names, allow the imagination to run wild, and at almost any given moment one will be passing residences where the greatest names in all of racing once stayed, sometimes for years on end, and sometimes with several "rival" race drivers living in the same house at the same time.

Picture, for instance, Johnnie Parsons and Jack McGrath rising on the morning of the 1950 race, eating breakfast in somebody's kitchen on 13th street, and then walking across to the track, anony-

---

Betty and Carl Otte on the front steps with sons Ron and John. (Otte collection)

mously intermingled with the bustling crowd. Picture the jubilation in that same house with the neighbors excitedly popping in and out a few hours later when Parsons returns as the "500" winner.

Picture Duane Carter on down 14th Street during the summer teaching his young sons, Pancho and Dana, and his stepson, Johnny Parsons, how to "dirt track" their quarter midgets around the school's baseball diamond.

Picture "500" aspirant Parnelli Jones sleeping on the couch in the living room of Jim and Betty Packard's house at 15th and Main, or a very young A.J. Foyt, dressed in t-shirt, light slacks, white socks and loafers, rocking on the porch of the same house in the early evening and then getting up to leave for the cafeteria with a bunch of others while the Packard children are entrusted to a Speedway junior high school student named Joyce DeWitt.

Picture Bob Veith and Johnny Boyd sharing a basement on 14th Street during their first summer in the area and being so broke that they sleep in until mid-morning in order to get through the day on two meals instead of three.

Picture the riotous quartet of Eddie Sachs, Howard Kelley, Don Freeland and Jimmy Reece sharing an apartment over the drug store on the corner of 15th and Main in 1956 and "Okie" Reece amusing the locals downstairs in the little restaurant each morning by routinely consuming a Coke and a bowl of chili for breakfast!

Picture seeing a "500" driver through a window on Main Street sitting in a barber's chair.

Picture seeing a race car being driven noisily down an alley or a side street and the police coming over for the umpteenth time to tell those responsible that they really aren't supposed to be doing such a thing.

Thousands of memories like that are forever etched into the minds of the people who experienced those days, and some still live in the area lamenting that life has changed somewhat.

John Otte grew up in Speedway. He is now the deputy fire chief for the city. His family goes back for at least five generations in this area, to the time when his great-great-grandfather farmed land near what is now 10th Street and I-465, long before the race track was even dreamed about. His mother remembers as a little girl in the 4900 block of West 15th Street having her parents take in race people in May. Earl Devore, runnerup in the 1927 race, was one. After she grew up and married, John's mother settled at a house on the corner of Norfolk and 16th Street and began taking in race people in 1947. John's parents would continue that for almost twenty years, and there were to be some pretty incredible experiences in store for a growing lad who was crazy about cars and racing.

OTTE: The first people to stay with us in May, when my brother and I were still quite small, were Ross Page and his son, and Freddie and Mabel Agabashian. Freddie and Mabel had a son and a daughter who were about our age, and after a couple of years they started renting a whole house instead. The Blakely Oil team were next, with Clint Brawner and Bobby Ball and the whole crew. Blakely Oil was pretty much of a big bucks team for those days, because they had two cars. They'd pull up with those cars on trailers and they had two or three Ford pickups all painted a sort of candy apple red, just like the race cars.

We had two bedrooms upstairs and one on the ground floor, so at race time my brother and I would move in with my parents downstairs and the drivers and the chief mechanics would have the room upstairs. Sometimes they'd buddy up in one room for part of the month, and then the wives would come in for the race.

Down in the basement we had cots set up for the mechanics. They'd all be lined up down there military style, but it was really nice. There was a shower down there and a sink and a stool. Everybody had an end table. We just kept getting more and more people each year, and the most we ever had was 17 in the house plus us!

We never got to know Bobby Ball that well, because he was very quiet. He was very nice but he just never said very much to us. He sure didn't seem like a race driver. He was tall and thin and had reddish-blond hair. He wore glasses and looked like a college

It's unknowingly prophetic that little John Otte would be driving a fire truck. How could he possibly know that he'd grow up to become Speedway's Deputy Fire Chief and be headquartered about two blocks from here? (Otte collection)

John Otte in 1987 as Deputy Fire Chief for Speedway, In., standing next to the real thing. (John Mahoney)

student. He always wore western- style clothes, which seemed really out of character for him. All of his shirts were silky and of western cuts and he wore Levis and cowboy boots, the real things with the designs on them and everything. He had one of the rooms upstairs, and his wife would come in for the race.

He crashed the Blakely Oil car in practice for the ''500'' and Clint decided not to rebuild it. Ball drove another car in the race. The Blakely car sat outside our house, wrecked and on the trailer, and in all the years race cars were out there this was the only time I ever remember anyone messing with any of them. The front of the car had been caved in and it had a sort of sports car-type grille. The spokes were all loose and I caught a neighborhood kid trying to pry one of those spokes out.

After Blakely, we had Dean Van Lines. In fact, we had the entire crew except for Al Dean, the owner. He probably stayed in a downtown hotel, but he was out at the house constantly and he got along real well with my parents.

Bruce Crower was part of the Dean crew in 1954. Later he became chief mechanic on the Helse Special, so we had that crew as well as Dean's. There was Dave Schneider, Ermie Emmerso, Bob Bubenik, Jack and Art Chrisman. A lot of them were big in drag racing, but I wasn't really paying much attention to them then. They were just guys staying at our house. I was more interested in the neat cars they were driving. They'd come back with Ford coupes with Cadillac engines in them and things like that. I was a car nut, so I'd always be buying magazines like Hot Rod and so on. Later on I'd be going through a magazine and here they'd be in photographs standing next to hot rods and dragsters. I'd run in and say, ''Hey, look, Dad, these guys stayed at our house!'' and my dad would just say, ''Oh sure, that's so-and-so.''

There was a midget driver named Bob Hornbrook who had moved to Arizona and became part of those crews. He stayed with us, and I still hear from him occasionally. Bill Cheesbourg had one of the rooms upstairs when he first came back. Later, he went to another family around the corner on Cadillac. My dad says that Bob Sweikert spent one night with us, although I don't remember him being there. That could have been in 1953, when he drove for Dean at the last minute. But the people coming over and visiting? Ohhhhhhh! That was happening all the time, but again it was just other guys coming in and out: Bob Christie, Al Keller, Jimmy Daywalt, Art Bisch, George Salih, Jerry Unser. Then Manny Ayulo stayed across the street, catty-corner to us. He was there for years. The Greenman-Casale team was over there too. George Amick was up the street.

My younger brother never really cared too much one way or another about racing and the race track, but they knew I did. They were always bringing stuff home. Hats, decals, jackets, T-shirts. Man, oh Man! I'd wear them to school. I had Dean Van Lines

T-shirts, I had Belond T-shirts. I loved that stuff. I had a bike that was just about the same color as the Blakely cars, and Clint gave me a Blakely Oil decal with a rocket on it to put on my bike. What I wouldn't give to have that fender back!

One year the Dean Van Lines Team wore heavy blue satin jackets that had red, white and blue knitted sleeves. I think my parents still have one of those hung up in a closet somewhere. Another time somebody brought home a whole box of Iskendarian Cam T-shirts

The 1947 Victory Banquet program signed by Rex Mays, Wilbur Shaw, George Connor, Mel Hansen, Harry Hartz, Pop Myers, Ted Horn, Walt Brown, Duke Dinsmore and Henry Banks, while the inscription at top right reads: ''To Carl and Betty, a swell pair— Freddy Agabashian,'' followed by ''Lower the rent''. (Otte collection)

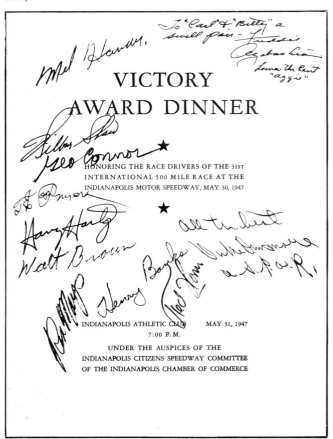

and I got a lot of heat over wearing those. Bruce Crower and Dave Schneider had their own cam company by that time, and of course they were both at our house! I think Bruce and Dave had gone to school together. Later on, I'm afraid, they had a disagreement and split. Then they went out and each formed their own cam companies. My own kid wears Crower Cam T-shirts now.

I don't have nearly the room to take guests in the house I own myself now, although we had Myron Stevens for several years, but we do have several people park their campers outside. In 1985 Bruce Crower parked out there and we were talking away for hours. After a while, my wife said, ''Well, wait a minute now, just how long have you two known each other?''

I said, ''I don't know. Bruce, what was the first year you came back with Clint?'' He said, '''54.'' So it was 31 years.

It was really very educational for me and my brother and made us aware of a lot of things, because we would meet people from different parts of the country who couldn't get over the difference between what they were used to and the Midwest. My mother always wanted them to feel like they were at home and she always told everybody that they didn't have to sneak their beer down into the basement. It was quite all right with her to have them leave it in the kitchen fridge. Anyway, she'd have about a dozen lawn chairs out in the backyard for relaxing in the evenings, and I remember being so impressed by Dave Schneider's reaction to a firefly. He'd never seen one before and he just couldn't get over it. Then there was a mechanic who I can just see now but I can't remember his name. He was impressed by our maple tree and how green it was. He had nothing like that out in Arizona. When he got ready to leave and his car was loaded up, the last thing he did was to get out a couple of flower pots and fill them with dirt. He then scooped a whole bunch of maple seeds from under the tree and I suppose he was going to take them back to Arizona and try and grow them. I think he was going to build a house out there. Things like that impressed me as a kid.

* * * * * * *

And then there is the matter of one other house guest, who came in with Brawner and the Blakely crew in 1953 and ended up staying through the entire summer for seven years at the Otte home.

He was to become more than a house guest. He was to become a part of the family, staying for months on end, lounging around the living room and watching TV, engaging in pranks, running errands, bringing home gifts and sometimes sitting in the kitchen with John's parents and talking far into the night.

He was a hero to thousands and thousands of race fans around the world and was even idolized by other race drivers. He was certainly idolized by John Otte, who for half of the first 16 years of his life would count the days until this beloved house guest would return for yet another summer of fun and frolicking around. His name was Jimmy Bryan.

For the uninitiated, Bryan was a strapping, bass-voiced six-footer from Phoenix, Arizona who incessantly smoked or chewed cigars. He first came to Indianapolis in 1951, and after failing to qualify for the race is said to have been so broke that he borrowed a

Christmas greetings from the Agabashians. (Otte collection)

House guests Mabel and Freddie Agabashian with daughter Joanne in 1947. (Tower photo from Otte collection)

cart and went through the infield picking up discarded drink bottles in order to collect the deposit.

He qualified for his first of nine consecutive Indianapolis races in 1952 (finishing 6th) and near the end of 1953 won his first Championship race at Sacramento. In 1954 he qualified a dirt car for the outside of the front row of the ''500'' and led quite a few laps of the race, leading as late as the 149th lap. Several things had begun to break on the car by that time, including the right rear shock, which ended up with Bryan suffering a severe pounding on the still partially bricked surface. He was eventually passed by defending winner Bill Vukovich, who was driving a lower ''roadster'' much more suited to Indianapolis. But Bryan hung on to finish second. He was so beaten up at the end of the race that the monstrously strong Bryan collapsed on the garage floor. A nurse came in to administer some first aid just as Bryan popped open an eye. ''How are you feeling?'' she asked.

''Well, I'm feeling just fine, baby, how are you?'' responded the laconic Bryan, whereupon he lapsed back into unconsciousness.

The injuries were such that Bryan had to pass up the next race at Milwaukee, but three weeks after that on the treacherous and rough Langhorne track, he won. He moved into the point lead for the Championship, added to it as the season wore on and then went on a rampage near the end by winning the last four races in succession.

At Indianapolis in 1955, Bryan dropped out while leading with a new roadster near halfway. With oil and smoke pouring from the blown engine, the colorful, T-shirted Bryan climbed on the back of the seat, removed his helmet and rode the tail of the car into the pits, bare-armed, bare-headed and steering with his feet!

Bryan also dropped from the point-rich 250 mile race at Mil-

After crashing the Blakely car in practice, Bobby Ball qualified for Bill Ansted (behind cockpit) and they pitted next to the pole-winning Cummins Diesel of Freddie Agabashian on race morning. Ball did NOT look like a race driver. (Otte collection)

Al Keller qualifies the Helse car in 1959. Dave Schneider and Bruce Crower are at either end of the group. Check out the partial sponsor on the side. (IMS)

waukee in August in which "500" winner Bob Sweikert placed third. It put Bryan too far behind to overhaul Sweikert for the 1955 Championship, but he didn't lose it without a fight. Of the eight other races on the "trail", all 100-milers, Sweikert won one, Johnny Thomson won one, and Bryan won the other six!

Bryan won back the title in 1956 and again in 1957, giving himself eighteen wins between October, 1953 and November, 1957. Nobody else was even remotely close.

In the closing race of 1957, on the dirt at Phoenix, Bryan had been nudged from the track on the next-to-last lap by a slower car while he was leading. He smashed through the wooden "retaining" fence, drove around on the outside of the track and came in at an opening where somebody else had "departed" earlier. He came down for the white flag, clenching the ever-present cigar between his teeth and reaching into the underpan, steering the car with one hand and throwing chunks of splintered fence out onto the track with the other!

He caught Pat O'Connor again in the final lap and won the race!

In 1958, Bryan curtailed his activity quite a bit and switched from Dean Van Lines to George Salih's team, which did not have a dirt car. Driving the little Belond Special with which Sam Hanks had won the 1957 "500", Bryan went on to place his own name among the immortals who have won the Indianapolis "500". Bryan was easy to idolize.

The Helse Special on its trailer parked out on Norfolk in 1957. Jimmy Daywalt drove it in the race. (Otte collection)

After he had stood in the cockpit of his car in the old Victory Lane at the south end of the pits and accepted the plaudits of victory, posed for photographs, drunk the milk and kissed Shirley Mac-Laine, he did something very typical of him. He climbed from the cockpit, laurel wreath still around his neck, and walked with the happy entourage trotting along behind him to the edge of the track. The other cars were still allowed to stay on the track and complete their own version of 500 miles in those days. While they were whizzing by, Bryan stood near the line and waved to the fans on the other side of the track, first with one hand and then the other. It is believed that no other "500" winner ever did that.

After the post-race victory celebrations had been completed in the Garage Area and a beer or two had been consumed, Bryan, still in his yellow Belond uniform, did what he had done hundreds of times before during the previous several summers.

The new winner of the Indianapolis "500" headed west on 16th Street to unwind at the home of the Otte family.

OTTE: You just can't believe what a wonderful person he was. I just can't find the words to describe him. He was so good to us kids. We worshipped him. He wasn't like a race driver coming to stay. He was like an uncle or an older brother. He was just like a big kid himself. We'd look forward all winter to him coming back and the first thing he'd do was romp around on the floor with us. All the kids in the neighborhood would come over and we'd gang up on him. Of course, we always lost.

My dad and I got into the Garage Area after the 1957 race and I was in several of the garages; Dean Van Lines, of course, with Bryan and Clint and the crew. They were third that year. We went down to Sam Hanks's garage. He'd won. He was sitting up on the bench all hot and tired and dirty and they put me right up there next to him while all of the well-wishers and friends and people from other teams were coming to congratulate him. It was the first time I'd been that close to a winner.

The next morning Bryan says to me, "I'm going over to the track. Hop in and I'll take you over." We walk in and just after we get to the Dean Van Lines garage a guard comes in and tells Bryan that I have to leave because I'm too young to be in there. There's an argument going on now and I don't know what to do because this argument is over ME. I don't want to be the center of attention. Finally it ends—the guard leaves—and I stay.

It wasn't like it is now, where getting into each garage is like trying to get in to see the space shuttle. All the doors were open. They were all friends. Everybody was going in and out to see everybody else. Every garage you went in had a fridge with beer and soft drinks and bread and lunch meat and jars of mayonnaise. I just

Al Singer, Al Dean, a very young Bruce Crower, Clint Brawner and Carl Otte pose with Jimmy Bryan after qualifying for the 1954 "500". Mr. Otte wasn't on the crew but was invited by his house guests to get in the picture! Bryan has inscribed "The best motel in the Midwest" just above the tail. (IMS from Otte collection)

tagged along with him for the rest of the day like that.

One time I was out riding around with him during the summer and we stopped to cash some winnings check or another at the Speedway State Bank on Main Street. He cashes the check and then gives ME the money. "Here," he says, "Hold this for me until we get home." I'm carrying this wad of hundred-dollar bills. We get home and I go to give him the money and he just tells me to go upstairs and leave it on his dresser. That's just the way he was.

When you go in the museum, along the east wall there is a portrait of every winner done as a pencilled sketch. The year after Bryan won, he came in the house one day and he was carrying about eight copies of the one that had just been done of him. It must have been right before the '59 race because Lue, his wife, was there. He left them on the dining room table and went upstairs. I went over and had a peek. Oh, MAN! I was drooling. She saw me and told me to just take one. I wouldn't do it. I never wanted to ask or beg for any of those sorts of things. I wanted one of those portraits so bad, but I just didn't think it was right to just take one, because maybe he had other plans for them. I didn't want to be a moocher.

The next morning I came down and he had autographed one and left it for me. Today that portrait is framed and hanging in my living room.

Here's another little thing that gives you an idea about how he was and how good he could make you feel. In 1957 he bought one of the very first Ranchero trucks and it was a beautiful thing. We were sitting out on the steps one evening, admiring it, and Bryan turns to me—and I'm still just a kid—and he says, "You know, John, I think that truck needs something. What do you think it needs?" I say, "I think it needs whitewall tires." He says, "I think you're right."

Next day, he goes down to Firestone and has them put a set of whitewalls on. That night we're out there again and he says, "You were right about the whitewalls, John. That's what it needed."

Bryan always had two or three cars parked outside. He brought the Dodge pace car home one day in 1954 and I loved that car because it had real wire wheels. In 1955 he had two Buick Centuries and they were both out there on the street. He'd usually give my dad the keys to cars he wasn't driving when he'd leave, and one time in 1957 he was going out the door and says to me, "Here, catch!" "What's this?" I ask.

"The keys to the Ranchero," he says. "Drive it while I'm gone."

"I can't," I laugh. "I don't have a license. I'm only 13."

"Well, give them to your dad, then. Have him drive you around. See you later."

Another time, he asked my dad if he could run some errands in our car, even though he had several of his own out there. The tires were about shot on ours. It must have been about four days later that

The 1954 front row of Bryan, Jimmy Daywalt and Jack McGrath pass some time with actress Marie Wilson and cowboy star Roy Rogers just before the start of the drivers' meeting. (IMS)

I happened to notice that we had new tires. I mentioned it to my dad and he didn't know what I was talking about, so he went out and had a look. Ole Bryan had taken the car down to Firestone, put a new set of tires on and never said a word to us about it.

And the fun we used to have? You can't believe the water fights. My brother and I had these little squirt guns we used to play with. One night Bryan comes home and he calls out of the car window, "Come here, kids. I've got something for you." We go over to the car and he brings out this great big thing in the shape of a gangster-type machine gun. It must have held a quart of water and could shoot thirty feet.

He shoots us through the car-door window, so we run into the house to get our squirt guns and begin a water fight, which of course we lost. We'd keep running out of water and have to run over to the garden hose to fill up and Bryan would come over, just laughing away and drowning us with this machine gun while we stood there.

He had a dinner to go to that night. He showered and got all dressed up in a suit and shirt and tie. We were ready for him. We got the hose behind the evergreens we had in the front yard. My brother worked the faucet and I had the nozzle. We tested to make sure it was set on straight stream.

Bryan comes out of the house all slicked up for the dinner and I'm out behind the tree. I yell to my brother to turn on the faucet and we let him have it just as he gets to the car.

Well, suits weren't made of polyester yet, so by the time Bryan gets back to the house all of his clothes have shrunk up and he looks like Little Lord Fauntleroy!

He goes to my mother and says, "Betty, look what those boys have done to my suit," and she says, "Well, you asked for it. I don't even want to hear about it. You got what you deserved."

Bryan had a dog, a huge German Shepherd he had bought in Phoenix which he would air freight back here in the spring! This was after he had a place up by Lake Shafer, but of course he would bring the dog with him whenever he came to stay with us. A German shepherd tends to be a one-man or one-family dog, so it would always take him a few days to get used to us again.

His name was Bobo. Bryan had named him after Bobo Olson, the fighter, for some reason. Anyway, there was a drug store just around the corner from us, just a couple of doors from Beck's, named Eddie's. They had a deal where you could get a dew-top ice cream cone for a dime, so Bryan would send us down there with Bobo and thirty cents so we could have a cone each. We'd go out on the sidewalk, throw Bobo's up in the air and he'd catch it before it could hit the ground and gulp it before you realized it.

One night we were down there and there were some older, bigger kids picking on us. Now Bobo had never paid much attention to us before, but I told him to sic one of the kids and he started off after him. Well, it was like water skiing down 16th Street without water or water skis trying to hold on to the leash and keep Bobo from getting that boy.

That was about the only time I got in trouble with Bryan—for telling Bobo to do that.

Sure, Bryan liked to romp around with the kids, but he also liked

"The Bike". This is the job that had several racing decals on the frame, while the front fender bore the Blakely Oil decal given John by Clint Brawner. (Otte collection)

John gets his picture taken in the cockpit of the Blakely car out in front of his house in 1952. (Otte collection)

Bryan tries in vain to stay with Bill Vukovich in the late stages of the 1954 race. (IMS)

to relax quietly in front of the television. You hear all those stories about how he used to carouse around, and I'm sure he did plenty of that, but I can tell you that he spent a lot of time, and I mean a LOT of time, just staying home and watching TV.

Well, we were in there one night and the kid next door had built a go-kart and he was running it up and down outside the house. This was back before the days of air conditioners. It was hot and the windows were open. It's about nine o'clock and getting dark. Bryan is getting annoyed because he's trying to listen to television.

"Come on," he says, and we go upstairs to his room. He gets out an M-80 firecracker. Now, we had the old wooden- framed screens that hooked at the top and had a hook and eye at the bottom, so we unhooked the screen and I kind of held it while he watched the kid driving the go-kart back and forth. We couldn't see him all the way, but you could hear him out in the road and coming up over the sidewalk. Then it would get a little quieter as he hit the grass along the side of the house. The houses were only about ten feet apart. Bryan wasn't saying anything, but then I realized what he was doing. He was counting to himself and timing how long it would take before the kid would come by. Apparently, he already knew exactly how long the fuse would burn! He puffs on his cigar, holds the fuse to it and then just stands there with the fuse going. The kid comes along on the go-kart, I hold the screen open and Bryan drops the firecracker. It lands right smack on top of the engine, and no sooner has it done so than it explodes! The kid doesn't lift his foot off the gas, but takes both hands off the steering wheel. The kart lurches over to the right and he drives right into the basement window of his own house!

Bryan and I run downstairs, and no sooner are we back in the living room than there is a knock on the back door. My Mother looks out and sees that it is the boy's mother so, knowing exactly what is going on, she tells Bryan he'll have to answer the door himself, which he does. "Well, howdy, Ma'm."

The next-door neighbor is surprised by it being him answering the door, so she just says, "Oh, yes, would you please ask those Otte boys to not throw firecrackers this late at night?" and he says, "Why yes, Ma'm, I sure will." He comes back in the room, slides down in the chair and just carries on watching TV. He loved those firecrackers!

He came back from being away at a race for a few days one time and he had just brought a brand-new 1956 Ford truck. He says, "Come out and see what's happened to my new truck." He opens up the door and from about where the seat bottom would be on down on the door was just charcoal grey. The only thing left on the seat was the leatherette. Back then they weren't all that fancy. They'd just have a heavy canvas oilcloth-type material for the seat. Well, all of that was gone. What happened was that he had had a bunch of fireworks under the seat and something had caused him to drop his cigar under there. Before he could do anything all of the fireworks went off and set fire to the material!

In 1960 Bryan bought a brand-new El Camino. Boy! It was navy gray and had a tanaho cover. Blackwall tires, gray rims and little hubcaps. And a great big 348 Chevy V-8 tri- power engine.

I had my driver's license by that time. One day—he was going off somewhere—he threw me the keys. "You drive it," he says. Here I was 16 years old and driving Jimmy Bryan's El Camino! Whenever

Carl Otte (back to camera) visits Crower, Bryan, Brawner and Al Dean. The man working on the car is unidentified. (IMS)

Bryan qualifies for the 1955 ''500'' and is greeted by Arizona Senator Barry Goldwater, who would run against Lyndon Johnson for President of the United States in nine years' time. Bruce Crower is top left, while on the right was a mechanic who came back in 1955 and then not again for six years. John remembers him as staying at the house for the month but did not recall his name. When he returned in 1961, it was as a driver, and in 1962 he finished 4th! It's a very young Don Davis! (IMS)

he went away after that he'd leave it with me. I even drove that car to SCHOOL!

I was going to Speedway High School by that time, which in those days was what is now the Junior High over on 14th Street. We had to park along 14th between Allison and Lynhurst and they had a rule that you could only drive to school if you lived over five blocks away. They'd go down on the road and check from time to time to see that nobody was breaking the rule. I was, of course, but I never did get caught. They'd be checking on all those junky-looking ''first'' cars lined up down there and they'd never even consider that a high school kid could possibly be driving that shiny new El Camino with the Arizona plate on it!

Bryan blows an engine while leading the 1955 race. (IMS)

Here's another thing, too, about Bryan to show that while he was no longer a kid himself, he hadn't forgotten what it was like to BE a kid. My brother and I had to take turns at mowing the lawn and my dad started getting on me because it was my turn and I hadn't done it. I hated mowing the lawn. He told me he wanted to see it done by the next evening, but when I came in after school I noticed that it was already cut. I thought that was kind of strange. Later on, my dad started to tell me that I had done an exceptional job and I was just about to tell him that it wasn't me when I looked and here is ole Bryan with his leg up over the arm of the chair trying to get my attention. He just looked at me, shook his head ever so slightly and put his finger to his lips. My dad didn't see that and Bryan just smiled and winked. He'd done it, of course, and we never did tell my dad.

I don't think anyone ever knew how badly that man was beaten up in the 1954 race. I know he didn't come home that night and he had to pass up Milwaukee the next week. Now we are talking about a STRONG man here. Bryan was like a bull. But his right leg was black and blue to the hip and his muscles had just turned into mush. He was just beaten to a pulp. Most of that summer he'd watch TV and sit on the big couch we had with his right leg up on it. That couch could hold three people. You'd see him kind of slowly moving around to try and find a comfortable position and I don't think he ever fully recovered from it. Any time after that you could always tell if he'd had a tough race or been on a rough track because you could notice a limp. When he came back from winning at Monza in Italy he complained about how rough those high banks had been. Now, this was three years after that '54 race, and yet I'd bet he walked with a limp for a month after that.

Sometimes he'd sit up late at night talking with my mom and dad. One night he was talking about how uncomfortable the uniforms were to wear and it gave my mom an idea. In order to make their

Coincidental to the accompanying story, talented artist Cynthia Engelstad produced this beautiful piece of art in time to present it to Clint Brawner at the track in May, 1987. She applied the finishing touches to it in the trackside hospitality room of Bill Simpson, located on the very plot of ground where the old Victory Lane once stood. It shows the 1955 Kuzma being worked on by Brawner, Don Davis, Lloyd Chrisman, and Art Chrisman, while the inserts are of Bryan and Brawner.

Breakfast for Champion

Jimmy Bryan, who's won just about everything worth winning in his last year of auto racing, including yesterday's "500", ate lone this morning. His wife, Louella, wasn't feeling well after yesterday's excitement. They're staying with friends, Mr. and Mrs. Carl Otte, 5440 W. 16th.—Times photo by Raymond Bright.

The Indianapolis Times visited the Otte household the morning after the race to take this shot at the kitchen table. John points out that the use of the sports coat was very un-Bryan- like! It came off right after the picture was taken. (Otte collection)

This was Bryan's transportation from the Otte's back steps over to take 3rd on the morning of the 1957 "500". (Otte collection)

uniforms fire-retardant back in those days, the drivers used to dip them in 55-gallon drums filled with water and mix in some chemical solution. Then they'd hang them up to dry. Sometimes the chemical would dry in blotches and it could become very uncomfortable during a long, hot race. It used to bother Bryan. My mom worked at American Art Clay, right across from the track, and there used to be a cleaners next door, so she started taking his uniforms in there and they would do something to them to make them more comfortable for him to wear. He always appreciated that and as I say, he was just like one of the family.

I don't remember exactly how Bryan went over to the track on race morning in 1958, but in '57, I know that he rode over on a mini motorscooter. I have a picture of that. In '58 I'm sure someone must have taken him over. Lue came in for the race. She usually did. I never ever heard her call him anything other than just plain "Bryan," by the way.

Angelo Angelopolous, a sports writer for the Indianapolis News, was with us a lot for a day or two because he was doing a feature story that appeared in True Magazine. That was unusual, because Bryan usually kept quiet about where he stayed. The neighbors knew he was with us, but he didn't want the press coming over and bothering us or him. He liked to just take care of all of that at the track. I'd say he was protecting us just about as much as we were protecting him.

Lue came down that morning wearing a black and white check- ered outfit. A lot of the neighbors kept coming in to wish him good luck and then off they went.

I never actually saw him take the checker when he won the race because my dad and I were running back to the garage area. We wanted to make sure we were already back there when he came in.

Later that afternoon when he came home, he still had his yellow Belond uniform on! Again, I'm sure somebody must have brought him and Lue home and dropped them off. Lue got on him about cleaning up to go out and then she went on in the house and upstairs. Bryan came and sat down on the grass with us kids and just kind of

This was the next-to-last year for Borg-Warner to bring in a Hollywood actress for the festivities. Some of them weren't that crazy about the assignment but bright young Shirley MacLaine seemed really to enjoy herself. (IMS)

Bryan is chased by George Amick and Johnny Boyd late in the 1958 "500". They finished in this order but not this close. (IMS)

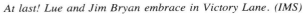

At last! Lue and Jim Bryan embrace in Victory Lane. (IMS)

Jim and Lue relax in the Belond garage a few minutes after the checker had fallen. (IMS)

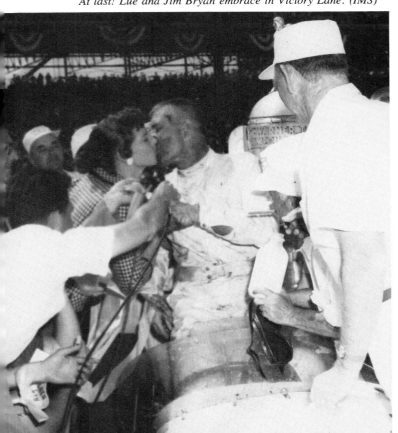

Bryan accepts the first-place check of $105,574 from Tony Hulman, assuring the Ottes that Jim will continue to be good for the rent. (IMS)

lay back on one arm and played with us and the dog. People could park on 16th Street in those days and the cars probably went down about as far as where it turns on to Cunningham. Well, the funny thing was that a lot of people were still walking back from the track to their cars, right by our house, and nobody looked at him. Who would ever pay attention to just another guy in a stained yellow uniform? Probably he was just some crew member or another! Here's all these people who have come from wherever to see the Indianapolis ''500''. They're walking back to their cars and there, just sitting on this lawn they're strolling by and paying no particular attention to is the man who just WON the race they've been to see!

And for all I know, George Amick and his crew, who placed second and who were staying about eight or ten houses further up from us on Norfolk, were probably out on their lawn doing the same thing.

It's quite acceptable to take a picture of your house guests before they go out for the evening, especially when they look so nice! Although already in possession of the pace car, Jim and Lue are just leaving to go down for the Victory Banquet. (Otte collection)

The 1958 Clymer ''500'' yearbook is tough enough to find as it is. How about this one with Bryan's AUTOGRAPH on it? (Otte collection)

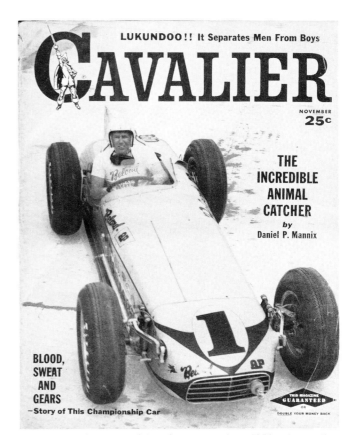

Bryan on the cover of Cavalier, November, 1958. (Otte collection)

Bryan on the cover of Sports Illustrated, May 27, 1957. (Otte collection)

The '58 pace car parked on Norfolk the day after the race. Just what Bryan needed was ANOTHER car! The two parked on 16th Street are his also. (Otte collection)

Bryan at the track in 1960 in typical fashion, unselfishly spending a minute or two with a kid who'll probably remember the encounter for the rest of his life. (IMS)

This winner's portrait is autographed: "To John Boy, now a young man." It hangs today, framed, in the Otte living room. (Otte collection)

About the only down side was the fact that the win didn't come with Clint. Foyt was his driver by this time. Clint had his own place in Speedway by then, but all of the Dean crew were still with us. Even to this day, Clint is like family to me, and it just seems that it really should have been his win too.

* * * * * * *

Bryan spent less and less time with the Ottes, other than in May, because he had taken the place up by Lake Shafer. He still had his room at the house and would stay from time to time throughout May and whenever else he needed to be in town. He stayed on after the 1960 "500" and surprised the Ottes along with everyone else when he announced he was going to drive at Langhorne. He had quit driving any Championship events after his 1958 "500" win and competed only at Indianapolis, plus selected stock car races and sports car events, for the next two seasons. In the meantime, Rodger Ward, the new National Champion, had an aversion to competing at Langhorne and he steadfastly refused to return there. Car owner Bob Wilke and chief mechanic A.J. Watson decided to take the number-one dirt car over there anyway and invited Bryan to drive it. In spite of having been away from Championship dirt tracks since winning the November, 1957 Phoenix 100, a full two and a half years earlier, Bryan accepted.

He qualified for the outside of the front row, but flipped end over end through the infamous "Puke Hollow" on the very first lap of the race, and the great Jimmy Bryan was fatally injured.

OTTE: This sounds a bit like a Twilight Zone thing, but whenever he was going anywhere, he'd always say, "See you in a couple of days," or, "I'll be here when you get back from work," or something like that. When he went to Langhorne, he turned around, waved, and said "Goodbye".

I'm not kidding. It was weird. Just "Goodbye". I'm sure it was the first and only time I'd ever heard him say that. He headed east on 16th, waving out the window, and that was the last we saw of him.

My folks had a cabin down in Brown County and we went down there for the weekend after he left. A friend of mine had gone down in his car and we had just come in from water skiing when my dad came over with tears in his eyes and told us what he had just heard on the radio.

My folks remained down there, but I wanted to go home right away, so my friend drove me.

I still had the keys to the El Camino in my pocket. That was the LONGEST trip I ever took.

Even though he'd been spending a lot of his time up at the lake, there were still a lot of his things around the house and in his room. We had to pack it all up. THAT was tough. He still had a couple of helmets around there. Some trophies, pictures, clothes, knick-knacks people had sent him. There was one of those Revell kits of a Kurtis roadster that someone had done as a Dean Van Lines Special and given him. There was a portfolio of photographs, a photo essay someone had done on him. We packed everything in boxes and loaded it into the cars he still had there. There was the El Camino I had been driving, plus a white '60 Ford Thunderbird hardtop. For a while, the plan was that Clint Brawner and I were going to drive the cars back to Phoenix and then Clint was going to put me on the plane home. It ended up that I didn't go, because I was still only 16 and my parents thought I was a little young to be driving halfway across the world.

That was it for us as far as race drivers were concerned. We still had crew members. But no race drivers. I didn't go to the 1961 race, but I was over at the track for practice quite a bit. Crower was a crew chief for Lindsey Hopkins that year. They were running two cars. Jack Beckley had Tony Bettenhausen and Bruce had Wayne Weiler. The day before the first qualifying day, Bettenhausen was killed testing the Doug Stearly car for Paul Russo. Crower was with us as usual, along with several of the Hopkins crew, so it was off to another funeral.

Lue Bryan never came back. She remarried, a couple of times in fact, and we didn't hear from her for years. One race morning, it must have been '65 or so, my mother answered the phone and it was Lue! She had been thinking about us a lot but

200

Tony Bettenhausen, not yet (and never to be) an Indianapolis winner, has that fact rammed down his throat (in good-natured fashion) by a display of winner's rings from Sam Hanks, Bill Holland, Troy Ruttman, Johnnie Parsons, Rodger Ward, Lee Wallard and Bryan. (IMS)

never could bring herself to call. Finally she did. Right on a race morning.

* * * * * * *

It would seem a shame for this to end on a sad note, and so it won't. Does John Otte have one special memory about Jimmy Bryan that stands out for him above all of the others? He most certainly does.

OTTE: Bryan had this 1957 Mercury stock car that he owned himself. All of the factories got together after the 1956 season and put a ban on participating in stock car racing anymore. They shut down all of their teams and gave all of the equipment over to the teams and drivers who had been running for them and just said, ''Here. We're out of it. You take it and run it

The old Otte household in 1987. The family hasn't owned the house in several years, but OHHHHHH, the memories! Yep, that's the front lawn where Bryan relaxed and played after the '58 race. That's his bedroom right of the chimney, and next to the drain pipe on the house next door is the basement window into which a certain go-kart crashed after being bombed by a certain firecracker dropped from the Otte's upper window by a certain house guest. (John Mahoney)

201

St. Christopher's school with the church on the left. The telegraph pole marks the spot where John was "delivered" to school. (John Mahoney)

Bryan and Troy Ruttman with Bryan's stock car. The stock car figures in this story's final anecdote. (Otte collection)

JIMMY BRYAN
5

John and Sally Otte with their sons, James Bryan and Michael. John says of Mike: "I was working on calling him Anthony Joseph but Sally was already coming out of the anesthetic, so I didn't quite get it done!" (Otte collection)

yourself if you want to."

So Bryan ended up with this Mercury. A Bill Stroppe Mercury. He'd run it whenever there wasn't a conflict with a Championship race. He didn't even have a trailer for it. He'd just hook up a tow bar and pull it to the races.

It was sort of aquamarine blue and it had a red and white interior, which I could never figure out. And military-type shoulder harnesses in olive drab! It had his name over the door and the numbers and a few decals. He was going to sell it and he wanted $500 for it!

Can you imagine that? Five HUNDRED dollars for Jimmy Bryan's stock car! "Dad, let's buy it," I pleaded.

"Now, what would I do with a thing like that?" reasoned my Dad.

Well, here it was parked out on Norfolk heading north one day and Bryan decides that he is going to DRIVE it over to the track. I wasn't in high school yet. I was still going to St. Christopher's, which was about a block and a half down the street. "Here, help me do this," says Bryan.

He has a pair of mufflers which he attaches to the exhaust pipes coming out from under the doors and with a couple of coat hangers we wire them up under the car.

"It's getting a little late and I'm going to have to leave for school," I tell him. "Hop in," says Bryan!

You couldn't open the doors. They were wired or welded shut or something, so I climb in the window like the NASCAR drivers do now. The front seat is a bench-type seat, but the passenger side is missing. I crouch on the floor and Bryan climbs in the driver's side and fires it up. My god, the NOISE!

I don't know why we bothered with the mufflers. We are hollering back and forth but it is so loud that all you can do is lip read. He clamps his cigar between his teeth, turns around to look out the back window and backs the Stroppe Mercury off Norfolk and out into 16th.

There's about twelve kids standing outside St. Chris, and they look up when they hear all of this noise. They can't believe this thing coming down the street. It pulls up next to the walkway and I climb out the window! What a way to go to school! I'll tell you, I was a big man on campus that day.

* * * * * * *

And that is just some indication of the influence a great "500" champion had on a boy as he was growing up, and why John Otte had absolutely no hesitation at following the vow he made to himself years ago in naming his first son James Bryan Otte.

The ways of the world and the ways of racing have changed now, so that things don't happen like that around Speedway any more. And that's a shame.

A very special person. (Otte collection)

The author had toyed with the idea of a story along these lines for quite a number of years, and upon the final completion of this would like to very sincerely thank John Otte for unselfishly sharing his wonderful anecdotes and for loaning some of his treasured memorabilia for use in these pages. We conclude with an irony. There is, in another section of this publication, a feature concerning crew member-turned-land developer Charlie Patterson, who transformed an ignored, overgrown plot of ground into the spectacular Gasoline Alley, where several of the Indy car teams and related businesses are now housed. When Carl and Betty Otte moved to Brown County in the early 1970's and sold their house, the purchaser was the very same Charlie Patterson. Several of Charlie's family still live there today—DCD.

These were A.J. Foyt's first substantial tire marks in 21 years. (Strauser)

"500" TRIVIA

by Bob Watson

The fact that A.J. Foyt has started in 30 consecutive races at Indianapolis is even more amazing when one considers that 202 drivers have made the starting field only once and an additional 93 drivers have managed to make the starting field on only two occasions. For the record, there have been 572 different starting drivers in the history of the "500."

* * *

Mario Andretti has started from the pole position at Indianapolis on 3 occasions, 1966-67-87. Mario's 1987 qualification average of 215.390 mph was 49.491 mph faster than his pole speed of 1966. This is the widest margin in Indy history by which a driver has qualified on the pole two or more times. Mario's 20-year stretch between pole position starts is also an Indianapolis record, breaking Bobby Unser's 9-year gap (1972-81).

* * *

The 1987 starting field not only contained a record 9 former winners who represented a record 18 previous victories at the "Brickyard," but it also contained a record 19 former lap leaders of the classic. The 1987 field was also the most experienced Indianapolis 500 field in history, with the 27 veterans in the 33-car line-up accounting for 260 previous starts at Indianapolis.

* * *

Between the time Tom Sneva recorded the first 200 mph qualification lap at Indianapolis in 1977 and George Snider's third lap qualification accident in 1987, there had been 666- 200 mph qualification laps recorded at the speedway. Amazingly, none of those 200 mph laps were ever recorded on a qualification attempt that ended in an accident, except for the last two, which were recorded on George Snider's ill-fated run.

* * *

Absent from the 1958 starting field were Sam Hanks, winner of the "500" in 1957, and Don Edmunds, winner of the 1957 "Rookie of the Year" award. Nineteen fifty-eight marks the only time that a starting field did not contain at least one of the current champions of these two categories since the rookie award was established in 1952.

* * *

Harry Hartz is the only driver to have posted five top-4 finishes in his first five starts at Indianapolis. Hartz finished 2nd, 2nd, 4th, 4th, and 2nd, from 1922 thru 1926. Bill Holland and Roberto Guerrero are the only other drivers to have posted four top-4 finishes in their first four starts. Holland finished 2nd, 2nd, 1st, and 2nd, from 1947 thru 1950. Guerrero has finished 2-3-4-2 in his only four starts at Indianapolis.

* * *

It is a well-known fact that when Al Unser, Sr. led the final 18 laps in 1987, he tied Ralph DePalma's all-time record of 613 leading laps at Indianapolis—a figure which had stood alone since 1921. What is not as well known is the fact that DePalma had actually stood alone at the top of the all-time lap leader list since 1912!

* * *

The first participant to be killed in the Indianapolis 500 was riding mechanic Sam Dickson in 1911. The last survivor of the 1911 inaugural event was riding mechanic Col. Edward Towers, who died almost 75 years later. Ironically, both men were members of the same racing team (Amplex). The oldest living participant of an Indianapolis 500 is 1919 relief driver Reeves Dutton, who turned 100 in February, 1987.

* * *

Mario Andretti is the only driver in Indianapolis history to have been the fastest qualifier of a starting field in each of 3 decades. Mario was the fastest qualifier, starting from the pole position in 1966, 1967, and 1987, and was the fastest qualifier in the 1976 field, starting from the 19th position.

* * *

A.J. Foyt has started the "500" from the 4th position on three occasions. Those three occasions were 1967, 1977, and 1987, when A.J. made his 10th, 20th, and 30th anniversary starts at Indianapolis. For the record, Foyt's finishing position figures for those three years are 1-1-19.

* * *

Al Unser's victory in 1987 was the first by a non-"pole position day qualifier" or "first period qualifier" since Johnny Rutherford in 1974 and Sam Hanks in 1957.

* * *

Louis Schneider holds the Indianapolis 500 record for the widest span between finishing positions, by virtue of a first-place finish in 1931 and a 42nd-place finish in 1933.

* * *

Mario Andretti and Tom Sneva have each started from the first position three times and each driver has started from the last-place position once. Andretti and Sneva have also finished first on one occasion and each has finished last on one occa-

Veteran Texas midgeteer Tubby Stewart was on Foyt's crew this year and brought with him the long absent Bill Homeier, runner-up in the 1953 AAA Midget standings, a two-time "500" starter and relief driver for 5th-place-finishing Walt Faulkner in 1955. (Mahoney)

sion. They are the only drivers to have completed this bitters-weet cycle at Indianapolis.

* * *

Nine former winners started the 1987 "500," but only two were running at the finish. The seven that didn't finish represent the greatest number of former winners to have dropped out of an Indianapolis 500.

* * *

The fastest race lap and the fastest leading lap in Indianapolis history was turned in by Bobby Rahal on lap 200 in 1986. Rahal's time was 43.031 seconds and his speed was 209.152 mph.

* * *

Starting from the front row in 1987 were Mario Andretti, Bobby Rahal, and Rick Mears. The 1987 front row is only the third front row in Indianapolis history to be comprised entirely of former winners. The 1987 front row, however, has the distinction of being the only front row comprised entirely of former winners who each recorded an Indianapolis victory in a different decade: (Mario Andretti-1969) (Bobby Rahal-1986) (Rick Mears-first win, 1979).

* * *

In 1986, a record seven second-generation Indy 500 drivers were among the 33 starters in the field. Those seven drivers were Michael Andretti, Gary & Tony Bettenhausen, Jr., Geoff Brabham, Pancho Carter, Johnny Parsons, and Al Unser, Jr.

* * *

Mario Andretti's 170 leading laps in 1987 is the third highest total by a driver in a losing cause. The only other drivers to have led more laps in a non-winning performance were Ralph DePalma, leader of the 1912 event for 196 consecutive laps, and Parnelli Jones, who led for 171 laps in 1967.

* * *

On only two occasions have the first two starting positions been occupied by the winners of the two previous races. In 1927, defending winner Frank Lockhart started from the pole and Peter DePaolo, winner of the 1925 race, started from the second position. In 1986, defending winner Danny Sullivan started from the second position and Rick Mears, winner of the "500" for the second time in 1984, started from the pole.

* * *

There have been five starting fields that did not contain a former winner (1911-12-13-15-16). Mauri Rose was the only former winner in the 1946, 1947, 1948, and 1949 starting fields. The only former winner in the 1958 starting field was Johnnie Parsons, winner of the 1950 race! The 1928, 1934, and 1952 starting fields also contained only one former winner.

* * *

Race day preparation includes placing the fuel tanks in the pits.
(IMS-Duffy)

Two-time "500" winner Rodger Ward comes back every year.
(Katsoff)

The first and last-place starting positions in 1987 were interesting, in that each was filled by a former World Driving Champion. Mario Andretti, the 1978 World Champion, started from the pole, and two-time World Champion Emerson Fittipaldi started from the 3rd position. Mario Andretti and 1964 pole sitter Jimmy Clark are the only former World Champions to have started from the pole at Indianapolis.

* * *

Altogether, there have been 6 drivers who have started at Indianapolis after winning a Grand Prix World Championship. Those 6 drivers are: Jimmy Clark, Jack Brabham, Denis Hulme, Graham Hill, Emerson Fittipaldi, and Mario Andretti. World Champions Jackie Stewart, Jochen Rindt, and Alberto Ascari started at Indianapolis, but not after winning a World title for the first time.

* * *

In 1986, Michael Andretti became the first driver ever to lead the opening lap with a speed in excess of 200 mph and Bobby Rahal was only the second winner to do likewise for the final lap. This is the only time the "500" ever started and ended with lap leader speeds in excess of 200 mph.

* * *

The 1987 "500" marked the third consecutive year that the top lap leader of the race did not win. The only other three-year stretch in which this occurred was from 1927 thru 1929.

* * *

In 1980, Johnny Rutherford, the fastest qualifier in the field, won starting from the pole. Tom Sneva finished 2nd starting from the 33rd position, and Gary Bettenhausen, the slowest qualifier in the field, finished third starting from the 32nd position.

* * *

In 1985, Pete Halsmer qualified at 204.634 mph and was the "first alternate" for that year's race. Halsmer was the first "first alternate" ever to post a 200 mph qualifications average.

* * *

Nineteen sixty two "500" runner-up, Len Sutton, who simply looks nowhere near his age returned for the first time in many years and saw many friendes including Linda Vaughn. (Walker)

On three occasions a driver has managed to lead the same "500" in two cars. In 1923, Howdy Wilcox led 10 laps in his original car and 41 laps in relief of Tommy Milton. In 1924, co-winner Joe Boyer led one lap in his original car and 24 laps in relief of L.L. Corum. In 1941, co-winner Mauri Rose led six laps in his original car and 39 laps in relief of Floyd Davis.

* * *

The late Mark Donohue's race record for the 190-lap distance, Jerry Grant's race record for the 180-lap distance, and Gary Bettenhausen's race records for the 130-140-160-170 lap distances were all established in 1972. Not one of these records were broken until 1986, when all six records were finally un-seated during the running of that year's race.

* * *

In 1986, there were 170 official qualification laps recorded at the speedway. There were also 8 additional laps that were recorded on disallowed runs. All 178 laps were at 200 mph or above. This was a "first" for qualifications at Indianapolis.

* * *

Some records seem to take forever to break. Just ask A.J. Foyt. It took A.J. 30 trips from Houston to Indianapolis to become the oldest starting driver from the state of Texas ever to compete in the "500." At age 52, Foyt was only about a month older when he competed in the 1987 race than was fellow Texas Jim McElreath when he competed in the "500" for the last time in 1980.

* * *

The leader of the opening lap has started from the pole position a record 29 times. Second best is 17 times each from both the 2nd and 3rd starting positions. The last time a driver led the opening lap from a non-front-row position was in 1967, when Parnelli Jones led the initial lap starting from the 6th position.

* * *

There have been five occasions when the first and last place finishers of a race started from consecutive positions (1926-54-55-66-81). The only time the first two starting positions were involved was in 1981, when Bobby Unser won starting from the pole and second-place starter Mike Mosley finished last.

* * *

There have been 18 individuals who have held the title of official starter at the Indianapolis 500. Fred J. Wagner was the official starter for the initial "500" in 1911 and held that position through the 1912 race. Pat Vidan served as official starter of the "500" for a record 18 years, starting with the 1962 race. Duane Sweeney took over the flags from the retiring Vidan in 1980 and has held the post of official starter to the present day.

* * *

In the entire history of the "500" a new one-lap qualification record has been established 75 times and a new four-lap mark 73 times. 1987 marked the first time in six years that a new standard was not set in either category.

* * *

In 1976, there were four ties in qualification: Bill Puterbaugh and Al Loquasto (182.002); Jan Opperman and Spike Gehlhausen (181.717); Larry McCoy and Larry Cannon (181.338); George Snider and Bob Harkey (181.141).

Danny Sullivan discusses a PC-16 handling tendency with the car's designer, Alan Jenkins (left) and with Penske's Derrick Walker. (Wendt)

OVER A DECADE
OF EXCELLENCE

1973
Kurtis Cars, Pocono and Ontario 500's; Profiles of Swede Savage, Sid Collins, Art Pollard, and Fritz Dusenberg; Pace Car History. 8-1/2" x 11," 160 pages, 250 plus photos. Limited Quantity left. Softbound only............CH073S $100.00

1974
Articles on 1924 and 1954 races; Sampson Schroeder; car profile on 'The Riley;' Ontario and Pocono; Times and Averages 1911-1973. 8-1/2" x 11," 160 pages, 250 plus black and white photographs, 18 pages of color photos.
Softbound CH074S $14.95
Hardbound CH074H $20.95

1975
Profiles on Bobby Unser, Dan Gurney, Don Brown, and Myron Stevens; Winners; Harry Miller and his cars; The New Cosworth. 8-1/2" x 11," 224 pages, 400 plus black and white photos, 100 plus color photos.
Softbound CH075S $14.95
Hardbound CH075H $20.95

1976
New Cars at Indy; 'Thunder and Lightening' Sprints; Profiles on Ralph Ligouri, Herb Porter, Wally Meskowski, Chris Economaki, Janet Guthrie; The Dusenberg. 8-1/2" x 11," 224 pages, 350 plus black and white photos, 150 plus color photos.
Softbound CH076S $14.95
Hardbound CH076H $20.95

1977
CRA Sends Its Best; Tribute to Sid Collins; 1937 Race; Foreign Driver Profiles; Odds Against The Brickyard; The Riding Mechnics; Indy Incidents. 8-1/2" x 11," 224 pages, 350 plus black and white photos, 150 plus color photos.
Softbound CH077S $14.95
Hardbound CH077H $20.95

1978
Tony Hulman; Speedway Safety Patrol; Clint Brawner; "500" Festival Queens; Car owners. 8-1/2" x 11," 240 pages, 400 plus black and whites photos, 150 plus color photos.
Softbound CH078S $14.95
Hardbound CH078H $20.95

1979
Studebaker at Indy; Jackie Stewart; 60 Years Ago; Winner's Scrapbook; Profiles on Bill Alsup, Art Sparks; Baseball and Racing. 8-1/2" x 11," 224 pages, 400 plus black and white photos, 100 plus color photos.
Softbound CH079S $14.95
Hardbound CH079H $20.95

1980
1941 Winner Restored; 'The Greatest Debacle in Racing;' Tire Tests and Other Oddities; The Cummins Diesel; Grant King, Car Builders; The History of Ground Effects. 8-1/2" x 11," 224 pages, 400 plus black and white photos, 100 plus color photos.
Softbound CH080S $14.95
Hardbound CH080H $20.95

1981
The Hearing: A Re-Reversal; Ron Burton, artist; Dennis Torres, photographer; Jules Goux, 1913 Indy Winner; 20 years of Car Design; Jud Phillips. 8-1/2" x 11," 224 pages, 350 plus black and white photos, 100 plus color photos.
Softbound CH081S $14.95
Hardbound CH081H $20.95

1982
Profiles on Roger Penske, A.J. Foyt, Desire Wilson; The Six-Wheeler; 20 Years Ago; The High Cost of Racing; Pit Safety. 8-1/2" x 11," 224 pages, 300 plus black and white photos, 100 plus color photos.
Softbound CH082S $14.95
Hardbound CH082H $20.95

1983
The Meyer Family; Dick Greene; Patrick Racing Team; Personal Cars of Pro Drivers; Norm Hall. 8-1/2" x 11," 224 pages, 300 plus black and white photos, 100 plus color photos.
Softbound CH083S $14.95
Hardbound CH083H $20.95

1984
New records; Mears/Penske win again; Detailed accounts of race, practice and qualifying; All 33 starters in color; All cars that missed the race; 8½" × 11", 244 pages, hundreds of color and black and white photos.
Softbound CH084S $14.95
Hardbound CH084H $20.95

1985
Danny Sulivan's incredible "spin and win"; Garage Area nostalgia; Johnnie Parsons tribute; Art Sparks; History's persistent drivers who never made the lineup; 8½" × 11", 224 pages, hundreds of color and black and white photos.
Softbound CH085S $14.95
Hardbound CH085H $20.95

1986
Relive Rahal's glory days, a tribute to Jim Trueman, the "fiery" Bill Simpson. Recapture the month of May with the annual collector's item. Feature stories, statistics, driver bios, the Speedway daily facts and much, much more. 8-1/2" x 11", 224 pages, hundreds of color and black and white photos.
Softbound   CH086S $14.95
Hardbound CH086H $20.95

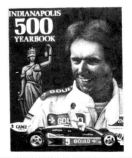

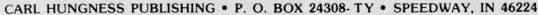

CARL HUNGNESS PUBLISHING • P. O. BOX 24308- TY • SPEEDWAY, IN 46224
MASTERCARD and VISA accepted   Indiana Residents add 5% sales tax.
Postage & Handling $2.00 per book, $8.00 maximum per order.

A TRADITION OF HORSEPOWER

Budweiser

Bud KING OF BEERS

VALVOLINE

Bud KING OF BEERS

1

RED ROOF INNS

sleep cheap!

GOODYEAR

HORTON

sleep cheap!

Bobby Rahal. '86 CART PPG National Champ.

Is motor oil just motor oil?
Not to these guys.

According to USAC Rule 108, Sub-Paragraph B, once the Indy 500 starts, not a single drop of motor oil can be added.

For the past five years, under this rule, 75 percent of the drivers who started at Indy chose Valvoline. And that includes last year's winner, Bobby Rahal.

Valvoline. Motor oil is <u>not</u> just motor oil.™